South

O F

Freedom

South

OF

Freedom

BY

Carl T. Rowan

With a New Introduction by Douglas Brinkley

Louisiana State University Press
Baton Rouge and London

Dedicated to
MY WIFE, VIVIEN,
and to
Faith in Humanity,
Two Sturdy Leaning-Posts
in a Shaky Civilization

CONTENTS

PREFACE

IT has been said for decades that "there is nothing new about the race problem." Perhaps not. Perhaps there has been nothing new about the problem since men first learned to hate. Yet the problem stays with us, despite all the noble things men have said. Never was it more with us, nor in a more sinister way, than in these times of international gloom, when hatreds seem everywhere and differences in men, both racial and ideological, would seem to govern our fate. After more than three centuries, America's race problem still is a creeping miasma that overshadows our economic lives, frustrates our social lives, and enshrouds our sexual lives in curiosity and untold fear.

This book is about the Americans—white and black—who live under the shadow of the problem. It is about their struggles—on the one hand to maintain the old order of segregation and racial caste, and on the other hand to establish a "New South." I have tried to tell of the "little things" that circumscribe the lives of black folk. I also have told of our gains. This is a balance-sheet of American race relations: it tells how far we have come and where we still must go.

I have written this book because I do not believe that man was born to hate and be hated; I cannot believe that the race problem is an inevitable concomitant of democratic life. If I have said nothing new, perhaps I have said it in a different way that will bring something to the makings of men. If this be impossible, I still hope that the old things that I have written will produce new understanding among the millions of Americans who know so little about the problem.

I am grateful to the editors of the Minneapolis *Morning*

Tribune, who shared with me the belief that Americans ought to have such a report. Because they opened the *Tribune's* pages to a series of articles in which portions of this book first were printed, this book is possible. To all others whose help and guidance enabled me to complete this book, I give my sincere thanks.

CARL T. ROWAN

Minneapolis, Minnesota
December 1951

INTRODUCTION
Douglas Brinkley

It was August 3, 1952, and the Twin Cities were in the grip of a heat wave, the temperature in the mid-80s for the sixth straight day. In a one-bedroom apartment at 2900 Portland Avenue, the celebrated twenty-seven-year-old Minneapolis *Tribune* journalist Carl T. Rowan and his wife, Vivien, rose early to read local newspapers, brunch with friends, and then drive down to the newsstand on Hennepin Avenue to purchase the Sunday New York *Times,* which arrived there in corded bundles at midday, railroaded in from Chicago. Alfred A. Knopf, Inc., had just published Rowan's *South of Freedom*—an autobiographical road narrative based on a six-thousand-mile tour by bus, car, and train through the segregated South in early 1951—and the young African-American reporter was anxious to see if his first book had been reviewed in that week's *Times.* To his astonishment and horror, it had been.

The review appeared on page 3, under the heading "The Bitter Search for First-Class Citizenship," with the critical evaluation penned by Hodding Carter, the pseudo-liberal editor of the Greenville, Mississippi, *Delta Democrat-Times.* Rowan's heart sank upon seeing Carter's name, for he had severely criticized the Washington County editor and other civil rights gradualists in *South of Freedom* as being almost as much the enemy as Senator James Eastland of Mississippi and other avowed racists. Rowan was understandably devastated that the *Times,* playing its own racial politics, had assigned his book to a "freedom-for-you-sometime-soon" gradualist like Carter, whom Rowan had lampooned by name. "It would be simple to write a report embracing the popular theory of gradualism," Rowan noted about "fake liberals" such as Carter. "The theory finds easy acceptance when it is someone else's freedom that is to come later." By contrast, *South of Freedom* attacked the problem head-on, in the same devastating fashion Harriet Beecher Stowe's *Uncle Tom's Cabin* had taken on slavery a hundred years earlier, with Rowan dissecting the evil of Jim Crow laws that governed almost every aspect of life for African-Americans below the Mason-Dixon line.[1]

The review justified Rowan's consternation. Though Carter found Rowan's anti–Jim Crow arguments "moving and sincere," he gave the impression that the book was written by what some might have called an "uppity Negro" in a hurry, a shanty-raised Tennessean who had been spoiled by the racial egalitarianism of social democratic Minnesota. "Had I been older, or more mature, I might have read those words as an indication that a proud, relatively old white man in Misisippi was caught in a war between his heart and mind and the realities of publishing a paper in one of the most benighted States in the Union," Rowan reflected years later. "But I was not old, or truly mature, so I went to bed that Sunday night in August '52 thinking how Hodding Carter's last description of my book was that it was a 'bitter report of a loyal and perhaps unquietly desperate American, who will not find in his lifetime full acceptance as a first-class citizen everywhere in his country.'" As Rowan tossed and turned, finding it impossible to sleep, he had one simple, straightforward rebuttal to Hodding Carter's words: "Like hell I won't."

Born in the dying coal-mining town of Ravenscoft, Tennessee, on August 11, 1925, Rowan was a child of the Great Depression in the worst sense. Raised in utter squalor across the street from a junkyard in McMinnville, the neighboring town to that of his birth, he constantly feared being gnawed by rats while sleeping (a nightmare that became reality for his sister). Young Carl's winter coat

1. The term *Jim Crow* derives from a song-and-dance routine by Thomas Rice in a mid-1880s black minstrel show. The U.S. Supreme Court gave its approval to Jim Crow segregation in the 1896 case of *Plessy* v. *Ferguson*, in which the court held separate but equal facilities to be constitutional. In practice, southern states never provided equal facilities to blacks—only separate ones.

was so tattered that his friends dubbed him "Strings." To lift himself out of such stark poverty, Rowan developed a protective armor and inner strength based on the Christian assumption that somehow life would get better. Though he graduated from high school literate, this did not immediately improve his fortune. Rowan understood from an early age that to break the shackles of discrimination and prejudice, he would someday have to spit in the eye of Jim Crow. "The remarkable thing about this country," Rowan believed, "is that even in an era of grotesque bigotry there were roads of escape." By the time he was nineteen he had already shattered a major race barrier: he had become an ensign in the U.S. Navy during World War II, traveling aboard fleet tankers in the North Atlantic and receiving accolades despite the color of his skin. Proud to have personally contributed to the crusade to crush German and Japanese totalitarianism, Rowan was inspired by the words of General George C. Marshall: "Fight for the dignity of the individual." Rowan's main goal after the war—besides getting married—was to make sure that all Americans, regardless of race or gender, were considered equal under the law, were granted the basic dignities that genuine democracy purported to offer—even in the ex-Confederate states.

Imbued with a touch of the firebrand, Rowan and a whole generation of African-American servicemen were detemined to overturn racist Jim Crow laws just as surely as they destroyed the racist Nazi regime. Undeterred by what white gradualists such as Hodding Carter thought, Rowan believed that someday he *would* be a first-class citizen everywhere in the South. Determined to bring democracy to Dixieland, African Americans of Rowan's generation sought bold new strategies. Enthralled by Mahatma Gandhi's success in leading the Indian masses in peaceful demonstrations for independence, the Congress of Racial Equality (CORE) decided to put the philosophy of nonviolence to work. After much training and brainstorming, black and white members of CORE entered segregated restaurants, took counter seats, and refused to leave until they were served. They did not shout expletives or retaliate if attacked: nonviolence had become their *modus operandi*. After the Supreme

Court outlawed segregation on interstate buses in 1946, CORE members set out on a "Journey of Reconciliation" to test whether the laws were being obeyed. Blacks rode together with whites on buses throughout the Deep South, enduring humiliations and harassment with stoical dignity.

While CORE was practicing civil disobedience in Greyhound stations and blue-plate cafés, major battles were being waged in courthouses and legislatures. President Harry Truman boldly integrated the armed services in response to pressure from black veterans, and he established a civil rights committee, which in early 1948 issued the landmark report "To Secure These Rights," calling for the elimination of segregation in all forty-eight contiguous states. Already half a million African Americans belonged to the National Association for the Advancement of Colored People (NAACP)—established in 1910 by Harvard-educated sociologist W. E. B. Du Bois and others—whose relentless lawyers were forcing local governments to improve black schools. Then, in 1950, NAACP lawyers began building the case that would force the U.S. Supreme Court to overturn the doctrine of "separate but equal" in the area of education and would mark the beginning of the modern civil rights movement: *Brown* v. *Board of Education* (1954). African-American protests against segregation, which had been voiced for decades, were finally being heard.

It was during this simmering period, which roughly coincided with Truman's presidency, that Carl T. Rowan entered the civil rights fray in dramatic fashion as an earnest reporter. In 1947—when Rowan graduated from Oberlin College in Ohio with hopes of becoming the next Ernie Pyle—there were no black broadcasters or screenplay writers or accomplished journalists. The American mass media was uninterested in reporting honestly about the race problem in the South, and the handful of writers who occasionally did—such as Lillian Smith, Jonathan Daniels, Ralph McGill, Harry Golden, and Ashley Montagu—were white. But there was a group of African-American-owned newspapers, such as the Norfolk *Journal and Guide*, the Pittsburgh *Courier*, the Baltimore *Afro-American*, and the Chicago *Defender*, that reported lynchings, commonplace beatings, and the frequent jailing of southern blacks, on a regular basis. In 1950 no more than five African Americans could claim to be mainstream general-assignment reporters, and none was writing much that was truly informative about race relations. What was missing was an African American with a keen eye and the gift of writing to penetrate the Deep South and expose the brutality of Jim Crow in a sober, reflective way worthy of the most objective New York *Times* reporting. Rowan, hired by the Minneapolis *Tribune's* white integrationist publisher John Cowles, Sr., would soon prove equal to the task.

At first Rowan covered the Twin Cities back-page beat like any other rookie reporter, astounded to encounter naked racism in every corner of metropolitan life, including the Radisson Hotel on Seventh Street, which refused to register the world-renowned contralto Marian Anderson as a guest unless she promised to ride the freight elevator and not enter the dining room. Though postwar Minnesotans considered themselves progressive on the race issue, Rowan quickly learned that blacks, Jews, and Native Americans were by and large still treated as second- or third-class citizens by the white establishment.

But Rowan was determined not to be the "token Negro" on the *Tribune's* staff, covering only "black events" as if he were incapable of writing up City Hall scandals or Mississippi River floods. Rowan intuitively understood that if he were to make it as a big-league print journalist, he would have to move in the same circles and get the same assignments as the white staff. But he added a caveat, following it like gospel: "Your determination not to become a token Negro reporter must not deter you from telling decent, thoughtful Americans some truths that only you can tell them." Rowan understood that the "truth" regarding racism in 1950 was hard for white citizens to comprehend, for they had worn blinders on the issue since the days of Christopher Columbus. Assiduously, he searched for an opening to expose American racism in print, until a grand notion came to him. Why not write a series of unvarnished reports from Dixie on black/white relations for the Minneapolis *Tribune*?

In an act of hubris he would never regret, Rowan drafted a

memorandum to his managing editor, Paul Swensson, a first-rate
newspaperman, proposing that the *Tribune* send him to the South
to report on the legacy of Jim Crow. To his astonishment, Swensson,
along with executive editor Bill Steven, thought it an inspired idea,
one that would change the face of American journalism, and they
approved a travel budget for a series of eighteen articles under the
provocative title "How Far From Slavery?" Rowan was beside himself with cautious joy: "I left town knowing that while fate may have
smiled upon me, I was the only one who had to survive travel into
my native Tennessee; into a brutally racist city, Birmingham, Alabama; into Gene Talmadge's Georgia; into a troubled New Orleans
and a violent Monroe in Louisiana; and into a Southwest smoldering
under the passions of legal assaults upon segregation in universities
and other public facilities." The *Tribune's* cub reporter was truly
heading "south of freedom."

Flying from Minneapolis to Louisville to Nashville in January,
1951, Rowan began his six-week odyssey in his hometown of Mc-
Minnville, startled to see how little civil rights progress had been
made south of the Mason-Dixon line. "Buttressed by self-caution
and the feeling that I knew my way around the devious halls of Jim
Crow, I returned to McMinnville, to the familiar gravel streets that
I had walked for almost two decades," Rowan wrote, using his old
haunts as prose launching pads for his trek. Things were so bad in
central Tennessee that Rowan soon realized he wasn't going to have
to preach about the evils of racism—all he had to do was report
the truth. Not only were African Americans still ordered to use
separate restrooms, water fountains, restaurants, waiting rooms,
swimming pools, bus seats, and libraries, but they were often refused treatment at hospitals, dying on the doorstep from lack of
medical attention. And just sleuthing around McMinnville in sport
coat and necktie, with notebook in hand, was enough to raise whites'
eyebrows. "Come home, again, nigger, and we'll have a delegation
out to meet you, and it won't be no brass band," read one of the
hate letters Rowan received after his arrival. In the all-white neighboring town of Crossville, Rowan was greeted with a placard hanging from a tree at the city limits: NIGGER DON'T LET THE SUN SET

ON YOU HERE. At least a dozen times during his sojourn, Rowan feared for his life, particularly as he pushed the limits of Jim Crow to see how far they would bend. And he learned early in his journey not to generalize about the South, for a "Negro can do things in one town that he would be killed for seventy-five miles away."

Upon leaving McMinnville, Rowan headed to nearby Columbia, where race riots had recently grabbed headlines, and then to Alcoa, an area regenerated by the New Deal's TVA rural electrification program but still degenerated by Jim Crow paradoxes. Surprisingly, the most dehumanizing events occurred in Washington, D.C., where segregation was vigorously enforced. Whether he visited one of the Senate office buildings or Nedick's hamburger stand or the Y.M.C.A., the young reporter was shunned because his skin was black. "Washington," Rowan surmised about what would someday become his home, "leads the nation in segregation and discrimination in many respects."

Humiliating experiences in the nation's capital taught Rowan that segregation was a religion and that to even think of challenging the warped logic of white supremacy made one a heretic. Rowan rode with whites on a Georgia railcoach, beating Jim Crow, but in Macon he was nearly arrested for trying to purchase a newspaper in the "white" waiting room at the station. In Miami he entered a hotel and matter-of-factly asked for a room, only to be met with a bewildered expression. Racial segregation was all most southern whites understood. The apartheid system was beneficial to African Americans, whites believed, because it gave them a sense of hierarchical place: the bottom of the heap. Wherever Rowan traveled—even in supposedly cosmopolitan cities such as Charleston, New Orleans, and Atlanta—obsessive worship of Jim Crow dominated all aspects of civic life. "Atlanta is racially segregated by law and custom, and the human straightjacket that this imposes was as evident in Atlanta as elsewhere," Rowan wrote about the supposed citadel of the tolerant "New South." Everywhere Rowan went in Dixie, he encountered bigotry and ignorance, blanketing the region as thickly as kudzu.

When Rowan returned from his assignment, the Minneapolis

Tribune printed his eighteen articles (February–March, 1951), creating a nationwide journalistic sensation. Anecdotes about Carl T. Rowan's journey into the belly of the beast appeared in all the leading black newspapers. White intellectuals who had championed Richard Wright's *Native Son* and *Black Boy* were now touting Rowan's razor-sharp prose. *Time* magazine called his articles "a perceptive well-written series on segregation and prejudice in the South as only a Negro could know them." *Editor & Publisher* considered the "How Far From Slavery?" reports "a significant readable glimpse into the American race problem as only a Negro sees it." And, most important of all, fifty-nine-year-old Alfred Knopf flew from New York to Minneapolis to offer a $1,500 advance for a book based on the articles.

Success came pouring in from all corners for the journalistic Horatio Alger who dared to tweak Jim Crow. Not wanting to lose their ace reporter to a bigger daily, the *Tribune* upped Rowan's weekly salary from $80 to $92. Civic groups and churches began offering him $35 to deliver a single speech on the "Negro Problem." Lincoln University in Jefferson City, Missouri, cited Rowan for "high purpose, high achievement, and exemplary practice in the field of journalism." The Sidney Hillman Foundation presented him its annual award and a $500 check for "the best newspaper reporting in the nation in 1951," while, incredibly, the white Minneapolis Junior Chamber of Commerce named him Minneapolis Outstanding Young Man of 1951. "I was in heaven," Rowan recalled as he started the nine-month process of turning his articles into *South of Freedom*.

Though the core of the book emanates from Rowan's *Tribune* series, a great deal of additional material and intellectual reconsideration went into *South of Freedom* to make it a modern classic. It is not merely a compilation of newspaper articles but a fully realized autobiographical narrative. Although Arna Bontemps in the *Saturday Review* compared *South of Freedom* to Richard Wright's *Native Son* and Ralph Ellison's *Invisible Man*, in many regards Rowan's book was built on Du Bois' *The Souls of Black Folk*. Often *South of Freedom* reads like a sociological polemic, a "balance-sheet of

American race relations," as Rowan phrased it. But at other times the Tennessean abandons the social scientist posture and allows pure prose poetry to pour out of his pen as if he were Thomas Wolfe in search of America: "A bright moon splattered the lumpy earth; the ghostly light reflected off naked bushes that shivered in a slight breeze. To my mind, still accustomed to crusty piles of snow that would hide Minnesota earth for months to come, the illusion was one of heat waves rising from sun-baked soil in August. The highway was like a brightly polished corridor that suddenly pitched off into spacious darkness when the road dipped over a steep hill or curved stubbornly with the terrain."

As a "road book," *South of Freedom* shows just how wide the racial gulf between Jack Kerouac and Carl T. Rowan was. If in *On the Road*[2] Kerouac headed South in a burst of Whitmanesque Romanticism, listening to Lester Young jazz, smelling magnolias, and "digging" black culture, Rowan's highway narrative is devoid of reckless joy, offering only overcrowded ghettos, sharecroppers' shacks, and loudmouthed bigots. Kerouac and Rowan were living in two different Americas just as surely as white and black southerners were. If Kerouac found existential freedom driving down the Great American Road, Rowan found paranoia, constantly worrying about race-baiting police, white citizens' councils, and lynching trees. "The last thing I had in mind was to romance the South like Kerouac," Rowan noted. "My task was to expose harsh injustice."

Nearly half a century has passed since Carl T. Rowan wrote *South of Freedom*. During the ensuing years he went on to become one of America's most recognizable journalistic figures: author of numerous books and articles, a nationally syndicated columnist for the Chicago *Daily News* and the Chicago *Sun Times,* and a regular pundit on any number of Washington-based television shows. Professional honors came cascading down on Rowan, and included his serving as John F. Kennedy's Ambassador to Finland; as Lyndon B. Johnson's director of the U.S. Information Agency, replacing the

2. Kerouac wrote *On the Road* between 1948 and 1956, but Viking Penguin did not publish the autobiographical novel until 1957.

venerable Edward R. Murrow; serving as president of the Gridiron Club; becoming biographer to Supreme Court Justice Thurgood Marshall; and earning fifty-six honorary degrees, the great majority from "white" universities. For almost fifty years Rowan has played many roles on the American stage, but he has never been Ralph Ellison's "Invisible Man."

When one harkens back to that warm August afternoon in 1952, when Carl T. Rowan read in the New York *Times* that he would not in his lifetime become a "first-class citizen everywhere in his country," one can only celebrate the inaccuracy of that prediction. Not only did Jim Crow die, but Rowan became a first-class citizen of the world, a special confidant of presidents and prime ministers alike. What Hodding Carter had failed to comprehend was that by writing *South of Freedom* Rowan had obliterated "Jim-Crow-of-the-mind," freeing himself to become a first-class reporter, which was what he always wanted to be. Rowan had dissected the segregated South so thoroughly, so devastatingly, that the astute reader knew it would only be a matter of time before the racist pillars of segregation would start to wobble and fall.

The landmark *Brown v. Board of Education* ruling came a short eighteen months after *South of Freedom*'s publication, as if Rowan were a harbinger of the coming civil rights movement. And though now best viewed as a historical document in the struggle for African-American equality, *South of Freedom* remains, as *The Nation* stated in 1952, "a book every American should read." It serves as a dramatic reminder of how far America has come in establishing democratic justice, and how far we still have to go before equality becomes a reality.

Eisenhower Center for American Studies
University of New Orleans

South

O F

Freedom

CHAPTER I

MY NATIVE LAND

I REMEMBER 1943 as the year of the "great rebellion." For it was in the summer of 1943 that my mind, heart, and soul rebelled and ceased being part of a green, small-town Negro youth, well-schooled in the ways of his native South. During that summer, I broke all mental ties with my home town; yet, physically, I was still very much a part of McMinnville, Tennessee, a farm-industrial community of about five thousand persons, at the foot of the Cumberland Mountains. It was a foolish and rather dangerous predicament for a young Southern Negro.

As I remember that Summer, I realize how fortunate I was to get out of McMinnville. Obviously, I had lost my usefulness to that middle-Tennessee community; and I cannot remember McMinnville ever being of particular usefulness to me. I had returned to McMinnville after spending my freshman year at Tennessee Agricultural and Industrial State College in Nashville. I felt that even in those nine months of college life I had outgrown my narrow life in McMinnville. I betrayed my feelings easily, much to the irritation of whites whose lawns I had mowed, whose windows I had washed, or whose basements I had scrubbed in past years.

During my year at Tennessee State, I had passed tests given by the United States Navy and was promised the opportunity to earn a commission, something the Navy had given no Negro at the time. After being sworn in at Nashville, I had returned to McMinnville, an apprentice seaman in the Naval Reserve. I was on inactive duty, awaiting assignment to what, in effect, was to be officers' candidate school.

3

For nearly eighteen years, practically all my life, I had lived in McMinnville. I had mowed lawns, swept basements, unloaded boxcars of coal, dug basements, hoed bulb-grass out of lawns, and done scores of other menial tasks that fell to Negroes by default. Until 1943, I did these jobs because almost all McMinnville Negroes did such jobs; the community expected it of us. In 1943, with Negro manpower already swept away by the draft board, I could see that I was expected to handle a greater-than-normal share of such jobs. But my year outside McMinnville, and my status as a Navy man, created revulsion within me and an air of haughtiness not designed to make me popular with the white citizens of my home town.

The Navy had put me outside the jurisdiction of draft boards, so, unlike many "rebellious" Negroes of the South, I could not be railroaded into the Armed Forces as punishment for offending some staunch citizen by rejecting his dirty chores. The Navy already had me, and I would be around until the Navy decided I should move elsewhere. I felt that, for the first time in my life, I was out of reach of all McMinnville and all her twenty-five-cents-an-hour jobs.

I became self-employed. I had learned to weave cane bottoms and backs for chairs in a shopwork class at Bernard High School, where the instructor had charged chair owners a very modest amount and the pupils did the work for sticks of peppermint candy. Since Bernard no longer was doing such work, I had a corner on the market. I tripled the charges and notified the "antique furniture" set that I was in business. Soon I had enough chairs piled up at my home to keep me busy most of the summer.

Tennessee summer days were not made for work; in fact, many a resident has doubted that they were made at all, but that they sprang to life from the caldrons of hell. In any event, I dressed more like a Southern Colonel than a Southern Negro, and spent the days reading. Occasionally I strolled through town, driving town and military policemen almost crazy in their efforts to understand how an apparently able-bodied Negro male had escaped the draft board. In three months they stopped me at least thirty times, demanding to see my draft-registration card.

That I was stopped so frequently was partially attributable to my conspicuous dress. Any Negro in a small Southern town is viewed with suspicion if he wears a tie and suit on weekdays, unless he is the principal of the Negro school, or perhaps a minister. I wore suits, which, though secondhand, were new to McMinnville. I had got them at the State Tuberculosis Hospital in Nashville, where I worked the summer of 1942 to earn tuition funds. I had left McMinnville for Nashville that summer—with seventy-seven cents in my pocket, and my clothes in a cardboard box—aboard a Mc- Broom Lines truck on which I had wangled a ride from the white driver. I remember him only as a good Joe who drove me out to the college campus because he figured I could stand to save the bus fare.

At the hospital I carried food to the patients, bussed and washed dishes, swept ward floors and screens, and did almost everything but wash the nurses' feet. But I needed the thirty dollars a month—desperately. Occasionally, a doctor would complain that he had outgrown a suit. He would pass it to me, suggesting that I find someone who could use it. That was a fairly simple assignment. These suits made me one of the best-dressed freshmen on the Tennessee State campus; and but for my Naval Reserve card would have made me one of the best-dressed McMinnvillians ever jailed on a vagrancy charge.

After loafing through the blistering days that summer in McMinnville, I worked while the community slept. I weaved cane far into the cool night-hours, when the town was so silent that the rustle of wind in the pear tree behind the house was like the echo of a thousand chorus-girls, simultaneously swishing their taffeta skirts.

Early mornings, shortly after crawling into bed, and in the

daze of half-sleep, I could smell boiling coffee and fried white salt-pork, and hear the splatter of hot grease as eggs were dropped into a frying-pan. Soon my father would be off to his job, stacking lumber at a near-by mill. And the rest of my family would be up, some heading for what work they could find, and my two younger sisters off to play. I would sleep until the sun's merciless rays curled the tin roof and drove me out of bed.

But morning after morning, before I arose, one or more cars pulled up in front of the house. A voice, obviously of a white person, would ask youngsters playing near by if "Tom Rowan's boy" lived there. "Yessir, Carl Rowan lives there," some child would reply, and, without further instructions, a clattering horde of kids would stampede into the house and to my bed to say: "Some white man wants you out there."

This irked me enough; but the whites always came with a half-demand, saying: "Somebody *has got* to do this job for me," and they irritated me until I acquired a smart-aleck disposition that was not part of my true nature. I had begun to love independence, and it pleased a part of me that I could not name, or even place, to be able to say that "Tom Rowan's boy" didn't *have* to do the job.

A man named Hunter, whose lawn I had mowed scores of times in previous years, several times for ten cents an hour, had me awakened early one morning. "Boy, they (he didn't say who) tell me uptown that you ain't doin' nothing. We're going to have a lawn party, and I gotta have my grass cut." With what now strikes me as boldness verging on recklessness, I told him that I had been so busy lately that I planned to hire someone to mow my lawn. He looked at my house, which sat about two feet off the gravel street, those two feet of yard containing not one blade of grass. He gave me a stare of contempt and drove away.

With reluctant thanks to man's greediness and inclination to war, I got out of McMinnville before I so provoked the whites as to jeopardize my physical well-being. One morning in late October I was ordered to active duty. On October 30, 1943, my secondhand clothes in a borrowed suitcase, I boarded a Jim Crow train and left the past and present of a life that I had begun to abhor. I had received more than the call of the United States Navy; as it turned out, I was answering the call of opportunity, for my hello to arms was farewell to the South in which I had been born and reared.

That I was leaving by Jim Crow train meant little to me then. Jim Crow was all I had known. For all the years that I had lived in the shadow of the Cumberland Mountains, two things were always certain: racial segregation and a steady stream of moonshine liquor out of the hills. I was a small-time youngster, off to a big-time war, riding the train for the first time in my life; and except for an accidental journey into Alabama aboard a lost bus, I was leaving Tennessee for the first time. Caught in a maelstrom of excitement, I could get little disturbed about Jim Crow—even when I was refused a Pullman berth from Nashville to St. Louis, despite a Navy order. The ticket-seller told me none was available, and, even after my "great rebellion," I had not acquired the habit of challenging the word of a white man—not even after watching several whites get berths after my request was rejected. I took my first-class ticket and boarded a last-class coach, as Negroes had done for years.

I propped my head on my hand and dozed that Autumn night as my dirty, smoky Jim Crow coach rolled across Kentucky and southern Illinois. I was bound for Topeka, Kansas, and a Navy V-12 unit at Washburn Municipal University. There I found that I had crossed from my world of bare black feet on red clay and white perspiration on black brows into a strange new land. I had been snatched completely from a life of segregation; I was in a unit of 335 sailors, 334 of them white.

Part Two

In 1951, nearly eight years later, I returned to McMinnville. It was the opening of old wounds. It was like rolling
back time. I found that Negro youths still leaned against the
First National Bank Building, where I once leaned hour
upon hour. We had no place to go, nothing to do except wait
for a white man to come along and offer twenty-five cents an
hour for whatever job had gone without white takers.

There was the colored section of town. It was the same
squalor, the same unpainted dwellings huddled close to narrow, hole-filled streets, some of which town officials had
named, with apparent sincerity, "African Avenue," "Egypt Alley," and "Congo Street." The same paths led through weedy
backyards to smelly wooden privies.

There, on Congo Street, was the little frame house in
which I had lived during my early teen-age years. To the rear
of it was a row of privies, and in front of it had been a junkyard. I recalled hot summer days when I sat on the rough
oak front-porch with my brother and sisters. On those sultry
afternoons we would watch the mountains, waiting for them
to belch up the rain that we knew was coming. As the downpour rode across the distant fields like a wind-driven silver
wave, we young dreamers would pretend that this was a
magic puff of rain that would cleanse McMinnville of junk-
yards and privies, pave Congo Street and give it a new name,
and transform our frame house into a stone mansion with a
huge brick chimney.

Upon returning, I found the house still frame. It was partially wired for electricity and had an outdoor hydrant for
city water, two improvements over my days there. I had carried water from a neighbor's house at the end of the water-
supply main, more than a block away, or fought off black
gnats while filling my bucket at Hughes's spring. But the

privies still were there; and weeds and wild cane had hidden remnants of the junkyard in a veritable wilderness. Weeds and time had even choked out two peach trees that I once robbed with great delight. It appeared that McMinnville Negroes still were waiting for that magic rainstorm to wash away deprivation and human wretchedness.

But I did not return to *expose* McMinnville, or the South. You do not expose racial hatred and social and economic injustices any more than you expose a fresh dunghill; you tell Americans that it exists and wait until the wind blows in their direction. I returned to McMinnville, to my native Dixie, to keep a promise to a white Southern sailor who found in 1943 that he was a stranger in his native land. I was to pay a debt to this sailor who had helped to keep me from being a stranger when I so abruptly left the world of segregation.

I had reached Topeka with no idea as to the nature of my Navy unit. Although the Navy had promised me the opportunity to earn a commission, I knew that it was notorious for restricting Negroes to mess-attendant duties. I also knew that the Navy followed the segregation pattern of the South, which I had just left, so I expected segregation at Washburn.

I reached the campus and stared up a long, tree-lined driveway at the University buildings. It was a warm night, with the kind of breeze poets write of, and sailors and their girls lined the driveway like Burma Shave signs. I saw that they all were white sailors, and I wondered, as I walked toward the nearest building, where the back road was. Because of my background, I thought they must have reserved another road for Negro sailors and their girls.

I walked into a building as white sailors observed me with ill-concealed curiosity. I asked where I should report, and was directed to the Administration building. The looks on a few faces made me feel as if I had barged into a ladies' restroom. I paused under a street light and re-read my orders. Thus assured that at least I was at the correct school, I reported to the Administration building. A chief petty officer named

Pappas and a Lt. Beuhler gave me an extra-warm welcome. As Pappas stepped near me to hand me a slip with my house, room, and bunk numbers on it, he whispered: "I don't think you'll be *lonely* here."

Then I sensed that I was a lone Negro in a white unit. The First National Bank Building was gone. I had nothing on which to lean. It was like losing a raft after drifting out from shore: I would either sink or swim.

But the white sailors and I found that the things we had in common far outweighed our differences. We all hated early-morning calisthenics, Friday afternoon drills, and Saturday inspections. The color of my skin became less important daily. When Charley Van Horn of Coffeyville, Kansas, learned that he was to be my roommate, he quipped: "I'll be too damned busy trying to memorize Ohm's law and pass this physics course to count the pigment in your skin." That is how it was.

For Noah Brannon, a religion student who planned to become a chaplain, it was not so simple. Brannon came from near Brownsville, Texas, where prejudices run a bit deeper, perhaps, than in Coffeyville. But Brannon loved music, and that is where we found our common ground—he at the piano and I above him, singing "My Ideal," "Star Eyes" or some other popular song. We quickly became piano pals.

But I was the first Negro whom Brannon had known on an equal basis. One day he said to me, with the startled expression of a man awakening in the darkness and feeling a stranger in bed with him: "Carl, where is that overpowering odor they told me all Negroes have?"

Laughter spread to every muscle of my face. I thought Brannon's first racial question was exceedingly funny. Then I saw the utter sincerity of his expression as he awaited my answer. I bit my lip to recall laughter and wipe the smile wrinkles off my face. I offered a serious reply:

"If I don't have such an odor, Noah, I must have lost it in

the shower room. I'll bet that could happen to anybody—of any race."

Brannon shook his head as an admission of naïveté. I soon learned that he was even more misinformed about Negroes. "Until I met you, Carl, I didn't even know Negroes had last names. Honestly," he went on as I gave him a look of disbelief, "we always called them 'Aunt Susie' or 'Uncle Charlie'!"

I explained to Brannon that, for decades, the South had refused to accord to Negroes the dignity of the titles Mr. and Mrs. A large segment had refused to acknowledge the Negro as participant in the institution of a family, so in the minds of these people Negroes could have no family name. "Is it possible that you grew up in an area of such great darkness, and among people who wanted to keep you misinformed?" I asked, trying to emphasize the human and regional background of something that had struck my friend only as "peculiar" at the time.

Brannon expressed amazement when I told him that in Mc-Minnville I could not get a drink of water in any drugstore unless the fountain clerk could find a paper cup. (I found on my return that this is still the custom; no Negro drinks out of a glass.)

One afternoon in June 1944, nearly eight months after we had met, Brannon abruptly stopped playing "I'll be Seeing You." I had been ordered to a new station, and I could see that before we parted he wanted to get something off his mind. He turned to me and said: "You plan to be a writer after the war. Some time, why don't you just sit down and tell all the little things it means to be a Negro in the South, or anyplace where being a Negro makes a difference. It all was right there before my eyes, but I'd never have known it. You probably can't get a drink of water in a Brownsville drugstore either.

"If you're a Southern white person, you see these things and you don't. You're taught not to care. It's something that exists because it exists. Don't preach, but tell it all," Brannon pleaded, "for there must be many people in the South with big hearts but so little knowledge of this thing."

I promised Noah Brannon that some day I would tell Americans of "the little things" about being a Negro in America, and seven years later I had not forgotten. Because Brannon's words kept haunting me—and because a secretary made a typing error—I was able to keep my promise.

In December 1950, I asked for a change in my days off at the Minneapolis *Morning Tribune*. The change was approved by City Editor Bower Hawthorne, but in revising the work schedule his secretary unwittingly gave me an extra day off. I knew that I was to work that extra day, but the assistant city editor who made story assignments did not, and he was somewhat surprised when I reported for work. He had assigned someone to each of the immediate news events, so I retired to the library to do research on a story for the following Sunday. As I rambled through the files of the *New York Times*, stories about Negroes and happenings in the South kept staring out of the pages at me, reminding me of my promise to Brannon. I stopped my research and wrote Hawthorne a memorandum, suggesting that I be allowed to return to the South to gather data on Negro life for my report to all of America's Noah Brannons.

There was much more to tell than I had been able to discuss with Brannon, I told Hawthorne. There was much about being a Negro in the South that I had not personally experienced. There were new things happening in my native land, things that I should be able to interpret because of my Southern birth and background. I proposed that I be allowed to write a series of articles on the South, to tell the story as it is seen by a Negro who has lived it; to tell it not in terms of the statistician or the politician or the professional ranter on either side of the fence, but in the human terms of the men, women, and children who live and are the South. I suggested that I start by revisiting McMinnville and that I go on to scores of cities, towns, and villages throughout the South and the District of Columbia.

Despite the *Tribune's* well-earned reputation as a champion of racial justice, I feared that my three-page memorandum would be laughed off. Both the race question and the South were explosive subjects, and, with a few notable exceptions, had been given only cursory treatment in the daily American press. I took a copy of my memorandum home. When my wife and I had finished laughing at what we considered my audacity, I had built up a dread of going to work the next day. But I went to work and was surprised. Hawthorne had liked the idea, as had Managing Editor Paul Swensson. Executive Editor Gideon Seymour agreed that there was much America's Noah Brannons ought to be told. But I knew that Seymour would remember a day in August 1948, when I talked to him about a job on the *Tribune*. I was about to receive my master's degree in journalism from the University of Minnesota's School of Journalism. I had walked into the *Star* and *Tribune* personnel department and asked for a job, the way any other applicant would have done. I wanted the same kind of job that any other applicant would expect. That was how Seymour wanted it: we both agreed that the only terms on which I would work for the *Tribune* were that I be just another newsman, that I not be a specialist in so-called Negro news. Seymour did remember that day, and he mentioned it, because he figured—correctly —that there would be readers who would accuse the *Tribune* of exploiting the fact that I was a Negro. But we agreed that the project was more important than all such accusations, so he approved the assignment, with only libel laws and truthfulness to limit what I could write. His sole plea was that I try to stay out of jail. I knew then that for the first time a daily metropolitan newspaper was going to print a Negro's account of Negro life in the kingdom of Jim Crow.

So on January 11, 1951, I returned to the South, where the color of my skin counts above all things. I returned to a

South that had undergone many changes since Noah Brannon and I shared torch tunes and laughed at racial myths that antedate slavery. I wondered just how much change had taken place since my childhood. Certainly, I would find the Negro better off in some big and some small ways. Aided by the federal courts, he had made much progress toward equality of educational opportunity on higher levels; yet I knew that complete equality still was far away. In other fields —employment, health, and equality at the hands of the law —progress had come at snail's pace.

But this progress, made largely during and after World War II, had stirred Southerners proudly to proclaim a New South. They spoke of ferment within the South, and self-styled Southern liberals swore that out of this social upheaval was to emerge a new day for the Negro in Dixieland.

"Will I find a New South?" I asked myself as once again I turned my face toward the land of mint juleps, cotton rows, and peanut patches. I looked at democracy and civilization, caught in the shadows of their gloomiest hour, and I hoped that I would find a New South. I hoped that I would find the social turmoil of a white South casting off the mental shackles of belief in white supremacy; and a Negro South casting off old, uncertain fetters in preparation and demand for a new day. Together, I believed, they could lift the South out of its decades-old social and economic morass, and give American democracy a sword of unity to help cut the threads of international despair.

CHAPTER II

JOURNEY INTO DOUBT

I took a plane as far South as Nashville, but before I got that far across the Mason-Dixon line (which is more an attitude, locked in the minds of men, than a geographical boundary) I saw plainly that the Old South is not dead. At the Louisville airport I went to a candy stand. One white soldier was there, and the attendant waited on him. By this time, other whites reached the stand. The attendant passed me going down the counter and waited on whites. When she ignored me going up the counter, I walked away. This was the old racial protocol system that I had known since my childhood. I knew that I would be served only after all whites had been waited on. I was acutely aware that once again I was in Dixie, land of my birth and childhood.

Were there any doubts, my arrival in Nashville dispelled them. I had flown through Nashville in 1945, and at that time there was no segregated seating in the airport. This time, as I stepped into the building, I noticed a sign on the wall just above two chairs. It read: FOR COLORED PASSENGERS ONLY. There also were four toilets, one for white men and one for colored men; another was marked WHITE LADIES, and yet another, COLORED WOMEN. I took a picture of these signs, doing it as slyly as I could. Then I laughed a puzzled laugh of dejection, and walked out of the airport.

I entered the airport office of the Hertz Drive-Ur-Self System. I had asked the airline to see that I had a car waiting. "I'm Rowan of the Minneapolis Tribune," I said to the attendant. "I believe you have a car waiting for me."

"You . . . you're Rowan?" he replied.

15

"That's right, Carl T. Rowan. I believe Eastern Air Lines wired from Chicago."

The attendant glanced at my identification and began to write on some forms. He tossed some keys to a Negro porter who sat near by, and ordered him to "bring up car 42."

A few minutes later I was driving a 1950 Chevrolet. I was surprised—but the Hertz agent didn't know it. I was laughing—laughing at the serious "Oh, no!" that I got for an answer when I jokingly asked the porter if car 42 came equipped with a time-bomb.

The Jim Crow signs in the airport and the courteous Hertz attendant were typical of the unpredictable South that I had known. They illustrate what it is like to be a Negro. It is a life of doubt, of uncertainty as to what the reception will be, even from one building to another. It is this doubt that permeates Negro life in the North as well as the South. In the North, the doubt is created by whites who circumvent democratic laws by subterfuge, in the South, the doubt springs from the fact that, because few statutes exist that are favorable to the Negro, the white man's mood and spoken word become law. Whatever the Southern white man decides for the Negro has the sanction of tradition, and against tradition there has been little legal recourse.

As I drove that rented car through cracker-barrel hamlets and along highways that snaked across fields laden with shocks of dead cornstalks and cotton plants browned by winter's chill, I realized that I had come face to face with doubt. Doubt as to which filling-station would allow me to buy gasoline and also to use the toilet. Doubt as to which restaurant would sell me food, even to take out. Doubt as to which cities forbid Negroes to ride in white cabs, and whites to ride in Negro cabs. I remembered that in order to give my report to America's Noah Brannons I was to cover some six thousand miles of Southland. In five weeks I was to visit towns and cities in thirteen states and the District of Columbia. For my own safety I would have to erase some of the doubt.

I would have to remember to wear a tie on the bus from Nashville to McMinnville. In that area, a Negro fares better if he looks educated and willing to demand the few rights he possesses. I would have to remember *not* to wear a tie in several small towns in Georgia, Mississippi, South Carolina, Louisiana, or anywhere in the Deep South. A Negro can get killed in those areas for "dressing and acting like white folks." Americans who doubt this will have forgotten the name of Robert Mallard, an insurance salesman who was lynched at Lyons, Georgia, in November of 1948.

Mallard's only crime discovered thus far is that he drove a car and wore a suit when white Toombs County men wore overalls.

I knew that on highways, where all-white patrols enforce the law, I must always be prepared to smile meekly and question nothing should patrolmen stop me.

I remembered June of 1946, when, after release from active duty with the Atlantic Fleet, I returned to Tennessee for two weeks. In Nashville four GI college students and fellow McMinnvillians asked if I'd like to ride in their car to McMinnville. I accepted the invitation. About twenty-five miles out of Nashville we met a car with two highway patrolmen. "I'll bet a dollar they turn around," said R. C. Brown. Before anyone could accept the wager, I looked out the rear window and saw the brake lights flash red on their car. Paul Bates, our driver, slowed the car down to ten miles below the speed limit.

The patrolmen soon caught us and ordered Bates to stop. We sat silent as the patrolmen got out. One said to Bates: "Boy, we got a tip that y'all are hauling liquor."

"No, sir. Where did you get any tip like that?"

"That ain't for you to know. All you boys get out."

I pushed my suitcase out before me and stepped onto the highway. As the last man got out, one patrolman pulled the rear seat into the street. No liquor.

"You, boy, what you got in that grip?"

It had been a long time since I had been called "boy." Evidently this patrolman did not know that, in getting my Navy commission, I had become a gentleman, by act of Congress; and that people—even white people—had called me mister since I last was in Tennessee. I didn't think it was the time or place to apprise him of such happenings, however. "Clothing," I replied in a voice that was high-pitched with anger.

"Zoot-suit clothes?" he continued.

"Just plain old everyday clothing."

"Aw, surely some of you black boys can dance," the patrolman said.

The eyes of five Negro veterans met silently. I knew that we all thought the same thing. One smart word and they might shoot us, and then swear that we "acted biggity." On the other hand, the five of us could cram their pistols right into their toenails—but we still would lose in the long run. We stood silent, staring eye-to-eye at each other and the patrolmen.

"You boys git," said one with finality. "Guess you boys ain't the bootleggers."

I looked at my unsearched suitcase and at unsearched parts of the car where hundreds of bottles of whisky could have been hidden. But Bates had it all figured out: "They weren't looking for any liquor. They just wanted to have a little fun."

By 1951 it was just another memory, if an unpleasant one. It was simply another item in my frame of reference for the South. And as I recalled the incident, I was not stricken with fear or thoughts about the danger of my assignment. I felt fortunate in having had the experience, because I would be prepared if it happened again. That is, I would be prepared to answer if addressed as "boy," to smile if a white man insulted me under circumstances where he obviously was in power, and even to dance a little jig should I encounter two armed patrolmen bent on having some fun.

Part Two

Buttressed by self-caution and the feeling that I knew my way around in the devious halls of Jim Crow, I returned to McMinnville, to the familiar gravel streets that I had walked for almost two decades. I returned to frame houses with decaying foundations, to yards barren of grass, and even the tiniest hovel with the farthest-away privy had its nostalgic meaning. Some were houses where human beings—people I knew—lived like rats, and where rats outnumbered the people. Some were houses I knew by the starred flags of World War II, which still hung dusty in windows. They were houses where my schoolmates lived, or once had lived.

Beside one house, youngsters in skimpy, tattered clothing played hopscotch on squares marked off in the earth. As one lad hopped, he held up a foot, and I could see that he had put pasteboard inside his shoe to cover a hole. I could have told him from personal experience that linoleum lasts longer than pasteboard. This was in 1951, when Americans, speaking of economics, would tell you that "times were good." But a youngster hopscotching with holes in his shoes was not part of a New South, this was the McMinnville I had left.

I went to a dumpy little café that townspeople call "The Slobbery Rock." That name aptly describes the shaky old structure, which sits on a rocky ledge just two blocks from the heart of downtown. A jukebox blared out a blues tune. High-school youngsters of fourteen to sixteen, and a drunken woman of at least fifty-five, dragged across the sawdust-strewn dance floor. The air was thick with greasy smoke, heavy with the mingled odors of laborers and schoolgirl perfumes. There, at The Slobbery Rock, gathered ninety-nine per cent of Negro McMinnville's youth, out for their weekend entertainment.

As I sat at a grimy table, covered with a wrinkled oilcloth,

I watched gamblers, bootleggers, and harlots ply their trades. But I knew I had not gone slumming. That was *my* club ten years before. From 1938 to 1942, weekend after weekend, I was at The Slobbery Rock, or in the adjoining poolhall. My mother still may not know that at fourteen I was the "colored Willie Hoppe" of our town.

When I was a youth, Negro youngsters had two choices for away-from-home entertainment. They went to one of the two segregated movies, where they sat in a balcony not even provided with a restroom; then they either went home or to "The Rock." It takes no sociologist to guess which course they usually chose. McMinnville did have one other Negro café, but it was too small for dancing and usually closed very early. There was a skating rink—barred to Negroes. There was a tax-supported swimming-pool—barred to Negroes.

My return reminded me of days when I swam in the Barren Forks River with my buddies—Buford Hunter, Franklin Woodley, Paul Officer, all good swimmers. Often, after a heavy rain, the river was muddy. You could squeeze a handful of water and watch the red residue settle between your fingers as the water oozed out. Still, we swam in it, for it was a recreational gift from nature. We would swim a half mile upstream from our rendezvous and tread water under the bridge carrying the highway to Camp Forrest and Tullahoma, Tennessee. On the shore near the bridge was the city swimming-pool, where whites frolicked in blue, chlorinated water. We sometimes splashed near by for hours, masking our resentment behind wisecracks.

Woodley might look longingly at the pool's blue waters. "Where there's life, there's hope," he would quip, more out of sarcasm than optimism.

Hunter would cease splashing the murky water and add: "Yeah, and where there's a tree, there's a rope."

Those two quotes are an old Southern proverb, familiar to almost every Negro man in the South. What they meant in our case was that the white men of McMinnville thought they were "protecting Southern white womanhood" by barring us from the pool. And, though it all seemed silly to a few guys who simply loved to swim, we knew that as long as "Southern white womanhood" frequented the pool, our chances of swimming there were slim indeed.

The situation was more than silly to us. We found it funny, in the sense that the Negro has learned to laugh at the whims of the dominant race, rather than allow them to subdue his mind and soul as well as his body. So, laughing gaily, we would file up the weedy riverbank to the highway and climb the steel rails of the bridge. We would stand on tiptoes atop the structure, flexing our muscles, peering at the water some sixty feet below. Then the white swimmers would see us, and some of the girls would run toward the bridge to see the "daring divers." When we had lured the girls from the pool (we knew the boys would follow) we would peel off like fighter planes and knife into the mudbath below.

Each would emerge with the same proud observation: "Not a soul seems interested in that pretty pool with the clear, blue water. Must be that awful chlorine that stings the eye. Anyhow, a swimming-pool is too confining." Then we would splatter downstream, having rationalized away any bitterness at discrimination in recreational opportunity.

But we could not rationalize away the effect of this recreational discrimination any more than we could use our minds to wipe out the effect of second-rate economic opportunities. Our swimming-place provided a crude sort of catharsis in our half-empty lives, serving as a recreational area, as a picnic ground, and even as a gambling-spot.

I remembered the first time I ever shot craps. I couldn't have felt more guilty if I had sneaked loaded dice into the game. I knew that to hear of me rolling dice would fairly shock a few citizens who looked at me as "Little Mr. Good Boy." After all, I had gone to church school for the seventh and eighth grades, and it was generally decided that I would become a preacher, for I could give book and verse for almost any line in the Bible.

But McMinnville citizens underestimated what the desire to please a young lady—on a $1.75-a-week job—can move a young man to do. I had started my first steady job at one dollar a week, considering a dollar better than nothing. I got a raise to $1.75 when I started going mornings before school to wash a few dishes and build a fire before my employer got up. I also backed the car out as part of my job, until one morning when I relieved a massive maple tree of much of its bark, at the same time relieving the car of its right taillight and bashing in a fender. This did not cost me my $1.75 job, since I had forewarned my employer that I couldn't drive. He had elected to gamble so as to dodge the morning chill.

By Christmas of 1939 I had saved about ten dollars. But a fuzzy, red-white-and-blue sweater had caught my fancy. When I got it and some shoes and pants at the Federated Store, my Christmas reserve had dwindled to nothing. I had exactly five cents left, and still no gift for a young lady whom I was inclined to like in those days. I dreamed of a Cashmere Bouquet set that I had seen in the J.C. Penney store window, and wondered where I would get forty-nine cents with which to buy it.

Along came the Devil in the guise of a buddy, who informed me that a few of the fellows planned a small crap game on the riverbank behind the slaughter pen where cattle were killed and cleaned. My dreams of surprising that certain girl wiped out my memory of everything from Genesis to Revelations. I joined the boys, and, as the Devil would have it, won close to two dollars. Even though my heart was shattered when an older rival who taught school gave the young lady a seven-dollar bracelet, I thought I had learned a big lesson: there were easier ways to get $1.75 than to build fires, wash dishes, and mop floors six days a week.

Eventually, something between Genesis and Revelations

won—or it could have been that the dice began to roll the other way and I realized that work was an easier, surer way. But I could sympathize with the underpaid, undereducated riverbank gamblers. I realized that you don't have to look for grime and trouble, or have an inclination for them; they wait constantly to prey on the weak and unprepared, or those without opportunity. I had realized the meaning of those hours on the First National Bank Corner, waiting for work, or those nights sitting on a sidewalk, "shooting the bull" because there was nowhere to go. They were lost, idle hours; and I had seen clearly that nothing fits idle hands like a pair of dice, or brass knuckles, or a pistol.

The McMinnville of 1951 was little different, I found. "The Rock" was still "the place to go." There was one new place, Harvey's Bar B-Q Stand. Harvey's was clean and the food delicious, but a resentful Negro community talked of boycotting it because the place, run by Harvey Faulkner, a Negro, was segregated. Negro youngsters complained that when they asked for straws in their soft drinks they were told none was available. On the other side of Harvey's, however, whites sipped through straws.

"Worst insult of all," said a Negro teacher, "are the signs put up on the colored side: NO DRINKING, NO CURSING, NO MATCHING." Faulkner had put up no such signs on the white side.

I asked Faulkner why he ran a Jim Crow place. Most cafés run by whites bar Negroes entirely, a few allowing them to enter by the back door for food to take out. A Negro ordering hamburgers at the Serv-All (sic) must stand on the street and wait until they are cooked. Harvey Faulkner knew all this as well as I. He leaned on the counter, studying my question; then, as if the answer had popped out of nowhere, snapped: "I've got to live; white folks represent nearly half my trade."

What McMinnvillian could condemn Faulkner? He had set no precedent; Negro McMinnville had done that in many ways. Had not Bernard High School annually set aside front seats for white guests who came to see our closing-of-school plays? Had not the Church of Christ reserved many of the front seats for whites who came to its tent revival? I stood in Harvey's, on the colored side, peeking around the counter into the white side, and I realized that his Jim Crow establishment was just another sacrifice offered up to the Southland's deity, segregation. Faulkner, like myself and millions of other Negroes, had made concessions to Jim Crow in adjusting his life to the South's double standard. The signs on the colored side of Harvey's were a manifestation of that double standard. In a few misty seconds, I seemed to recall countless incidents in my relatively short lifetime that were manifestations of that double standard.

Against this background, I could understand Faulkner's decision, even if I could not justify it. He had learned the who, what, when, where, and why of the South the same way I had, and the nucleus of every lesson was strict compliance with the mores of the particular community; above this there was neither justice nor common sense. That made running a café something like going home from school—the way I went home from school in the early thirties. You learned to put up a partition so white and black hands never lifted a glass from the same counter, though it be the same piece of wood, and you learned the same way I learned the ABC's of Dixie race relations: words like nigger, redneck, darky, peckerwood, shine, cracker, eight-ball, snowflake, and any combination of these with bastard or sonofabitch. The way I learned them, these were third-grade words.

McMinnville's Negro school was located in such a way that a group of white children had to pass it on their way home from their school. They met homebound Negro children, and each afternoon there would come the chant:

"Eeny, meeny, miny, mo; catch a nigger by the toe . . ."

And a Negro youngster would reply:

"We've got cheese at home; all I need is a *cracker* to go with it. . . ."

Since no group could clearly establish dominance by hurling epithets, the issue was resolved into who should use the sidewalks, and the conflict assumed physical proportions. Young fists, propelled by hatreds of past generations, hatreds no youngster could give reason for, would fly at young faces of opposite color, churning blood from noses and feeding grist to the mills of hatred for another generation. But this could not go on indefinitely—not in McMinnville. White parents apparently complained to the school superintendent, who called the Negro principal. Soon, a swollen lip betraying me as a participant in the strife, I stood before the Negro principal with several schoolmates.

With the wisdom of a man who has been burned, lecturing children against playing with fire, the principal explained that we could not win. "If the whites want the sidewalks, get off. Walk in the street," he ordered. With those words, words I dislike to remember, "peace" came to McMinnville to the extent that nobody fought over sidewalks. This was because a few youngsters walked in the street; the indomitable among us climbed fences and went home across fields rather than face the youngsters for whom we had had to give up the sidewalks. Twenty years' time has enabled McMinnville to decide that, though in passing they need not nod the "Good morning" that is typical of that small Southern town, whites and blacks may share the sidewalks. "Peace" remains with McMinnville in that sense.

It is this capacity for change that has made McMinnville a "good Southern town," in the words of her Negro citizens. They mean that for a quarter century there have been no lynchings, no race riots. Policemen do not "pick on" Negro neighborhoods. There are no Ku Klux Klan pogroms, no bigots shouting in the streets that all Negroes must be shipped to Africa. In that negative sense—because it *is* better than a lot of small Southern communities—McMinnville is a "good town."

But McMinnville is a peaceful town, I found in 1951, because, in the words of a former river-buddy, "no Negro in his right mind" would show up at the city swimming-pool with trunks and the intention of swimming. And McMinnville Negroes still do not go to the tax-supported public library, ask for a book, and sit down and read. If Negro pupils want books, their teachers must go get the books and bring them out to the pupils. Skating is still something Negroes do on sidewalks or not at all. And when a street is blocked off for square dancing, Negroes watch from a distance.

Part Three

I was walking along McMinnville's Main Street, reminiscing. Passing Stiles's store next to the railroad trestle, I tried to remember who ran it back in the days when, in one year, it seems I must have carried out a thousand gallons of coal oil (kerosene to city slickers), a nickel's worth at a time. Coal oil and Irish potatoes were my favorite purchases, because I always could get nine cents' worth of potatoes and four cents' worth of coal oil and pocket the two pennies toward movie fare, come Saturday. And then, late on Saturday, I would confess to my mother, explaining that I always got as much oil for four cents as I got for a nickel, that if there was any difference it was hardly enough to wet the wick of our lamp, and that, anyhow, no amount of coal oil could make fire out of that slate which we bought as a rather unreasonable facsimile of coal.

I walked on, past the McMinnville Grocery store, remembering the last years of the depression, when eggs were a penny apiece there, but our pennies always were scarcer than hens' eggs. And how a nickel's worth of mixed sausage from the McMinnville Grocery and a nickel loaf of day-old bread from the bakery across the street would make a passable meal for a family of six, but only because your mother knew how to take that sausage grease and some flour and make a skillet of gravy that was at least filling, if neither appetizing nor nourishing.

And there was the Piggly Wiggly store, where jack-salmon fish used to be ten cents a pound, and my father yielded to some compulsion to buy a few pounds every Friday night. (That was when "times were getting better," and he could earn two dollars for stacking lumber ten hours a day.) In those days, fish became almost as unpopular around my house as white salt-pork (known to McMinnville Negroes as "Hoover's ham"), and I vowed that some day I would ban from my table anything that had bones or scales and couldn't clean itself.

I wondered what had become of the auburn-haired, pop-eyed but rather cute white girl who was a clerk in Piggly Wiggly's for a short while. I remembered her small role in my life, and trembled a bit.

It must have been the summer of 1940 when I met her. I had agreed to deliver the Chattanooga *Evening Times* for a few days when my uncle pleaded with me to do so, on the grounds that my cousin, Richard, was ill. It turned out, however, that Richard simply was sick of carrying newspapers, and I was stuck with the route, as I had feared. The *Evening Times* was new and fighting for circulation in the area, so the regional manager, a man named Williams, started prodding me. He told me that there should be twice the forty-two subscribers then listed on my route. He showed me a watch, a sweater, a money-changer, and several other prizes that I could win by getting new subscribers. I got busy, even venturing out of the Negro neighborhood. Soon I had a hundred and twenty-five subscribers, the watch, the sweater, the

money-changer, and the notice that I was included with the
Times's "star" newsboys, who had won a trip to Chattanooga.

Two or three white carriers and I were driven to Chattanooga by Williams. We were shown through the newspaper
plant. Because I had got so many subscribers so fast, I had to
make a little speech to the other newsboys on how to be a
good salesman. Then they lined us up and took our picture
for that afternoon's paper. I felt like the personification of
Horatio Alger's wildest dream.

At lunchtime we were taken to a downtown restaurant
where we were to be treated to a fine meal. I filed into the
restaurant with the other newsboys, with whom I was chatting gaily. I was the only Negro in the group. I had
not learned to watch little conferences behind restaurant
counters, so the first hint I had that my glory trail had ended
was when Williams sat beside me and put his arm around my
shoulder. "I hope you won't feel bad, Carl, but they say you'll
have to eat in the kitchen," he said softly, as if trying to keep
the other boys from hearing.

"I don't see why," I said, my voice cracking faintly. I indicated that I would leave the group first, realizing at the same
time that I had less than enough money for bus fare home.
Many of my subscribers were more reluctant about paying
than they had been about subscribing, so I had not been getting rich as a newsboy.

"Please, Carl. Just for me. Don't make a scene. I'll never
get you into this sort of thing again."

I crept into the kitchen and toyed over a plate of food. I
had lost my appetite, both for the victuals and the Chattanooga *Evening Times.* I was ready to quit my job, and so informed Williams on the way home. I promised to continue
until he could find a replacement.

I delivered my papers the next day, still in a cloud of resentment. I reached a white neighborhood where everybody
took my paper except one family that I had been unable to
woo away from the Nashville *Banner.* An auburn-haired girl,

who must have been about fifteen, was sitting on a red coaster-wagon in the front yard of the holdout family.

"You take an awfully nice picture," she said as I walked into the yard next door.

"Pardon, miss," I said, a bit startled, but knowing that she referred to the group picture of newsboys in the paper the afternoon before.

"I say you take an awfully nice picture. I saw it in yestiddy's Chatt'nooga paper. We don't take it, but I read it next door. I like the funnies in it. I like Dan Dunn 'bout the same as Dick Tracy."

"Well, er, thanks for the compliment. My mother likes Dan Dunn, too. Guess I've got an extra here." I gave her a copy of the paper.

It took weeks for Williams to get a replacement for me, and I continued to carry the *Evening Times*. Almost daily this girl, whose name I never asked, would meet me in front of her house. She smiled and talked sweetly, and I would give her a paper whether I had an extra or not. After I quit the newsboy route, I would pass her on the street and she would pause for a few sentences of chatter about nothing in particular. That fall I saw her working in Piggly Wiggly's on a few Saturday mornings when I went in to buy candy, grapes, or fig bars. She always tried to wait on me, chatting much too much for me to feel secure. My colored buddies soon began teasing that "the little pop-eyed clerk in Piggly Wiggly's has got hot pants for Carl!"

I was concerned about this banter, but not alarmed until one summer afternoon in 1941, when we were standing on the First National Bank corner. This girl, whose eyes were not the only well-developed parts of her body, walked by and stopped to tell me that she thought she would get to go to college the fall after next.

The guys were silent until she walked away. Then one asked, amid laughter: "What the hell are you, Rowan, her counselor?"

I answered by joining in the laughter, hoping to silence them by appearing unaffected. Then one rhyming character started singing:

> The whites caught Rastus the other night
> Bending over a damsel white;
> They pinned old Rastus 'gainst the wall,
> Now Rastus got no balls at all.

There was a roar of laughter, and I participated as heartily as the rest. But I was frightened. I had heard grownups talk about one Negro citizen who had never married. They swore that he had been caught with a white girl near Sparta, Tennessee, in White County of all places, and that four white men whipped and castrated him. After that, the story went, he had no need for a wife. Then, I heard the street-corner know-it-alls talking about venereal diseases. A "mixed" case of syphilis—that is, syphilis acquired through intercourse with a person of another race—was supposed to be the "most deadly kind of all." I turned these things over in my mind and concluded that I would have absolutely nothing to do with that babe. Jumping Jehoshaphat, no!

"Hell, fellows, I don't even know the girl's name," I pleaded when the laughter died down.

"Naw, but you sure seem to have her number," snapped a young wit, who promptly was rewarded with more laughter.

I knew that they would continue until all aspects of the subject were exhausted. The guys got a big kick out of knowing, or suspecting, that interracial sexual activity involving a white woman was going on. We all felt that almost all the customs and laws of the town and the South were designed to prevent such activity. The white man succeeded in keeping us relegated to the poorer jobs and the balconies of the movies, and we had to take it; so it gave us great pleasure to see that the system had failed in the realm of sex, which the white man held most sacred. And always, when the bank-corner gang got on the subject of interracial sexual activity, a couple of the fellows who worked as yard-men would commence tales about how their boss was "anemic and 'through'" but his wife was not; and how it was safer for the wives to fool with them "'cause they know we can't afford to talk." Qne Negro would relate how his boss's wife started by asking him to lace her corset, which he began to do with trembling hands. As the story progressed, she wanted it laced tighter, and ordered him: "Put your knee in my back"; and this intimate tugging always made it "more conducive to unlacing the corset than to lacing it."

Listening to those guys first gave me the idea that white and Negro men were no different except for color. I had a buddy who shined shoes at a barbershop. I helped him several times, and often we sat in the back of the shop by the hot-water heater and listened to white customers weave tales about the sexual prowess of their colored maids.

We never knew how much of this talk was pure imagination, but it made good listening because we knew some of it was true. A select group of our gang had laughed for weeks that very summer, when we would crawl atop a garage late at night so that we could peek under the shade into an apartment above a little shop where a white woman and her Negro lover carried on illicit relations. There was living evidence, too, that the tales told by some of the white men were more than fiction. Negroes considered it general knowledge that one young woman had left town at the insistence of her boss's wife. This rather prominent white woman had caught her husband in bed with the Negro housegirl. To complain publicly would be to penalize herself as well as her husband. She simply frightened the Negro girl half to death and insisted that she go to live with Northern relatives. But since her Negro yard-man was wise to what had happened, the incident was no secret, at least not to the guys on the bank corner.

We didn't have much faith in the theory of the late Senator Bilbo of Mississippi that segregation statutes prevented interracial sexual activity and, consequently, "the mongrelization of the human race." We knew that many McMinnville citizens, like those in other Southern towns, were living the most phony, hypocritical sort of life as regards sex. The white man himself had perpetrated the myth that all Negro men are of superhuman capabilities between the sheets, and there always would be white women curious and willing to taste the "forbidden fruit." Likewise, white men whose appetites were whetted by barbershop tales never had shown any reluctance to sample the "not-so-forbidden fruit."

Considering all this, a friend of mine thought me quite a prude not to explore the interest that the little pop-eyed girl seemed to have in me. Although I had found that female smiles and taunts stirred the same passions in a male no matter what the color of the tempter, I never could wipe from my mind the street-corner verse about "Rastus," or the story of an alleged interracial incident in White County. Prude or not, I stuck to home base.

It was not until closing-of-school week that I learned that this friend had decided to rush in where I had feared to tread. From hints that I was slow to catch, he was doing very well, and one May afternoon he told me boldly that he had been meeting the young woman under cover of darkness and that, in his opinion, I had been a damned fool.

I think my ego was hurt a little. Although I could arouse no great interest in the girl, I didn't like to think that she so quickly could transfer her interest to another guy. I followed my friend that night. Sure enough, she met him on the riverbank in an area that had been cleared out the year before for baptism ceremonies by the Church of Christ. I crept through the bushes, peering wide-eyed at this violation of the Southland's most sacred law. When I tried to creep closer I stepped into a pile of what I rightly assumed was human feces, and before I realized it I had hurled a few expletives at whoever dared to do such a thing in a baptismal area.

I had startled the two lovers, and with the automatic response of a baby stuck with a pin, the auburn-haired girl screamed: "'Get up! Stop, you black sonofabitch! Jesus, he's raping me!"

We were a long way from the nearest home, so no one heard her screams. Yet I was bewildered momentarily. My buddy was practically ripping bushes up by the roots in his haste to get away. This was an extremely dangerous situation, dangerous for the entire community if it became generally known. I shouted my buddy's name, adding: "It's Carl; it's just me!" Then I looked around nervously to make sure it *was* just me.

My buddy paused some fifty yards away. He turned back hesitantly. "It's Carl; it's just me," I repeated, and walked toward the girl, who stood trembling and weeping almost hysterically. I was ashamed to have been a Peeping Tom. I hardly knew what to say.

"I was afraid they'd kill me. I thought they had come to kill me," the girl sobbed, trying to explain, in her shame, why she had cried rape.

It seemed an eternity before the tears, hysterical chatter, trembling hands, and rushing hearts settled down to normal. Naturally, the sensible thing would be for all concerned to keep their mouths shut about everything. We all realized that, and no military secret ever was better kept.

My friend had learned Lesson Number One about the mores of the South, in a most embittering manner. He sought revenge more than once by bouncing his fist off the chin of a half-drunk white man who was stupid enough to ask us if we knew where he could get "a nice colored girl." But my friend never forgot the lesson. When I saw him four years later, it still made him almost sick at the stomach to hear anyone sing the popular song, "Walking by the River."

Standing in front of the Piggly Wiggly store, thinking about the little auburn-haired girl, had almost plunged me into a trance. The memory alone had blistered my hands with tiny globules of sweat. I wiped them on the inside of my coat pocket, scolded myself for doing it, and walked on.

I almost turned into the Dixie Theater from force of habit. That was where I had spent so many Saturdays watching Hoot Gibson, Buck Jones, Tim McCoy—and even Hopalong Cassidy—at the expense of the self-kicked "kickbacks" from coal-oil and potato purchases. But there were a lot more ways to raise theater fare, and my closest pal, Bill Hogan, and I knew them all. Jim Martin's pawnshop gave four cents and two cents for quart and half-gallon canning jars, respectively, and either Bill's mother or mine usually could be relied on to make a slip some time during the week and leave their jars within our reach.

And, like the town's policemen, we knew who and where all the bootleggers were. These moonshine moguls paid a penny for pint bottles, a nickel for two empty half-pints, and a "cheater" (a half-pint bottle with an extra-high bottom, which reduces the bottle's capacity) was worth a whole nickel! My buddy and I walked the railroad tracks for what seems like a lifetime of Saturday mornings, combing through Johnson grass and pokeweed, and probing among the honeysuckle vines matted along the tracks' sloping banks, for "empties." When a fast nickel was needed we would wait near the house of a bootlegger who had bought a cheater. When a buyer (this was one activity that knew no racial bounds) entered who appeared already drunk enough to have the false-bottom bottle pushed off on him, we would follow that buyer away. We knew that almost momentarily the "Tennessee stump juice" would be gurgled down, where it would burn like acid in his already benumbed bowels. Our average at retrieving cheaters was remarkable.

Near-poverty was the father of ingenuity—and just the tiniest bit of crookedness—for Bill and me. Zinc, copper, aluminum, and old rags were reliable sources of movie income. We utilized that source to its fullest, for, with theater fare a dime, we often could hustle up enough additional money to buy fig bars or chocolate drops.

Negro women were wearing out a lot of washboards in those days, and the boards' zinc surfaces were salable. I often think of the times Bill and I stood by, waiting for either a washboard or a washerwoman to wear out. Those rubbing surfaces, along with the cast-off dippers, pots, and pans that we rounded up, often made an untidy pile of junk, for which we expected a tidy sum of money. But Mr. Cope, our buyer, knew our goal too well. Whether we delivered a handful or a sackful, he paid us just movie fare. It probably balanced out, but we only remembered being "underpaid" for the sackfuls. Bill and I knew that Mr. Cope stored his junk in a yard across from my house. We felt perfectly honest and justified in taking back half of the previous Saturday's sackful and reselling it to Mr. Cope. I often wondered if Mr. Cope didn't recognize some of that junk, but just wanted to keep two youngsters happy by seeing that they got show fare.

I stood in front of the theater smiling, actually laughing about the way I used to take a $1.98 pair of trousers and fairly iron the hell out of them, trying to make them hold a crease long enough for me to get to a party and be seen by everybody. As I laughed, I thought what power time has. It turns mediocre years into the "good old days," and takes the pain out of hours of tribulation, so that ten years later even a Negro can remember and laugh, if he has been lucky.

As I stood there, recollecting the past, I was slightly stunned by a voice that said: "Well, Goddam! Rowan! They're treating you all right up North, ain't they?"

I half-turned and faced a young white citizen whom I had known fairly well since the days when he was cutting fancy capers on the Central High football team in McMinnville. I shall not name him, for reasons that will be obvious. I reached out to shake his outstretched hand, staring into his eyes and at the fillings in his teeth as he looked me up and down, wide-mouthed.

"I say they're doing pretty nice for you up there," he repeated.

"I like to think that they're giving me a chance to do pretty nice for myself if I've got what it takes," I countered. Then, at his request, I ran through the events in my life since we last had seen each other. No, I explained to him, the Minneapolis *Tribune* is not an all-Negro paper. No, I went on, I don't just cover news about Negroes. When he repeated his exclamation that I was "doing all right," I asked him if I had done well enough to get on the first floor of the Dixie Theater.

My friend replied with a reason that I expected to hear many times before I got out of the South: he wouldn't mind me sitting next to him, but what about some filthy, stinking Negro? I told him, half jokingly, that I didn't think he meant it or he'd be out campaigning for a law that dirty, stinking people had to sit in the balcony, regardless of color, and that admission to the first floor be on the basis of cleanliness and odor test.

I was confident that my friend was honestly against racial segregation, and I expected him to laugh at my remark. He only looked puzzled. "What can I do?" he asked. "What can any one man do? The problem seems so damned insolvable. I just can't see what I can do." Before I could answer he was mumbling: "Minneapolis *Tribune* . . . *Tribune*. Say, you don't intend to criticize McMinnville in your paper, do you?"

"Criticize McMinnville? Heavens, no!" I replied. "I might mention some of McMinnville's situations, but that could hardly be criticism of *McMinnville*, for she is only a symbol, to me, of what hundreds of Southern towns mean to ten million Negro citizens."

"Man, if you criticized this town, your name would be mud," he warned. "We may have some faults, but we think we're pretty good white people. Why, some of our good citizens would burn every foot of ground you ever walked on."

"What would *you* do?" I demanded.

"You want the truth, don't you?" he replied. "I'd 'do like the Romans do'; I'd raise more hell than a castrated boar in sow heaven. But inside of me I'd be laughing my guts out." I winked at my friend and left to pack my bags. Although I had found my home town much the same as I had left it in 1943, I could leave with a flickering of hope. I could wonder if the fact that this young white Southerner showed signs of an aching conscience meant anything. I could wonder about the meaning of his admission that he would feel obligated to complain with the rest should I criticize McMinnville, although his would be a false complaint. I could wonder if his worry about what he could do as an individual represented the inner turmoil about which I had heard so much. I could wonder if he was a symbol of the inner conflict that was sup- posed to characterize the New South I sought.

CHAPTER III

LIFE, LIBERTY, AND LAW

THE sky was more than ominous. Low-hanging black clouds wrapped midday in a dusky gloom. I was sure that at any moment there would be a bolt of lightning, a loud peal of thunder, and that I, rented car and all, would be swept off the highway. So I mashed hard on the accelerator, trying to get to Columbia, Tennessee, before the sky caved in. As I sped along, I gazed almost continuously into the rear-view mirror; the last thing I wanted was entanglement with policemen. It was just as well, I thought, that the Hertz people put governors on their cars; I could only go so fast.

I thought of McMinnville, now scores of miles away, but only yesterday so close, so filled with poignant, if unhappy, memories. I wondered why, of all things, I had to remember such things as cold nights when I lay in bed and became constipated because nothing was more irritating than to squat over a privy hole on a midwinter night. But as much as I tried to cull "good old days" out of the past, I failed to ferret out a single day that wasn't stained with some memory of my have-not existence. I could recall only that it hadn't seemed so bad then, for mine was the kind of childhood that most McMinnville Negro boys had. There was the dubious comfort of numbers.

Suddenly I was jolted out of the past by a wave of water that splattered against the windshield. Nature had ruptured the biggest, blackest, wettest cloud.

I began to worry about how the rain would affect my plans for Columbia. I had problems enough without it. All I knew about that Maury County community was what I had read in

38

the papers, and most of that was far from enthralling. As to most Americans, Columbia to me was just a little Tennessee town, remembered because racial strife catapulted it onto the front pages of the nation's newspapers in February of 1946. With misgivings, I had convinced myself that Columbia should be included in my itinerary because what I would find in Columbia, just five years out of a race riot, ought to be indicative of what progress was being, or could be, made in even the most hidebound areas of the Southland.

I had been thoughtful enough to bring along a raincoat. Wearing the raincoat into Columbia would have one advantage: my camera would not be too conspicuous under its loose fit. However, I had not been sure how to dress for Columbia. I did not know whether I would be stopped by policemen if I drove about town in the car. I knew that small-town policemen often become suspicious of a strange Negro in a new car, and stop him, whereas they will not bother a Negro whom they recognize. In the end, I had decided to "dress up." to wear a suit and tie. But I would not go so far as to parade about town in the automobile. I would park it and walk through the sections I planned to visit. But the downpour was not going to make it comfortable for walking; and the raincoat would nullify whatever effect my suit and tie might have had.

I drove through the heart of Columbia, fixing the downtown area in my mind. Then I drove around the fringe of the business district until I found what I knew to be the Negro business-section. I parked my car and waited for the rain to stop. After a few minutes it appeared to slacken. I put on my raincoat, leaving the camera in the car, and walked the few blocks to the heart of town. Whom did whites consider to be the town's Negro spokesman? I would find that out first.

I stood under an awning in front of a downtown shop, protecting myself from the rain, which had all but ceased. It was a warm day, and I had unbuttoned my raincoat. This revealed the navy blue suit and red polka-dot tie that I was wearing.

I was not aware of their conspicuousness, however, until a battered old Hudson rolled down the street. A little girl of about six, with short, fuzzy blonde hair that would have made her look like a baby chick had her face been clean, leaned out the car window. Half-screaming, she pointed at me and exclaimed: "Momma, Momma, look at the pretty nigger!"

I looked to see if an embarrassed mother would grab her by her panties and yank her under the seat. Instead, the woman and two boys of about nine and eleven burst into hearty laughter. I became a bit nervous, and began pacing back and forth. I decided to walk to the end of the block.

As I reached the corner, a white man who appeared fairly well-to-do was getting out of an automobile. I asked him where the colored section of town was. He told me how to get to the Negro business-section, where someone would direct me to the house I sought. "Well, I really don't know what house I'm looking for," I continued. "Perhaps you could tell me what Negro citizen knows the town very well and could give me some reliable information about a former World War II shipmate of mine."

"You'll find a funeral parlor just where I told you to go. James Morton, the undertaker, will give you some reliable information," he replied.

He had said much what I expected him to say. I remembered that Morton was one of the twenty-five Negro defendants in the trial resulting from the 1946 disturbance. I thought it interesting, and perhaps significant, that five years later a white citizen would refer to this Negro, accused in 1946 of plotting a racial revolution, as a reliable citizen.

By now the fear and expectation of intimidation, the caution with which I entered Columbia, seemed unjustified. In 1951, the Maury County community appeared to be just another Southern town.

I walked the few blocks to East Eighth Street, which whites had given the opprobrious title, "Mink Slide." This street was the center of the conflict in 1946. On the left I could see

Morton's funeral home, and on my right was a row of shabby frame buildings that housed a honky-tonk, a store, a poolhall, a barbershop, and a few miscellaneous enterprises. They were the sort of places that mark any Southern town with a Negro population as large as Columbia's.

Barbershops have a livelier atmosphere than funeral parlors, and usually the people in barbershops are more informative. I decided not to call at Mr. Morton's place immediately. I would see what barber Sol W. Blair (I knew that he, too, was a defendant in the celebrated trial) and the people in his shop had to say.

I got my camera and ducked into the barbershop, out of what again seemed to be a cloudburst. I greeted the men in the shop, and they gave a sort of unanimous grunt in return. One man remarked to nobody in particular that it was "raining baby shoats" outside. I eased out of the raincoat, revealing my navy-blue suit, the trouser legs of which I had rolled above my ankles, the red polka-dot tie, and the Kodax Reflex camera that hung around my neck. Glancing slyly into a mirror, I watched the rotund barber and his guests size me up. The eternal barbershop argument apparently had been cut short by my appearance. I was sure they had been talking of something other than the weather. I wondered how I could take the conversational lead and ease into talk about the riot, something these people conceivably would consider a very unsavory subject.

A tall, thin-faced man with protruding cheekbones solved part of my problem. He offered his hand to me. When he was still six feet away I could tell that he had had a few shots of liquor to brace himself against the weather.

"You wid the Pittsburgh *Courier?*" he asked.

"Nope," I replied.

"You wid the Chicago *Defender?*" he continued.

"Nah," I said.

"The *Afro-American?*" he persisted.

"Nope, I'm just a guy who likes cameras. I'm on my way to

Nashville, but I remembered that a woman who used to live in McMinnville—that's where I grew up—probably lives here. All I can remember is Stella; can't think of her married name. I know she was living in Columbia during the 1946 riot."

"What was she doing in the riot?" asked barber Blair, showing interest for the first time.

"Oh, I just remember seeing her name in a few news stories," I lied.

Blair shrugged his shoulders as if to say he'd never heard of a Stella from McMinnville. I knew he was lying, for I had Mrs. Stella Grady's address in my pocket and knew that she and her husband were well-known Columbia citizens. Blair just wasn't talking until he found out my mission.

I had reached a verbal impasse. I began staring about the shop. On the bottom of a table was a pile of yellowing, obviously over-handled newspapers. From a picture on one I could tell that they were Nashville newspapers of five years back carrying stories of the Columbia incident. "I'll bet this is what I wanted to chat with the lady about," I said, aiming my remarks at Blair and pointing my finger at the papers. The wide-faced, heavyset barber turned toward the papers hesitantly, said nothing, and continued cutting hair. "Mind if I take a look?" I asked. He shook his head to say he didn't mind, puffing his jowls full of air and giving me another once-over at the same time.

I began thumbing through the papers. "What you wanta know about the riot?" asked Blair. Stepping near him as if to replace the papers, I mumbled in a voice only he and his chair customer could hear that I was a writer and a magazine had asked me to see if there might be a story in what Columbia is like five years after the riot.

"What magazine?" he shot back quickly.

"*Look*," I replied as snappily, anticipating his question.

"Well, I can sum the situation up in a few words," said the corpulent man, becoming loquacious now. I had set off the alarm inside him, and I could see that he was fully wound.

"You just tell them that before the riot Columbia was a hell-
hole, but that we've got a good city now. Used to be that
when a Negro went in a store uptown the clerks didn't see
him until he started to walk out. Then they *might* offer to
serve him. You go in now and ask for a pair of galluses and
those clerks will button 'em on you."

I could see that Sol Blair had not forgotten events that began on February 25, 1946. He would never forget so long
as he could point to the wall of his shop and show machine-
gun bullet holes that were souvenirs from the morning of
February 26, when policemen and civilians swept through
the Negro community with the devastation of storm troopers.
They had left only one mirror unbroken in the entire Negro
business-section. Hoodlums broke many mirrors by hurling
billiard balls. When they left the battered Negro section, only
the eight-balls remained on the ripped-up tables in the poolhall of J. W. Blair, Sol's father and the oldest businessman in
Maury County.

It all started when James Stephenson, a nineteen-year-old
Negro Navy veteran, knocked twenty-eight-year-old William
Fleming, white, through a plate-glass window. Fleming reportedly had slapped Mrs. Gladys Stephenson, James's mother,
after she expressed dissatisfaction with a radio-repair job
Fleming had done. Mrs. Stephenson and her son were jailed
on charges of assault. Fleming, only slightly injured, was not
arrested.

Tension mounted in the town of about twelve thousand,
nearly one third of whom were colored. Crowds of white persons began to mill about the Public Square, calling threats of
lynching the Negro couple.

"We went to post bond," Blair related, "but the magistrate
kept raising it in an effort to keep the Stephensons in jail. I
turned to Sheriff (J. J.) Underwood and said: 'Let me tell you
one thing, Sheriff, there won't be any more "social" lynchings
in Columbia.' They released the pair on a $3,500 bond."

By "'social' lynchings," Blair had referred to Columbia's

reputation. Two Negroes had been lynched within the last two decades, and in each case it had been an invitational affair. That is, the mob leaders had invited whites for miles around, including press representatives, to come out and view the proceedings. Columbia Negroes still were bitter about the lynching of seventeen-year-old Cordie Cheek. The youth had been slain after a grand jury returned a no-bill on a charge of molesting a white girl. It was considered general knowledge in the Negro community that the car which transported Cheek to lynching territory belonged to the magistrate who fixed bond in the Stephenson case.

Less than two hours after the Stephensons were released, about seventy-five men reached the jail and began kicking on the door. Underwood leveled a sub-machine-gun at them and ordered the mob to disperse. Two members were so drunk that they could not leave the jail. They were arrested on charges of disorderly conduct.

Negroes were convinced that there would be a lynching attempt that night, so, on the advice of the Sheriff, Stephenson was taken out of town. At dusk the white mob had grown. Shouts, rebel cries, and the firing of guns in the Public Square could be heard by Negroes who already were clamping down windows, bolting doors, and dousing lights in their business places. Darkness and an eery hush fell over East Eighth Street. Negroes, including more than 150 veterans, vowed not to "take it lying down." Having little faith in the city policemen, one of whom had struck Mrs. Stephenson over the eye when arresting her, the Negroes prepared to defend themselves.

At about 8.45 p.m. that February 25, according to trial testimony, city policemen started into East Eighth Street, allegedly to investigate a shooting. Shots were fired in the darkness, and, Negroes testified, they thought the whites had attacked. In an exchange, four policemen were wounded, one seriously. Mayor Eldridge Denham made an immediate appeal to Governor Jim

McCord, who rushed one hundred State Highway Patrolmen and four hundred State Guardsmen into Columbia.

These five hundred men wrapped a cordon around the Negro business-area and kept close vigil on the entire Negro community. At dawn on February 26 the patrolmen moved into East Eighth Street. The little barbershop got its bullet holes when, according to State Safety Director Lynn Bomar, the one hundred patrolmen "met resistance," and a machine-gun was used as a convincer.

Policemen and hoodlums spread wanton destruction throughout the Negro community in a "search for weapons." An insurance company's office was looted; record files were overturned and valuable contents were scattered. A physician's office was a shambles, with furniture damaged and decorations mutilated. Morton's Funeral Home was ransacked by vandals, who left no doubt as to their allegiance: they used plaster of Paris to scrawl the initials "KKK" on a coffin.

On February 28, two Negro prisoners (more than one hundred Negroes had been arrested as against four whites, although newspaper photographs showed whites walking the streets freely armed with sawed-off shotguns) were shot to death and one was wounded by policemen who were questioning them. The official explanation is that William Gordon and James Johnson were slain when Gordon reached into a pile of guns, managed to pull out one that matched bullets he allegedly had smuggled into jail, loaded the gun, and then fired on his questioners before they could detect his actions. The National Lawyers Guild investigated and called the killings "murder." Bomar boasted in the trial that he knocked down Napoleon Stewart (the third prisoner in the room), then placed his foot on Stewart's neck and, pointing a gun at his head, said: "If you move I'll kill you."

Ultimately, twenty-five Negroes went on trial charged with assault with intent to commit murder. An all-white, all-male, Lawrence County, Tennessee, jury found only two guilty. A motion for a new trial went uncontested by the state, and these two eventually were freed. As I sat in the little Columbia barbershop, I realized that at that very moment one of the twenty-five Negro defendants was stumping the Southland with a petition, asking Negroes to join him in denouncing Paul Robeson by declaring that they *would* fight for America against any enemy. In five years, things had changed considerably in Columbia.

Part Two

Sol Blair, O. C. Pulce, and the others in his barbershop agreed that there were some "lessons" in what had happened in and to Columbia. They agreed also that wise old Henry Harlan would know these lessons better than anyone. So, with Pulce as my guide, I drove out into the country, to this small-town Bernie Baruch, to ask what, if anything, mankind might learn from Columbia's conflict.

It was a most uncomfortable journey. The farther we drove the redder and muddier the clay road became. We sloshed past the plants of the Monsanto and Victor chemical companies, where many Negroes were employed and held membership in the CIO Mine, Mill and Smelter Workers Union. The relative economic security afforded by this employment had played no small part, I knew, in the 1946 decision by Columbia Negroes that they would not take lynching lying down.

Finally, we turned off the scarlet road and drove up a faintly discernible lane of deep black earth. Ahead of us was a thicket of majestic cedars, whose drooping boughs gave off a glow that seemed to help light the dreary day. When we came to a barbed-wire fence, Pulce untied a few wires and opened what served as a gate. I drove into a field that was grassy where limestone had not forbidden growth.

"We gotta walk from here," my escort said, "and it's sure one bitch of a day to go calling on Old Man Harlan. But you can't write no article about Columbia without seeing him. He knows of four lynchings in his lifetime. They lynched his grandson."

"Oh?" I said, half with a start, realizing that my reply was somewhat below the occasion. I parked the car on a rocky perch, rolled my trouser legs up higher, and set out in what had become a light, steady rain for the home of ninety-year-old Henry C. Harlan.

Harlan didn't come into town very often now, Pulce told me; and I could understand why. We negotiated a hill and a small brook by stepping from stone to stone. I still remembered how to crawl through a barbed-wire fence without leaving anything vital on a barb. But staying on top of mud, like walking on water, was outside my realm of achievement. Wet, sticky goo covered my shoes and oozed up around my ankles when the roots of dead cornstalks gave way under my weight. We were walking across open farm-fields, because a narrow road leading close to Harlan's house had been impassable for days.

Barking hounds brought curious Negro farm-families to their rickety wooden porches to observe the passers-by. I was just as curious, for it had been fifteen years since I had seen this kind of back-to-nature living. At each house buckets and washtubs were on the ground at the edge of the porch, catching the rainwater as it ran from the roof. This would serve both drinking and washing purposes for a few days. Pulce said the journey wasn't as far as it had been, which I took to mean that the next house was Harlan's; but already I was wet and muddy beyond care.

The gray-haired old man with the weatherbeaten hide was at the door to greet us, the fuss of a bitch terrior having served notice that guests were coming. After angering his eighty-four-year-old wife, Mary, by telling her that dinner could wait if he had a chance to talk about Negro life in the area, Harlan took a rocker and gave me a seat on the bed. This old man with the gnarled hands and frayed sweater, with trousers whose dirty front had been work-rubbed to a high gloss, had been born a slave on November 18, 1861, right on that land.

Harlan recounted incidents without gestures, recalling names and dates as though the events had occurred the day before. It was in 1927, he said, that fate jolted him with a bit of grotesque irony. He had walked across the fields chatting with a group of white men, exchanging ideas with them on how they might apprehend the individual responsible for raping a white girl. A few minutes later he found that the group had come to seize his grandson.

"The girl said she didn't think it was my daughter's son when they asked her to identify him. They said they would take him for safekeeping, anyhow," Harlan recalled. "The next morning we found him hanging. And a few days later they found for sure that another lad was the guilty party."

Henry Harlan talked on, above the objections of his wife, who asked him not to "say so much that they'll be out here a making trouble for us."

"There won't be no more trouble," Harlan said, as he cupped his hands around the pot-bellied stove, then suddenly arched his back to where his head almost touched the wall sign, which read: "Blessed are the pure in heart." "No, there ain't gonna be no more trouble. That's the one thing I learned from 1946. They know now that Negroes have guts. The Blairs and Mortons was the first Columbia Negroes ever to stand up like men. Blood was shed, but it paid off. I dare as to say times has changed. A colored man used to not have the chance of a sheep-killing dog. But 1946 changed that."

With the dismal music of rain on the tin roof and the heat from the pot-bellied stove, I could have curled up on Mary Harlan's bed and slept for hours. But I had seen enough of Columbia. I stepped into the miserable outdoors, dreading the muddy journey back to the car. With a sprightliness that belied his age and the hours of toil his old human frame had accounted for, Henry Harlan followed us off the porch. He shushed his wife, who was scolding him for going out without a hat or raincoat. Then he swept his arm out toward the hill.

"This is my land," he said. "This is all my land. They came out here telling me that I was old and they wanted to help me. I thought it was a friendly gesture, but now they want to take some of my land to pay for the 'relief' I never asked for. Look at that rock quarry up there—on my land. They're pulling dollars out of my land. I'm not gonna take that laying down."

Old Henry Harlan was in the twilight of life, but he had lived to see the dawning of liberty in Columbia. I left that dreary old country-land, with its muddy fields, baying hounds, and barbed-wire fences, hoping that he would live long enough to find that there can be justice under law. He, who lost a grandson to a friendly mob; and a gentleman I met earlier, named Meade Johnson, who lost a son in the questionable jailhouse episode, could find solace in the Columbia story. For, despite the apparent hopelessness of it all, Columbia's Negroes had come out ahead. No amount of persecution had been able to hold back progress. It still was impossible for a tyrant or a mob to twist a rope of sand, or make water run up hill.

CHAPTER IV

THE SUN RISES IN THE EAST

THOSE Tennessee nights hadn't changed; they still fooled you. I had returned for my luggage and a final glimpse at my home town, and as I stood on McMinnville's Main Street, across from Brown's Hotel, it seemed exceptionally warm for one a.m. on a January morning. Perhaps it was because I had carried my bags for several blocks. McMinnville is the kind of town where even the owls are asleep at such an hour, let alone taxi-drivers. I had panted up to the corner just in in time to board the Tennessee Coach Lines bus, bound for Knoxville.

I half-stumbled aboard with my luggage, pushing a large suitcase down the aisle with my knee as I moved toward the rear of the bus, where, according to state law, I had to sit. I removed my topcoat as a sort of automatic response to the beads of perspiration on my brow. I leaned forward from the rear seat and looked out at the night. A bright moon splattered the lumpy earth; the ghostly light reflected off naked bushes that shivered in a slight breeze. To my mind, still accustomed to crusty piles of snow that would hide Minnesota earth for months to come, the illusion was one of heat waves rising from sun-baked soil in August. The highway was like a brightly polished corridor that suddenly pitched off into spacious darkness when the road dipped over a steep hill or curved stubbornly with the terrain. The bus clung to the road with leechlike tenacity, and the monotonous swaying and the hoarse purr of the engine soon lulled me to sleep.

Somewhere just outside Crossville, Tennessee, my shivering

50

awakened me. A heavy frost and a biting chill had settled over the countryside, which now tossed back silvery reflections to the bright heavens above. The bus had become uncomfortable for dozing passengers who had removed their topcoats. I stepped from my seat and reached into the rack for my coat. As I began to fumble in the semidarkness, the driver flicked on a light for me. I got my coat and lifted my hand toward him as a gesture of thanks. I had ridden scores of buses in the South, many times on that same route, and drivers showing such courtesy to a Negro passenger were rare. It was the first time I had ever observed such an act.

The driver's almost insignificant little gesture was important to me. It brought to my mind a bus trip on that very same route, when I saw what I considered a significant crack in the pattern of the Old South. In 1947, shortly after my graduation from Oberlin College, I was in Tennessee for a couple of days and had stopped in McMinnville for a few hours. I stood at the station awaiting the bus for Knoxville. When it arrived I was surprised to see that a white schoolmate, Dick Sanders, was a passenger. Sanders, a native Tennessean, and I had been good friends in school. We had been allies in many a card game, and had split many high-low poker pots.

McMinnville is one of two major rest-stops between Nashville and Knoxville, and new passengers do not board until old passengers have returned to their seats. As I stood in line for those ten or fifteen minutes while the passengers were snacking, I wondered what Sanders would do. Would he want to ride with me? Was he sufficiently conscious of law and custom? I would find it a bit humiliating if he offered me a seat beside him near the front of the bus. If he did, should I accept it and await the rebuke that would certainly come from the driver? Or should I explain that I couldn't sit beside him, and then move humbly to "where I belonged"?

I entered the bus and found Sanders standing in the aisle. Apparently he had given up his seat beside someone, for no

double seats were empty. To sit with me, Sanders would
have to move to the rear. That is what he did.

As we made small talk about college days and plans for the
future, I kept an eye toward the front of the bus. The driver
got in, looked the passengers over. His eyes paused momentarily on Sanders, but he said nothing. During the first forty
miles of the trip, however, I noticed that a white woman
who sat just behind the driver kept turning uneasily to observe us. After forty miles of fidgeting, she said something to
the driver. Immediately, the driver glanced into his rear-view
mirror and swerved the bus to the side of the road. "Here
it comes," I thought, as the driver walked toward us.

"You can't sit there, fellow. You know whites and colored
can't sit together on this bus. That seat is for colored," the
driver told Sanders.

With a look of great embarrassment, which I had learned to
recognize in Sanders only after he had succeeded in a gigantic poker-bluff, my friend whispered in tones of confession:
"My father was white." Both the driver and I quickly got the
implication, and the driver, looking flustered, replied: "Oh,
oh, oh." He returned to his seat and apparently satisfied the
complaining passenger by describing my companion as a mu-
latto.

I wiped the stunned look from my face, smiled, and continued to chat, now more comfortably, with Sanders. When we
reached Knoxville, we stood waiting for the driver to get our
bags out of the trunk. As Sanders took his, he said to the
driver: "Say, I forgot to tell you back there that my mother
was white, too."

First the driver appeared embarrassed, but he quickly
smiled, then burst into laughter as Sanders winked and the
two of us walked away.

As I sat thinking about that day, watching the majesty of
night hurtle by as the bus plunged on into the Smokies, it
seemed that only the driver and I were awake. My thinking
was interrupted when I glimpsed a dull glow that played

hide-and-seek behind the hills as the bus moved around hair-pin turns. As the light grew nearer, I realized where we were. We were about to enter Crossville, which I remembered primarily because of a sign posted on a tree at the city limits: NIGGER, DON'T LET THE SUN SET ON YOU HERE!

The passengers were awakened by the screeching of the brakes as the bus stopped at the Crossville station. They stirred and yawned, and then looked about to see who was watching as they stretched their arms skyward. This was the other major stop before Knoxville, so many passengers got off to stretch or get a cup of coffee. Two Negro passengers got off and walked down a corridor to the kitchen, where they could get food or coffee. Since the sun had long set, I decided to remain aboard the bus for the stop.

From McMinnville to Crossville was a short journey, but those miles made a lot of difference. They showed why it is impossible to generalize about the South. A Negro can do things in one town that he would be killed for seventy-five miles away. Whatever inequities existed in McMinnville, a Negro still could walk the streets after dark. Negroes could live in McMinnville, whereas Crossville barred them from residence.

I watched the crowd in the café, thinking how easy it was to pick out the Crossvillians. A stoopshouldered, red-faced man clad in overalls sat drinking coffee, and I was sure he was chewing tobacco at the same time. He talked incessantly to a stringy-haired girl behind the counter. She giggled continuously. I wondered how it was that I could sit and watch a girl laugh and not get the feeling that she was mirthful and friendly. I thought of the sign at the edge of town, wondering how it was that the people who put it up, and my friend, Sanders, could grow up in the same state, 150 miles apart. Unable to resolve the problem, I pulled my topcoat over my head. I would sleep my way into the area that had been regenerated by the Tennessee Valley Authority, into a land whose limp veins had been filled with industrial power. I would see the atomic center at Oak Ridge, and the great aluminum-production center of Alcoa, Tennessee. There could be no doubt that they were part of a "new, industrial South." They were turning out vast supplies of products for the defense of democracy. I would see if they were building any democracy to defend.

Part Two

The Adge Shockley family knows what the "new, industrial South" means to the Negro, if that industry opens its doors generally to Negroes. It had meant a lot to the Shockleys; I knew that when I saw the comfortable but unpretentious home they were buying in Alcoa. They had a private, indoor toilet, running water, electric lights, and a heating system adequate for eastern-Tennessee winters. Shockley's children were well-dressed, apparently well-fed, and they attended school regularly.

"I don't have to fake deafness or turn my head in shame when one of my three boys asks for a nickel now," explained Shockley, who was in his early thirties. Then this friendly, quick-minded Negro smiled and reminded me that he had known less prosperous days. "After all, Carl, you know what things used to be," he said. I did know. Shockley and I both grew up in McMinnville. His brother-in-law and I were high-school classmates. While the Japanese were attacking Pearl Harbor, I sat in Shockley's two-room bungalow in McMinnville, listening to Sammy Kaye's Sunday-afternoon radio program.

Shockley, his wife Josephine, and their first child lived in a frame bungalow on the grounds of the Burroughs-Ross-Colville lumber mill, where he worked. The bungalow had no indoor toilet or plumbing. It was partially wired for electricity, and its running water was a spring that it straddled.

"Those days, I got one pack of cigarettes a week—on payday," Shockley continued. "That day I also bought enough Bull Durham roll-your-own to last a week. Can't say anyone was overfed." Again he reminded me that I knew. I did. For while Shockley worked at the Burroughs-Ross-Colville lumber mill, my father worked at the Smith and Walker lumber mill. Their pay was the same—whatever the federal government had set as the minimum at the time.

With memories as vivid as if it were the day before, Shockley and I talked of torrid summer days when he, my father, and other McMinnville Negroes stood atop stacks of oak timber, literally bathing them in sweat bought at two dollars a day. Those mills were the only industrial employment open to Negroes, and twelve dollars a week earned there fed more family than did seven or eight dollars earned for a week's work as a domestic.

Early in 1942 Shockley made the decision that thousands of Southern Negroes now are making: to get out of places like McMinnville. "I started pinching pennies," he relates, "and smoking Bull Durham one more day a week. Another lumberworker agreed to sell his wagon and team of mules and he and I would head for Detroit."

Shockley never got to Detroit. Someone told him that the Aluminum Company of America was hiring Negroes at its booming wartime plant in Alcoa. Shockley gambled with bus fare and got a job. He bundled up his wife and two children and "headed for greener pastures."

The pastures are considerably greener. Shockley averages about sixty dollars a week now. Were he in McMinnville, his best job would be at a lumber mill, where he would get the government-required seventy-five cents an hour. He would have no guarantee of the number of hours he would work; he would have no fringe benefits such as family hospitalization, pension, or even sick leave. Though Shockley, my father, and many others have left McMinnville, there are Negroes still who sweat atop those lumber stacks and faint in the summer sun. They are jobless for unexpected periods when the plants shut down. Then they join the standees on the First National Bank corner, waiting for someone to come along with a job offer. Probably fewer than five Negro men in McMinnville earn more than thirty-five dollars a week.

Many families other than the Shockleys had moved to Alcoa. Their improved status was evident in more than the neat, middle-class houses and the well-kept lawns I saw. "We haven't had a case of colored juvenile-delinquency here in five years," said A. V. Smith, the city manager. This seemed incredible, even after giving Alcoa the benefit of doubt. Yet, McMinnville could claim no such record for five years; or for one year; or for a month. Alcoa, with about 2,000 Negroes in its population of 6,486, is approximately the same size as McMinnville.

Smith cited two reasons for Alcoa's record. He pointed to "better jobs, and the expanded recreational program for whites and colored." The recreational program is segregated, so that some Negroes must walk blocks to "their" area although a "white" area is in their neighborhood. Nevertheless, the expanded program has been beneficial.

For Negro children Alcoa has a large grammar-high school with seventeen teachers. A new gymnasium, two classrooms, and a lunchroom were added in 1950. The facilities are not equal to those for whites, but they are about as nearly equal as is possible under a segregated system. McMinnville has a Negro school about one third as large, with seven teachers. There is a small lunchroom, no gymnasium, and an inadequate recreational area. McMinnville Negroes have been waiting for a gymnasium since 1941, when the state ran a highway across the school grounds, cutting the football-baseball field in two. The McMinnville school is new, the old one having burned down.

With the inducement of the gymnasium and an active sports-program, along with vocational training and a school of which they can be somewhat proud, 521 pupils were enrolled in the Alcoa Negro school, 132 of them in high school.

This is more than twice the enrollment in McMinnville. It indicated that many McMinnville youth had quit school, primarily because they found it necessary to supplement their family income.

The principal of Alcoa's Negro school reported that for September of 1950 less than four students out of every one hundred enrolled were absent during the month. The average for white Alcoa schools was about the same—in fact, not quite as good—as for the Negro school. In McMinnville, Negro attendance is considerably lower than that for whites. It also is considerably lower than that for either whites or Negroes in Alcoa.

There is something basic in the difference between the Alcoa school and the one in McMinnville. That basic something is the key factor in all the differences between the two communities. I saw no indication that Alcoa Negroes were any more intelligent, capable, or willing to work than those in McMinnville. The fact that most Alcoans had moved from communities where their living standards were on a par with, or lower than, those of McMinnville Negroes seemed to show that the greater economic opportunity of Alcoa was the big difference. If anything, Alcoa Negroes had failed to utilize their economic strength to its fullest advantage and strike out for further gains.

That economic opportunity was the big difference I saw vividly when I revisited Sunday School at the Methodist Church in McMinnville. There was remarkable improvement in the building and worship-services. It was a church befitting a large city. "This ought to encourage a lot of youngsters to go to church Sundays, as so many did when I was a boy," I said to Mrs. J. E. Wood.

"Attendance was marvelous last fall," she replied, "but winter stepped in. Look at our town's youngsters . . . holes in their shoes . . . no underwear . . . no overcoats. When the weather turns bad they get neither to school nor to Sunday school."

Then this retired schoolteacher, who had given more years than I could remember to instructing McMinnville youngsters, sat silent, shaking her head. "The Jarman shoe factory . . . the hosiery mill . . . the cannery . . . the silk mill . . . the overall factory making army uniforms . . ." She rolled familiar names off her tongue as she thought aloud, and I knew what the names meant without her telling me: only one Negro worked in any of those firms—a woman janitor at the overall factory.

Mrs. Wood stared out her window past aged walnut trees at Bernard school, to which she and her husband had given their lives; knowing, I am sure, that it had been inadequate to the needs of the Negro community for decades. Occasionally, an uncoated lad would romp down the rainy street. Mrs. Wood still shook her head as I sat silent, thinking about the past and hoping for the future as I crammed my mouth full of the wonderful holiday pastries that I always seemed to find at her house.

"Carl," she half-whispered, "it would mean so much if someone would give us one plant—just one plant—that would hire Negroes at decent jobs and wages."

In Alcoa, some 140 miles farther east, where the dawn comes a little earlier, even in the realm of human affairs, the Adge Shockley family could remember, and they could say: "Amen!"

CHAPTER V

A SYMBOL BY THE SEA

I STOOD in the airport between Alcoa and Knoxville, wishing that I were buying tickets for two—for Noah Brannon and myself. I wanted to take Brannon to Washington, D.C., the nation's capital, and let him see me, a Negro, try to walk erect in that city. I wanted him to see how Washington is the magic boundary where the mores of train and bus passengers shift suddenly and decree that Negroes and whites who have ridden side by side must do so no farther south; or where northbound passengers who have ridden under conditions of untouchability feel free to change to a closeness next to intimacy.

I wanted Noah Brannon, and Americans like him, to walk with me through Washington and see that city, the symbol of a great republic, as a Negro sees it. I wanted them to see it as foreigners see it. I wanted them to realize that no reporter could give a complete story of segregation, discrimination, racial hatred, or any aspect of life as an American Negro without writing about Washington. I wished that America's Noah Brannons could see for themselves how Washington is the beginning and end of democracy as the Western world knows it—and how it is also the beginning and end of racial segregation in America.

But as I stood there in the airport I realized that if Noah Brannon were with me there would be little that *I* could show him in Washington. There we would walk separate paths. Where could we eat together? Where could we stay together? Then I remembered that I did not even know where I would stay. I rummaged through my wallet for a

59

newspaper clipping that I had brought from Minneapolis. The clipping, from the Pittsburgh *Courier*, reported that three Washington hotels had agreed to drop their ban on Negroes in order that a Vermont schoolteacher might bring his pupils to the capital without worrying about where Negro members of the group would stay. Among those hotels was the Plaza. I figured that if the Plaza had gone that far, perhaps I would be allowed to stay there. I telephoned the Plaza.

I talked with a man who identified himself as Showers, the night manager. I did not tell him that I was a Negro. He assured me that a room would be held for me. When I reached the Washington airport the next morning I decided to check on my reservation. Again I called the Plaza. "Yes, Mr. Rowan, we are holding a reservation for you," said a woman.

I walked out to a limousine and gave my bags to the driver. The starter opened the front door, offering me a seat beside the driver, although only one person was in the back, which had room for five persons. The inference was that if I must ride in a limousine I should ride beside the driver and not other passengers. Although this had happened to me several times in Washington, I had not been able to understand why there was less harm in my sitting beside a white driver than in sitting next to white passengers. I assumed that the driver, a hired hand, could least afford to complain. But this time I knew that sex had reared its lily-white head, for the sole passenger in the rear was a young white woman.

"Plaza hotel," I said to the driver.

"*Where?*" he almost yelled, although he had received similar instructions from the starter.

"Plaza hotel," I repeated with faked nonchalance.

I was taken to the Plaza, where a Negro bellboy took my bags, making no effort to conceal his surprise. As I walked through the lobby I could feel stares from all directions.

I identified myself to a woman at the desk. After smothering a look of bewilderment, she picked up what I thought was the reservations book. Holding one side up so I could not see the pages, she looked at the book for several seconds, then said she had no record of a reservation for me. When I protested that some woman had just confirmed a reservation when I called from the airport, she called a man who performed the same routine with the book. He gave his head a negative shake, adding: "And we are completely filled."

"Does anybody work here named Showers?" I asked.

"That's our night manager," said the man, "but he's gone. But I'm sure he wouldn't have made a reservation last night. Why, we've been filled for quite a while—two weeks." I thanked him and nodded to the bellboy, who picked up my bags.

"I thought you must be crazy when you stopped here," said the bellboy as we waited for a cab. I shrugged my shoulders and asked him how he liked working for the Plaza.

"If Negroes didn't work for Jim Crow places in Washington, there'd be an awful lot of starving Negroes here," he replied.

I was climbing into a cab when another bellboy came out. "They say you might try the Whitelaw," he said. I told the driver to take me to the Whitelaw. I wanted to see what they recommended for a Negro traveler.

The Whitelaw was a Negro hotel, where my bags sat on the sidewalk until I found the manager, who carried them in himself. I asked for a room with bath. After several minutes of conferring with a maid and a scrubwoman, the manager led me to a room. I found the bed unmade. Once-white curtains were dark with dirt. The lower half of the windowshade was faded, apparently by rain. I turned on the bathroom light and watched roaches and waterbugs run for cover. When I tried to flush the toilet bowl, which was greatly in need of a flushing, the contents ran over on the floor.

I walked out to the manager (there was no phone in the room) and complained mildly. He sent a cleaning man in with a plunger and a bundle of rags. I stood in the middle of the room, looking at the bed, the curtains, the man probing into the toilet bowl with a plunger while he scoured the floor by moving a rag back and forth with his foot. I took a few pictures and checked out—with a Negro taxi-driver telling me how lucky I was to get that room, because he "didn't even know they had rooms with baths at the Whitelaw."

As thousands of Negroes have been forced to do since World War II, I went to Carver Hall at Howard University and got a clean comfortable room at half the price I was being charged at the Whitelaw.

I had encountered a problem that I would face scores of times in the next few weeks. Once in the Deep South, I would have to stay at dirty, bedbug-ridden, brawling houses, most of them owned by whites and run by Negroes, all gleefully profiting from segregation, or I would have to rely on the hospitality of Negro citizens. With that choice, I knew I would cross the thresholds of the homes of a lot of doctors, teachers, and preachers. I would try to keep this at a minimum by leaving towns at night and riding Pullman, or by staying on campus in cities with Negro colleges.

Washington had been a problem to more than Negroes seeking lodging. It had been a problem to the United States government, which had had to apologize when an African foreign minister was refused admittance to a white hotel, when a Puerto Rican Senator was forced to sleep on a couch in a government office because hotels refused him, and in several other instances of embarrassment to foreigners.

Friends told me, however, that Washington had made progress in the preceding few years. The Statler, Willard, and Shoreham hotels sometimes accepted Negroes, principally in conventions, they said. They warned me, however, that it probably would be useless to try to get into those hotels without arriving from out of town with a reservation. I knew that I would return to Washington and then I would explore the policy of these hotels.

A few weeks later I wired the Statler and was told by return telegram that no room was available on the date I requested. I wired the Shoreham and received a wire confirming a reservation for me. I went to the Shoreham the day of my reservation and identified myself to the desk attendant. "I believe you have a reservation for me," I said.

"Rowan? I don't seem to find any record of a reservation for you, sir."

I started unzipping my briefcase. "I have a wire of confirmation that ought to make looking a little simpler," I replied, matter-of-factly.

"Wire of confirmation?" he repeated, as if a little surprised. "Just a minute, the steward is back here." He walked into a back room. He returned with a clean-cut young man, who glanced at the telegram I held, then walked to the card file that the first man had looked through to no avail.

"Rowan . . . Rowan. Here it is," he said and pushed a registration card and pen to me.

The first man talked by phone with someone elsewhere in the building as I registered. I could tell that he was discussing the wire confirming my reservation. The bellboy picked up my bags and we started to my room. As I turned the corner I heard the man on the phone exclaim:

"Well, I'll be a sonofabitch if that ain't the prize of the week!"

Part Two

"In the shadow of the Capitol" is the way the Plaza hotel is described in that institution's advertisements. As I rode away from the Plaza that January morning when nobody could find a reservation for me, I could see something else "in the shadow of the Capitol," a sight surely more world-advertised than the Plaza. I saw the wretched alley-dwellings of Temple Court, sprawling like a festering sore amid marble statuary and gleaming white domes. I saw evidence that a great many of Washington's 250,000 Negro citizens are besieged with problems much more pressing than that of finding a hotel room. Even though this population represents the greatest concentration of college-trained Negroes in the world, the community's basic problems are filth, poverty, squalid slums, and disease—problems more reasonably part of a less able, less literate community.

Although Washington is a short distance below the Mason-Dixon line geographically, its citizens argue that it is not part of the South. Washington was the capital of the North in the Civil War, they point out. Nevertheless, Washington leads the nation in segregation and discrimination in many respects. Let us assume that you, the reader, were a Negro in Washington. This is what the nation's capital would mean to you:

If you were downtown at lunchtime you could eat only at Union Station, in government-building cafeterias and at the Y.W.C.A. Cafeteria. You would be barred from the Y.M.C.A. Coffee Shop, however.

You would find that even some government cafeterias still "suggest" segregation. I went to the seventh-floor cafeteria in the Bureau of Internal Revenue building. There was a large, three-wing cafeteria that technically was open to all races. Near by, however, was a small room "for colored," to be used by Negroes who preferred it or were too timid to eat in the main cafeteria. There were about ten times as many Negroes in the "for colored" room as in the main cafeteria. Management contended that it was not to blame—the main cafeteria was open to everybody. Negroes, who had Jim Crowed themselves, argued that the fact that the separate room was maintained meant that they were not welcome in the large cafeteria.

If you, the Washington Negro, went to a 5-and-10-cent store for a snack, as I did, you would find that you must pay a premium for being American. The premium is that you must stand to be served. I walked into a store, unaware of this policy, and sat at the counter. I ordered two doughnuts and a glass of milk.

"Colored can't sit down," the waitress said hesitantly.

"Poor things," I countered, pretending not to understand.

"You're colored?" she mumbled, adding: "I mean, do you have your foreign credentials?"

"Foreign credentials? What you ask," I said sharply, "is whether I am a foreigner or an American. Yes, I am an American."

"Well, I'm sorry, sir," she replied apologetically, "but we are told that you people have to eat standing, or you can't be served."

I glanced at the whites who sat eating near by. Several of them had heard the exchange, but the few who appeared concerned only looked at me as if to say: "Well, you heard her. . . ." My jaws began to swell with anger and humiliation. I saw spots before my eyes. I thought I could feel cool beads of perspiration break out on my arms and hands as I gripped the counter.

"You mean that in the nation's capital . . ." I began, then stopped. The waitress still looked me in the face, and her eyes seemed to reveal genuine sorrow. I knew that to scold her was useless. She was merely a pawn in a long-standing Washington game. I walked away—to let the experience die like a bad dream.

I went to the *Tribune's* Washington Bureau offices in the National Press Building. There I learned that, in Washington, the bad dream of racial discrimination does not die; Negroes just go on, dreaming pretty much the same old dream.

"Say, Rowan, aren't you gaining weight?" asked a Bureau member who had been in Minneapolis a few months previously.

"Yes, a bit," I replied, "but I expect this Washington-enforced diet will whittle me down."

"Say, where *do* you eat here? Why, I can't even take you to lunch in the Press Club dining-room."

I pointed out the few places where Negroes could eat, explaining that most places either refuse you outright or insist that you stand at the end of the counter. "I'm afraid to eat standing," I joked, "because I'd eat twice as much, I'm sure. Then I *would* be gaining weight." I added that a drive against the stand-up rule apparently was succeeding in a few department stores in the 7th Street shopping area.

"Well, how about coming to my house for dinner tonight?" he said. "We ought to be able to dig up a chair for you to sit on there."

I left the Press Building and walked a few yards on 14th Street between F and G Streets, N.W. I saw that not a customer was in Nedick's orange-drink and hamburger stand. Since I had seen Nedick's places in New York City, I thought the policy-setting offices might be there, and if so, I could get food at this stand. At least, if I was turned down there would not be the humiliation of having to walk out amid the stares and sneers of patrons with more acceptable skin colors. As I stood there, concerned with choosing a place where the rebuff I expected would not be public, I felt that I partially understood Negroes who Jim Crowed themselves in the government cafeteria. They had yielded to an impulse to go where their feelings would not be hurt. Even I, a reporter more concerned with gathering information for my report than with my personal feelings, had done the same thing.

I walked into Nedick's and sat down. One girl looked up and continued sweeping trash into a dustpan. A second girl wiped counters. Finally, the second girl, a short, bumpy-faced brunette with a very pleasant voice, acknowledged my presence. As the words, "Two hotdogs . . ." slipped off my lips, she was explaining that she was "not allowed to serve you, sir."

"I beg your pardon."

"I'm sorry, sir, but I can't serve colored."

"Not even standing?"

"No, sir. I'm sorry."

"You're sorry. Then that means it isn't *your* policy, but your boss's?"

"Yes, sir."

"Thanks. I'm sorry to have troubled you. I didn't know. I'm just a stranger in town," I finished, then walked out, less angry than amused at the ultrapolite manner in which Washingtonians told me that I was brown, obviously of African descent, although to what extent would always be a mystery, and that because of this I could not buy a hot dog in their place.

You, the Washington Negro, also would find a tight policy of racial exclusion in places of entertainment. Except for the Playhouse, which changed its policy in 1951, no downtown theater would admit you unless you wrapped your head in a turban or spoke a foreign language, thus posing as an alien. I thought of trying the foreign-language gimmick at a movie house, but after mumbling *"Un billet, s'il vous plaît"* a couple of times, I lost my nerve. I was sure the box-office girl would laugh in my face, and that my former French teacher would drop dead to read about it.

You would find that you could sit in the audience at Constitution Hall but that the Daughters of the American Revolution would bar you as a stage performer. Their banning of singer Marian Anderson almost caused another American revolution, and in late 1951 it was reported that the group had agreed to allow another Negro, Dorothy Maynor, to sing in Constitution Hall. On the other hand, the National Theater, Washington's only commercial playhouse, saw nothing wrong with Negroes performing on the stage, although it would not allow them in the audience. Rather than change this policy under pressure of a boycott by Actors' Equity Association, the owning corporation converted the National into a movie house, and retained the racial bar.

One of the few entertainment places open to Negroes on an unsegregated basis is Griffith Stadium, baseball park of the Washington Senators. And Negroes only go there to root against the Senators when they are playing the Cleveland Indians, Chicago White Sox, or other teams that have Negroes in their lineups.

Negroes and whites get along in Griffith Stadium, which would appear to make worthless the argument that segregation is best because the "two races cannot get along." They also get along on busses and trolleys, where the two races are packed in together daily on a nonsegregated basis. There, by custom and law, the Negro is the white man's equal—except that he cannot work for the Capital Transit Authority. During World War II the transit company advertised for white workers in cities more than two hundred miles away. It recruited government clerks as part-time workers. Yet, both the company and the union were adamant against hiring available Negro personnel. Their argument was, and still is, that passengers will not tolerate a Negro operator.

So it goes through every aspect of Jim Crow in America's capital: the restaurant owner fears his white customers will walk out if a Negro is served; the hotel manager fears his guests will go elsewhere next time, and even the owner of a dog cemetery has his worries. In banning pets of Negroes, he conceded that it probably wouldn't make much difference to the animals, but the white owners of pets might complain.

Part Three

I asked a taxi-driver to take me to Burke's Court, and to the area of 9th Street, N.W., and a few other streets where I could look over some slum housing. He told me that I didn't have to go that far, that there were slums within walking distance of the Senate Office Building, where we then were. I told him to take me to Burke's Court and the other places anyhow, because the slums near the Capitol had been so publicized that Americans might get the idea they were the only slums in Washington.

The driver turned out to be a rather loquacious chap. Between the starting-point and what we settled on as being Burke's Court, he gave me a rather extensive fill-in on why the international situation is what it is. He had convinced me that the world would be much better off if a Democrat never had been born, and, as we swerved into an alley, he was about to convince me that Joe Louis made his biggest mistake when he put on boxing gloves for the first time.

"Burke's Court? Burke's Court?" he said to himself. "This ought to be it up here."

He drove slowly because the alley was a narrow, dusky little thoroughfare where decrepit old men and women sat half in the car's path, and ragged little urchins walked about, either oblivious or indifferent to the approaching automobile. It was exceedingly warm for midwinter, I thought. I had the window down, and I was sure that I could smell the stench of urine.

"You want me to stop?" asked the driver. "I'm sure this is it."

"Sure, stop," I replied. "Doesn't matter what street it is. People live on all of them. I think I'll snap a picture or two."

"Mister, if you go in some of these places you'll have to bathe in DDT. Ain't all this a Goddam shame?"

I didn't answer, continuing to adjust my camera. I was afraid the residents would resent my coming there "all dressed up" to take pictures of them in their pathetic circumstances. Already, fat women in dirty gingham dresses, and with babies much too large to nurse hanging on their hips, were leaning from windows and doors of their second-floor flats to see who the intruder was, and what he was doing. I got out of the car.

I left my briefcase in the taxi, partly to assure the driver that I would return, and then went to what I assumed was the rear of the biggest building. Behind it was a miniature junkyard. Old, battered automobiles, worthless tires, and scrap metal littered the yard.

"Be real quiet," said a grinning one-armed man, "and you may git a picture of a gopher loping 'cross the yard. Mister, they's some rats 'round here that can whup any cat alive."

He laughed to indicate that he had made a joke. I forced a smile and told him that I thought too much noise was being made by the youngsters playing among the debris for any rats to be stirring.

I focused my camera on the large, dilapidated building, which had a maze of washtubs, clothes lines, drying diapers and ladies' underwear, old blankets, pots, gourd dippers, and other crude or nondescript utensils hanging on the walls or on cords tied to posts. The number of tubs seemed to indicate the number of cubicles into which the building had been partitioned. They also seemed to indicate that little or no indoor plumbing was available to the inhabitants. It was a repulsive sight, and to watch the youngsters playing amid the wretchedness, apparently unaware of the sadness of their young plight, made it even more sickening. I felt like vomiting, but there didn't seem to be anything, not even a bottom, in my stomach.

I braced myself and walked over to chat with the one-armed man, hoping that he would invite me into his little shack. He did not, so I put on a burst of friendliness and leaned against the facing of his half-open door. I could peek in, but it was dark inside. The room stank with the mustiness of close, crowded living. I joked with him, and each time he turned his head I tapped the door with my foot to open it wider and let some light in.

"You live alone, mister?" I asked him.

"Naw, I got me a wife. She ain't home from the white folks' kitchen yet."

"Jesus Christ," I mumbled to myself, gritting my teeth to keep the words from escaping. "The 'white folks' sure ought to see where their cook lives!" I looked at the Benjamin Franklin heater with the missing leg. I thought the grate must be burned out, for ashes had spilled all over the stove apron and on the floor in front of the stove, in which there appeared to be no fire. The little plaster had fallen from the part of the wall where the chimney shot through. It seemed a miracle that the shack hadn't caught fire.

"Just got this one room?" I asked, noticing that one wall apparently was cardboard; I could read the word ZENITH in the semidarkness.

"Yeah. This ain't no whole room. Used to be one big room, but it's cut in two. I feel sorry for them folks next to us," he went on in magnanimous grandeur, "they got five people a livin' in thet side." He said his rent was twenty dollars a month.

I stepped out to take another picture of the big tub-laden building. As I peered down into the reflex camera I saw for the first time where the cardboard partition apparently had come from. Atop this rickety old building, where a wilderness of black faces, some snickering and some showing resentment, looked out at me, were several television aerials. Obviously, it was more than economic poverty that kept some of these people where they were: either they didn't care or they couldn't get other housing.

I knew where to find at least part of the answer: in the 1948 code of ethics of the Washington Real Estate Board. In that code is this paragraph: "No property in a white section should ever be sold, rented, advertised or offered to colored people. In case of doubt, advice from the public affairs committee should be obtained." Washington real-estate men told me that the board considers a neighborhood white if one half or more of its inhabitants are white.

Since 1948, however, the United States Supreme Court has outlawed "restrictive covenants," or pacts in which home owners are bound by contract not to sell to a member of a minority group. The court ruled that such exclusion clauses no longer may be enforced through the nation's courts. Nevertheless, the powerful pressure of real-estate interests, and considerable social pressure, prevent Washington builders or home owners from selling to Negroes. Because of this, Negroes are barred from expansion into the city's suburbs. Whites outnumber Negroes more than twelve to one in suburban Washington, but just over two to one in the city proper. Thus, Washington's 250,000 Negroes have piled up to where more than seventy per cent are crammed into a crescent-shaped area, of which the outer boundary is less than two and one-half miles from the heart of the city. This also means that Negroes live in seventy per cent of Washington's slum dwellings, although they form only thirty per cent of the population, according to a 1947 Bureau of Census housing study.

You, the reader, who for this chapter are a Negro in Washington, would find that your family would be two and one-half times as likely as a white family to live in a dwelling containing six or more persons. It would be four times as likely to lack a private flush-toilet; nine times as likely to live in a structure needing major repair; eleven times as likely to lack running water; ten times as likely to lack central heating, and eight times as likely to lack electric lights.

You, the Negro, would see this in terms of its demoralizing effect on your children: in 1947 more than two thirds of the Washington felons arrested were Negroes, and one third of these felons were juveniles under eighteen years of age. Why is this? I asked the Washington Council of Social agencies. A young woman handed me a chart showing the crescent-shaped area in which most Negroes live. Then she handed me a chart showing that this crescent contains the overwhelming majority of dwelling units with two persons per room. Then she showed me a chart that showed where Washington police make the majority of arrests of persons under eighteen; it was the same area of crowded, substandard housing. To make sure I got the point, she showed me an area on the population chart where Negroes live in more prosperous, less crowded circumstances. The chart of arrests showed that policemen made very few calls to that area.

You, the Negro, also would see the housing situation in terms of human lives. Tuberculosis, which reflects shortcomings in housing and diet more than any other major disease, snuffs out the lives of Washington Negroes four times as fast as it does whites. It kills Washington Negroes twice as rapidly as those elsewhere in the nation.

"Negroes die so often from tuberculosis in Washington because they are segregated by race in the worst jobs and dwellings," reported the National Committee on Segregation in the Nation's Capital, a group of nationally prominent citizens that conducted a thorough survey of racial prejudice in the District. This group reported in 1948 that "colored people who had moderate incomes and lived in adequate housing . . . had a lower tuberculosis death rate than did slum-dwelling white people." Their report, indicating that tuberculosis is not a racial disease, and that "bacteria are broadminded," was based on figures from the District Bureau of Vital Statistics.

I found that you, the Washington Negro, would get the unhealthy end of the stick in more ways than can be attributed to poor jobs or housing. The inequality begins at birth, when a Negro baby is twice as likely to die as is a white infant, and when the Negro mother is six times as likely to die in childbirth as is the white mother. It follows the Negro throughout his life, which will be ten to twelve years shorter than that of a white resident.

The Committee on Segregation said that "there is no reason to assume that it is more difficult for colored women to bear children than it is for white women. . . . This rate of maternal mortality indicates that Negroes in Washington do not get sufficient medical care . . . the facilities for them are inferior, and far short of their . . . need."

On December 8, 1950, Washington's voteless League of Women Voters reported after a survey that "there is some form of discrimination or segregation in all of the hospitals in the District of Columbia, with the exception of Freedmen's, which is all-Negro and maintained by the Federal Government, and two very small privately-owned institutions for Negroes."

Doctors Hospital; Sibley, operated by the Woman's Home Missionary Society of the Methodist Episcopal Church; and National Homeopathic, operated under the auspices of the National Homeopathic Organization and located in a colored section of the city, admit no Negroes at all. The strictness of this policy is shown in the following report from the January 1947 *Survey Graphic* magazine:

> *On a wintry morning of 1945, a colored woman in labor, unable to find a cab, set out in the company of her sister for the maternity ward of the Gallinger General Hospital. Reaching the vicinity of* [a] *church-supported hospital, the women discovered that the birth was so imminent that the expectant mother could not reach Gallinger in time. The sister rushed up the steps of the denominational hospital and sought admission for the suffering woman as an emergency patient. This was curtly refused and the baby was delivered on the sidewalk in front of the hospital. Its staff supplied a sheet to cover the mother and child until the municipal ambulance arrived to take them to Gallinger.*

Nine other private hospitals admit Negroes to segregated wards, or not at all, except in two instances. George Washington University Hospital, which formerly admitted Negroes only to its birth-control clinic, now sets aside no separate floor or wards for colored patients. Colored and white may occupy the same floor but not the same room. The isolation ward at Children's Hospital is nonsegregated, probably because of the unusual physical requirements of such a ward.

The Committee on Segregation reported: "In almost all instances, the segregated accommodations for Negroes are inferior to those for whites. At Casualty Hospital, colored patients are housed in an old, deteriorated building, and their visitors must come and go through the ambulance entrance, not the main entrance."

This means that most Negroes go to Freedmen's and Gallinger, where seventy per cent of the patients are Negroes. Both hospitals operate on insufficient funds, and the conditions under which Gallinger patients live have become a national scandal. In 1946 a survey group found "an inordinately high mortality" among infants there. In 1947 *The Saturday Evening Post* reported that Gallinger "puts the legs of its beds in pans of water to keep the cockroaches from snuggling up to the patients."

In 1951 I went out for a personal look at Gallinger. I walked in, and as no one seemed to care who I was or why I was there, I roamed at will through the building. I might easily have been a fugitive from a psychopathic ward, but no one seemed to care. I walked with an official air through colored wards, past doctors and nurses. In medical and surgical wards I had to turn sideways to get through; extra beds had been put in the passageway to accommodate the overflow of Negro patients.

I walked into the white wards, noting that there were many empty beds there. I pulled out my notebook and started to count empty beds as I walked. Then, for the first time, someone seemed to notice that I was out of place. "I guess you're looking for the colored wards," said a nurse. She started to give me directions.

"No, miss, I'm not looking for the colored wards," I said. "I'd be happy enough if you'd just show me the way out."

Part Four

I met a theater operator in the Senate Office Building. I asked him why his theater and others barred Negroes. "It's just public policy, fellow," he explained. "Hell, I'm no reformer. I'm just trying to make money. The schools are segregated and that's custom *and* law. If Congress hasn't guts enough to change that, why should I stick my neck out?"

Max Kampelman, legislative adviser to Senator Hubert H. Humphrey, Minnesota Democrat, informed me that I would get much the same answer if I asked any Washingtonian to explain why he practiced Jim Crow. They all would take me back to 1878, when Congress passed the Organic Act. This, with Public Law 254, passed in 1906, restricted Negroes and whites to separate schools. They would tell me that the government practices Jim Crow, and that Congress had set the pattern, and until Congress does something about it, Jim Crow is good enough for them.

For that reason, I was not surprised to find that segregation in Washington's public schools is a bristling controversy that has caused sharp divisions in the white community and aroused no little animosity among Negroes. I felt that I had found one definite sign of a "New South," for never had I seen a Negro community so aroused and prone to action over any issue.

The situation in Washington schools is much the same as that in the hospitals. Negro schools are so overcrowded that thousands of colored pupils can get only part-time training. At the same time, there is room for four thousand more students in white schools. Only recently, one out of seven Negro students could get only part-time schooling although there was a surplus of eight thousand seats in white schools. There was —and still is—a shortage of kindergarten space for Negro youngsters, with 2,500 recently on the waiting list; there were no whites waiting.

One example of overcrowding was at Cardoza Senior High for Negroes. It had a capacity of 845 students, but was operating on triple shift with an enrollment of 1,721. On the other hand, Central High for whites had 1,300 enrolled with a capacity of 1,950. Negroes protested vigorously, as did many whites, and demanded that Central (thirty years old) be turned over to Negro students. The request finally was granted, although School Superintendent Hobart M. Corning opposed the transfer.

When the transfer was approved, Corning allowed Central alumni to remove the cornerstone "for sentimental reasons." Central also was renamed Cardoza. This preserved the tradition that no Negro and white Washingtonian could claim the "same" school as their alma mater. But the transfer still left an excess of several thousand seats in white schools, and a shortage of about two thousand for Negroes.

I talked with Congressmen, businessmen, teachers, newspapermen, and citizens on the street, trying to determine what the dominant feeling is relative to the school situation. There seemed to be enough people against segregation to enable them, by sheer numbers, to force an end to it. The one big gimmick, however, is that the citizens of Washington have nothing to say about their schools. The schools are run by a Board of Education that is directly responsible to the federal government. The nine board members, of whom three must be women, are appointed by the District Court Judges of the District. These judges are appointed by the President of the United States. Thus, the people do not have even indirect control over the education offered to their children.

With the make-up of the board what it was in 1951, there obviously was little chance that the issue would be resolved within that body. Not even all the Negro members could be counted on to stand against segregation. A bigger handicap in the fight were some Negro teachers and members of the dual administrative staff. Aged Garnett C. Wilkinson, assistant superintendent for Negroes, was the prime Negro target of the anti-segregation movement. One board member complained that "Wilkinson approves every notion of Corning." A white businessman who opposed segregation quoted Corning as lauding Wilkinson "because he keeps the loud-mouth Negroes quiet." But the only thing anyone could definitely pin on Wilkinson was that he would not take a public stand; nor would he even comment among friends at his home. He is known to the Negro press of Washington as "the man who insists he never criticizes his superiors," which would appear to be a safe-enough philosophy.

Wilkinson is to retire in 1952, however, and I thought that announcement of this would create widespread joy among his critics. "The sad part of the situation," said a Washington *Afro-American* reporter who has followed the school wrangle closely, "is that, of the four candidates for Wilkinson's job, three are *known* to be 'Uncle Toms'; and a lot of people wouldn't bet a doughnut hole on the fourth one." (An "Uncle Tom" is a cringing, cowardly Negro who believes that "white is right." He has accepted his unequal status and the theory that he can gain only by appeasement, and not by demanding any right. He is willing to trade whatever he can deliver from the Negro community, be it votes or the ability to keep them divided, for a place in the "good graces" of his white boss.)

Nowhere does racial segregation take on a more wasteful aspect than in Washington, where a Congressional cry goes up almost daily for "government economy, except in defense matters." Yet Washington is where the school superintendent makes two speeches to teachers each September. The speeches are identical, but white teachers hear it at one session and Negro teachers at another. Washington also is where the school board sends deaf Negroes to Overly, Maryland, and pays one hundred dollars more yearly per pupil to send deaf whites to Gallaudet College. However, the board sends both white and Negro blind students to the same Overly school.

Washington spends about $126 yearly per Negro pupil and $160 per white pupil, according to the Federal Office of Education. The waste of the dual system would be even greater were as much spent for Negroes as whites. As it is, both Corning and Wilkinson expressed disgust when Negroes insisted that Central be turned over to them. Wilkinson had been campaigning for a new five-million-dollar technical school for Negroes. Although the Congress-sponsored Strayer report recommended some thirty-five million dollars' worth of new buildings, with twenty-eight million dollars of the money needed to bring Negro schools up to par, the proposed new building was rejected by Negroes on the grounds that to accept it as a Negro school would be to perpetuate segregation. Furthermore, segregation opponents said, it didn't make economic sense to build a five-million-dollar school to remedy an overflow of Negroes when there already were more than enough seats for all the District children if the schools were opened on a nonracial basis.

Opponents of Jim Crow won that round. Now they are carrying their fight to Congress, where the root of the trouble lies. Senator Humphrey promised to introduce a bill to end Washington school segregation.

I had seen the whole pattern of Negro life in Washington, and I was convinced that Congress, the President, and the federal government in general have a great responsibility in Washington. They set the original pattern that District citizens have expanded over the years, causing a degeneration to the present Negro position in the life of the nation's capital. During most of the twentieth century, the government has had a "closed door policy" toward the Negro worker, whereas during the last half of the nineteenth century Negroes served as Register of the Treasury, Auditor of the Navy, consul, Collector of Customs, and in many other important posts at home and abroad.

In the administration of William Howard Taft, however, Jim Crow got what apparently was its first administration sanction, and it soon permeated the District's entire official and social being. The National Committee on Segregation cited a 1927 report by the Washington branch of the National Association for the Advancement of Colored People, which stated that "Mr. Taft segregated the census takers in this city in 1910, restricting white workers to white and black workers to black."

The committee reported, however, that "segregation did not become general government policy until the presidency of Woodrow Wilson." With Wilson's election in 1912, a group of Southern Congressmen rode into Washington on a pledge to maintain and extend "white supremacy."

Senators Hoke Smith (Georgia), Ben "Pitchfork" Tillman (South Carolina), and James Vardaman (Mississippi) formed an organization known as the Democratic Fair Play Association, the purpose of which was to "put the Negro in his place." This group made President Wilson an honorary member and then set about its mission. Negro and white employees of the Bureau of Engraving were set apart at lunchtime. In 1914 the Civil Service Commission began asking each job applicant to submit a photograph. This stopped Negroes from getting top jobs. With two exceptions, every Negro in the auditor's office was demoted.

The South had seized control of the District Committees of the House and Senate, and Washington became the citadel of Jim Crow. To this day, the situation is about the same. In 1944 the late Senator Bilbo of Mississippi became chairman of the Senate District Committee. On May 8, 1946, in a campaign speech at Meridian, Mississippi, he said: "I wanted this position so I could keep Washington a segregated city."

All this led the Washington *Evening Star* to comment on September 4, 1946: "It must be viewed as one of the ironies of history that the Confederacy, which was never able to capture Washington during the course of [the Civil] War, now holds it as a helpless pawn. . . ."

In a sense, the Confederacy has not captured Washington. Washington has been surrendered by the lord of its overseers, the Board of Trade. That is no secret to anyone in Washington, government official or man on the street, I found. Representative Deane of North Carolina declared in the House in 1948: "It is the Washington Board of Trade which now rules Washington." Speaking in favor of a bill to give limited home rule to the District, he added: "When the Board of Trade cracks the whip, the District Government jumps. . . . Quite naturally the Board of Trade is against this bill."

The Board of Trade, which Deane called a "Glorified chamber of commerce," represents the real estate, business, and banking interests of Washington.

I had seen a lot of Washington, the capital that a free American Negro, Benjamin Banneker, helped survey and lay out after being appointed to the L'Enfant Commission by President George Washington. Today, nearly two hundred years later, Benjamin Banneker would find himself something less than a citizen in the American capital. He would get small consolation from the following tribute he received in a letter from Thomas Jefferson in August of 1791:

Sir:
. . . No one wishes more than I do to see such proofs as you exhibit, that Nature has given to our black brethren talents equal to those of other colors of men, and that the appearance of a want of them is owing only to the degraded condition of their existence, both in Africa and America. . . .

As I prepared to leave Washington, I was sure that Benjamin Banneker would feel much as did the Danish official who wrote, according to the National Committee, after visiting the American capital on a mission for his king:

> *It is no exaggeration to say that most of our people who come to your capital go home with what you call a bad taste in their mouths. I believe you should know that Washington today, despite its great outward beauty, is not a good salesman for your kind of democracy.*

CHAPTER VI

A CRY IN THE WILDERNESS

W<small>ELL</small>, this is *it*; this is where the men get separated from the boys," I told myself. I was about to move into the Deep South. Overnight I would plunge from Washington into the heart of the palmetto country, where Old South traditions run a deep and narrow course. I was going to a historic old city that glitters in the social timelessness of Old Spain and Colonial New England. I was going to talk with a white Southerner who had risen up in the camp of the white-supremacists and withered magnolia-blossoms with a stinging rebuke to the people of his state, declaring that it was time they rejoined the Union.

I was going to Charleston, South Carolina, to the home of United States District Judge J. Waties Waring, who, with his wife, had become perhaps the voice pre-eminent in the cry for Negro rights in the South.

I had written Judge Waring before leaving Minneapolis, asking if I might stop and talk with him. Whether the South willed it so or not, I knew that he was part of my story. I knew that Judge Waring was something new in the South, but I did not know whether he was indicative of the New South I sought; I was not sure that, in his newness, the Judge was still a part of the South.

I picked up two letters from the Judge at the *Tribune's* Washington Bureau Offices. Out of superstition, perhaps, I opened the first-dated letter first: Judge Waring would be happy to see me at his home, and he and his wife would be delighted if I would take a meal with them. I opened the second letter reluctantly, fearing that a change in plans had

83

made it necessary for the Judge to cancel his invitation. It was only a clipping that he had cut out of the Charleston *News and Courier*. The Ku Klux Klan was to hold a big rally at Aiken, South Carolina, the Saturday night that I was to arrive. "What a situation," I thought: "Me dining in the home of a white judge in Charleston while the Ku Klux Klan kicks up its heels near by." I was not unhappy that, because of a change in plans, I would not arrive in Charleston until Sunday morning.

I phoned the train station and asked for a Pullman reservation on the Atlantic Coast Line's Palmetto Limited from Washington to Charleston. I was told that lower berth 2, car R-500, would be held for me. I had succeeded in the first phase of an act that I would go through many times. Many a Negro has secured Pullman space or reserved seats on a train by telephoning, since race is not so discernible over the phone.

I went to Union Station to pick up my ticket and reservation. I told the seller my berth number to assure him that I knew what I was to get. I didn't think all this was necessary in Washington, but I was practicing for days to come. The seller made the usual phone call to confirm my space, but seemed to do all his talking about a pile of coal in somebody's basement. He expressed surprise that the Army already had moved it, and then gave me my tickets with no apparent reluctance.

I boarded the train that night with a group of Marine recruits who were bound for Parris Island. Several were from the upper Midwest, and I soon found myself discussing the merits of the Twin Cities compared with those of Milwaukee. I kept looking for the passenger who was to be in upper 2, but no one claimed the seat.

A sailor across the aisle heard me say that I was Charleston-bound, so he began talking with me. He was going to the Navy yard at Charleston. He was a former newspaper worker and I was a former sailor, so we had plenty to talk about. I told him that I had been a communications officer on two fleet-tankers during World War II, and that got us on the Navy's changed racial policy, which we discussed briefly.

"By the way, they've cut out segregation on trains, too, haven't they?" he asked.

I explained that it hadn't gone that far, that segregation was illegal only in interstate travel, and that Jim Crow still was the rule on unreserved coach-trains. "Of course, Pullmans never were segregated—if you could buy a ticket," I added.

The porter, who was preparing the sailor's berth, overheard me and broke in, half-whispering: "Oh, but they had their ways of segregating. Ticket-sellers had race codes, and they do now in lotsa cities. They'll talk to the reservations office about the 'woodpile,' 'in the coal bin,' and all that stuff. It all means: 'This traveler is a Negro; put another one with him if you can.'"

I remembered the ticket-seller talking about moving a load of coal from somebody's basement when I stood waiting for my tickets. "Who's in upper 2, anybody?" I asked the porter.

"Yeah, a military policeman," he replied. I could now understand what the ticket-seller meant when he said the Army already had moved "the coal."

I left the sailor and the porter discussing some of the humorous elements of railroad Jim Crow. I wanted to get dinner before the diner closed. Also, I was still a reporter; I wanted to see how policy in diners and coaches compared with the policy of my last days in the South.

I walked into the dining-car of the Palmetto Limited as it sped into the Southland. I sat at a table smack dab in the middle of the car. No longer were there two Jim Crow tables separated from the rest of the diners by a curtain. For me, a Negro journeying into South Carolina, this was new. I had ridden the same train in 1945, when I was an ensign running from port to port, trying to find my first ship.

The train was jammed full of passengers that morning in

1945, and as I approached the diner I saw that a long line waited. I peeked around the line, trying to decide whether to wait or give up breakfast. The steward motioned to me to come forward. "Ensigns don't rate this high," I thought. Then I remembered that, through one of the quirks of the segregation system, Negro ensigns could. All the passengers waiting in line were white. There was one empty Jim Crow table, forbidden to whites as the others were forbidden to Negroes.

I sat at the Jim Crow table reluctantly, but with the same chiding smile I once gave to white passengers on the Nashville-to-McMinnville bus, when I was the lone passenger on the long back seat and standing whites jammed the aisle but had to travel in misery because the seats beside me were taboo. As the steward reached up to pull the curtain and seal me off from the world of white diners, a voice said firmly: *"Don't pull that curtain!"* Startled, I glanced up and saw that a white, Navy shore-patrolman had spoken. He stared the befuddled steward in the eye and repeated the order.

The dining-car was so silent that you could have heard a fork hit false teeth.

"But this is South Carolina," protested the steward. "It's the law!"

"Damn South Carolina's laws," barked the shore patrolman. "You'll pull that curtain on no Navy men today."

I sat silent, staring downward, trying to hide the watery film that covered my eyes. Someone was fighting for *me* and winning. I ordered breakfast with a buoyant feeling, but I didn't want it. I couldn't eat. From the shore patrolman's first words something had begun to swell in me. I was full—clear up to the tonsils. I would have settled for a glass of water, a toothpick, and a Medal of Honor for an unknown sailor who had gone exceedingly far beyond the ordinary call of duty.

By 1951, the United States Supreme Court had done with finality what a shore patrolman with a .45 automatic strapped to his side had done for the duration of a meal in 1945. That a Negro was eating within view didn't seem to bother the other diners in 1945, and nobody seemed to care in 1951. A tall, unmistakably Southern, white gentleman sat at the table with me in 1951, and we managed to get through the meal without stabbing or spitting at each other. This gentleman, who appeared to have a mania for pulling out his vest-pocket watch, even exchanged a few pleasantries with me.

But there still was segregation in the coaches of the Palmetto Limited in January of 1951. I walked through a string of modern cars marked: AIR CONDITIONED, KEEP DOOR CLOSED. Then I reached a car that had no such sign on the door. "This is it," I said. I knew that it was the coach for Negroes only. It was a dirty, dimly lighted car. Filthy blue headpieces were on each seat. I walked through after midnight, stepping across water that had seeped from a cooler and mingled on the floor with milk and small bits of glass. A young mother had dropped her baby's bottle. The mother fumbled in the dim light as a portable radio played, not quite loud enough to drown out the snoring of a man who had removed his shoes and stretched himself across two seats. I walked back to my Pullman car. It was early in my journey, and I still could escape temporarily from Jim Crow by going to sleep.

Part Two

A splendid sun rose out of the sea that Sunday morning, giving Charleston's stucco walls a jewelry-shop gleam. The city, to the eye, fit the storybook lore of elegant women curtsying to debonair gentlemen with honey suckle-soft voices. "So it is this beautiful city that has ostracized the Warings?" I asked the Negro taxi-driver who had met the train.

"Man, they done everything but nail him to the cross, if that's what you mean by ostracized," he replied.

"Yeah, ostracized could mean that," I said, more to myself

than to the driver. I told him to take me to the home of the private family from whom I would rent a room for the night. When we reached the house I asked the driver how far it was to 61 Meeting Street.

"Just a few minutes. That's the Judge's home," he added, as if to let me know that I wasn't being so secretive by using the address rather than the name. "I'm just gonna hang around home, so if you need a taxi today, call me. I'm reliable." I told him to pick me up at half past noon.

Just before one p.m., the sacred dining-hour in Charleston, my taxi pulled up in front of the glistening gray-white Colonial home. I looked at the quaint fan-window over the door, which no white Charlestonian had walked through since 1947, when Judge Waring issued the now-famous ruling that Negroes must be allowed to vote in South Carolina's previously all-white primary. One of the federal agents who guarded the Judge constantly sat in a coupé in front of the house. I nodded feebly at the agent and rang the doorbell. When the maid responded—"Mr. Rowan? Judge Waring is expecting you"—I realized that for the first time in my life I was entering the front door of a white Southerner's home as something other than a servant. I had rung doorbells in Dixie before and maids had told me: "Boy! You will go to the back door."

Judge Waring, former captain of the elite Charleston Light Dragoons, scion of eight generations of Charleston aristocracy and son of a Confederate veteran, stood erect. He reached out to shake my hand while telling me: "We are very, very glad to have you with us. We've arranged it so that, if your schedule permits, you are to spend the day with us." I just stood and stared at this man who lived in the limbo of social ostracism, and I felt that his welcome was sincere. I was to spend the day with two persons who I thought must be the loneliest people in America.

This seventy-year-old judge had incurred the mightiest wrath of people whom his wife called "sick, confused and decadent . . . full of pride and complacency, morally weak and low." This charming, exuberant Detroit-born woman of fifty-five had sharply defined the line of battle, had admonished the Negroes of the South: "Get off your knees and fight for the rights you already have."

With unmistakable clarity, the Judge.himself had issued a challenge that incensed the South. In his 1947 decision he declared: "It is time for South Carolina to rejoin the Union. It is time to fall in step with the other states and to adopt the American way of conducting elections."

South Carolinians were "insulted." No "Southern gentle-man" would say the things that Judge Waring said, they shouted. "I meant to say it just the way I did," recalls the Judge. "I wanted to preach a sermon and see if I could arouse the decent people of the state to a realization that democracy cannot survive if we continue to have first- and second-class citizens. I knew that it would take more than a dust-dry opinion to arouse them from a decades-old sleep."

Thus he invoked statutes never before applied in Dixie, and the Democratic Party of South Carolina said it would yield and allow Negroes to vote. There was a tiny gimmick, how-ever: the prospective voter had to swear that he believed in separation of the races and was against the Fair Employ-ment Practices Act. To the amazement of Southerners, Judge Waring ruled the oath illegal. He declared with finality that Negroes must be allowed to vote, and he issued an injunction banning interference with that right by Democratic officials. He warned that he would sit in court on primary day and would punish any violator of his injunction.

This federal judge, appointed for life, independent of local politics and with the power of the Army and Navy behind him, sat in court on primary day as he had promised. South Carolinians fumed, but not one violated his order. Thirty-five thousand Negroes voted for the first time in their lives. From that day, in the tiniest poolhall and at the most remote country-crossroad in the state, J. Waties Waring was known as "the man who let the nigger vote." The name J. Waties Waring became anathema.

In March of 1950, twenty-one thousand persons signed a petition asking that the Judge be impeached. The South Carolina House of Representatives voted ten thousand dollars to finance impeachment proceedings. It also voted funds to buy the Warings one-way tickets out of the state. No legal basis for impeachment was found, so Judge Waring remained, a pariah in his native land.

Mrs. Waring walked the streets, and white children who hardly had learned to say "mommy" cried "witch." When the Judge walked the streets, friends and acquaintances of more than half a century gazed in store windows or studied cloud formations until he passed. "There was a stone wall of unpleasantness everywhere I went," Judge Waring recalled, so he began to relinquish the social ties of a lifetime. St. Cecelia Society, symbol of top social recognition in Charleston, had closed its sacrosanct portals to the Judge when he was divorced by his first wife. Now he had become the black, black sheep of his own family. Even St. Michael's Episcopal Church was crossed off the Warings' list "because it is segregated."

The unpleasantness had only begun. Wherever she spoke, North or South, Mrs. Waring denounced racial segregation as "vicious, evil and illogical." When Charleston learned that she was to deliver the address at the Negro Y.W.C.A.'s annual meeting in January 1950, citizens were up in arms. White Y.W.C.A. officials demanded that the Negro branch, headed by Mrs. Septimah Clark, a Negro schoolteacher, cancel Mrs. Waring's appearance. Mrs. Clark refused, declaring that she knew of no reason whatsoever why Mrs. Waring should not address the group. One white man blurted out the ugly rumors that South Carolinians had begun whispering about the twice-divorced wife of the Judge. This white man had "lived near her in Connecticut and might be able to tell you some things about her social past that would give you plenty of reasons to cancel her speech."

Septimah Clark was angered. "You could have lived next door to her," she snapped at the white accuser, "and she would have been so many miles above you socially that you wouldn't have known which door she used when she left home." That was strong, unexpected language from a South Carolina Negro, and it silenced the white accuser. Elizabeth Avery Hoffman Waring went on to deliver the startling address in which she said white-supremacists are mentally ill; the brutal words she used to describe them, right in their own bailiwick, were part of her "shock treatment."

South Carolinians *were* shocked, and they responded with a militant resurgence of the Ku Klux Klan. In March of 1950 a cross was burned on the Warings' lawn while the jurist was holding court in New York. A few months later a cross was burned on the lawn of a Negro family whose son had applied for admittance to the University of South Carolina. In August of 1950 a robed Klansman was killed in a Myrtle Beach demonstration in which a few hundred shots were fired. The dead man, disrobed, was identified as an off-duty law-enforcement officer.

Anti-Waring feeling became stronger and approached its zenith when word went out that Judge and Mrs. Waring were entertaining Negroes. When Mrs. Waring appeared on the television program, "Meet the Press," she was asked if she supported "social integration." Mrs. Waring replied: "I want the whole thing." Social integration, she explained, is purely voluntary and does not mean that anyone is forced to ask Negroes to their homes. "But I should be able to ask them to my house, and I have asked Negroes to my house," she declared.

So the rumors were true. The Warings were entertaining Negroes. And Mrs. Waring went a step further: asked about interracial marriage, she said that she felt a person ought to be able to marry whomever he or she pleased and could get to say yes, whatever their race.

This was a blow to the South's never-never region. The South Carolina Sheriffs' Association passed a resolution accusing the Warings of attempting to wreak vengeance upon Dixie. "These utterances, if followed to a logical conclusion," said the resolution, "could but lead to mongrelization and bring about friction of a violent nature."

The Warings found that in Charleston violent friction came much swifter than mongrelization. On the night of October 9, 1950, the Warings had unexpected callers who hurled bricks and a piece of concrete through a window of their home. When three shots were fired in their front yard, the Warings crouched behind the dining-room wall, trying futilely to get the FBI, whose offices were closed. They called the city police.

When the policemen arrived, according to Mrs. Waring, their leader stopped on the sidewalk and picked up a brick that had ricocheted from the door. "See, it's really nothing but a brick," he was quoted as saying. "There's really nothing to it."

Later Wilmer Thompson, a native Charlestonian who headed the FBI office, arrived with two agents. They had been summoned by John Fleming, a Negro bailiff in Judge Waring's court. "Thompson's attitude was about the same as that of local police," said Mrs. Waring. "You would have thought the Judge and I were responsible for what happened."

Four days later, the FBI's Savannah, Georgia, office announced that a complete investigation had been authorized. Attorney General J. Howard McGrath ordered deputy United States marshals to maintain a twenty-four-hour guard over the Judge, although he had not requested it. For Charleston police, the case was closed. They dismissed it as a "boyish prank." Judge Waring called it "disheartening and disgusting; typical of the savagery of Southern white supremacists."

Charleston got Mrs. Waring's comment the morning after the stoning. She walked into a hardware store where several whites were chattering busily over the events of the previous evening. They fell silent when Mrs. Waring asked loudly if she could see some mousetraps. She looked the traps over, then exclaimed in a voice that no one had to strain to hear: "You know, I'm about ten times as scared of a mouse as I am of the whole Ku Klux Klan."

This was the "witch of Meeting Street," the woman South Carolina hated, the woman whom, in her own words, Charleston whites were "afraid not to hate"—the woman who seemed so kind and gentle that Sunday afternoon when I called for dinner. She walked down the stairs with an elegance that even Charleston's *haut monde* could envy, and accorded me a welcome fit for a Cavalier. "Dear, now you entertain Mr. Rowan for just a little while," she said to the Judge. "I want to fix his steak personally."

We sat down to steaks that were larger than any I had seen since World War II days in Galveston, Texas, when a few shipmates negotiated a fair-sized gray-market meat deal. Despite the hospitable circumstances, I was uneasy as I began to eat. Surely some of the neighbors had seen me enter the Warings' house, and it did not take much imagination for me to envision a brick crashing through a window to indicate my unwelcomeness in the neighborhood. Or the "boyish pranksters" could wait until I left to waylay me and give me a physical lecture on where not to take my meals. My fears soon gave way to my passion for good food and my eagerness to hear more about these people who had welcomed me into their home. After dinner I sat for nearly eight hours, probing into the past and present, almost into the soul, of this Southern-born judge as he told of his change. Sometimes he spoke quietly, sometimes forcefully, and often with tears running down the crevice between his nose and slightly wrinkled cheek.

The loneliness that I had expected seemed nonexistent. "I

admit that I miss the shop talk," said Judge Waring. "I miss chatting about this Supreme Court ruling or that, or such and such a case. Socially, I miss no one. I lost small brains and I found larger ones. I have met Southern Negroes and Northerners of both races whom I would never have known except for this."

So it evidently mattered little that lawyers addressed the Judge only when they had to, and that associates spoke to him, if at all, only out of diplomacy.

I looked for sorrow, and if it was there it was well hidden. "We have become the symbols of the fight against this vicious evil," said Mrs. Waring. "The cause of the American Negro—indeed, it is the cause of American democracy—is so much larger than both of us. As symbols, we are proud to suffer."

Then the Judge looked out at the federal guard, himself the subject of much verbal abuse by whites, who called him "the lover of the nigger-lovers." Judge Waring, whose greenish eyes continued to shed tears, rubbed his fingers through the gray-golden hair at his temples and pointed at the guard. "I didn't ask for him. He follows me everywhere. It's a nuisance. Perhaps there could be nothing better than that the white-supremacists should kill me."

I gave the Judge a surprised, say-that-again look.

"No, I'm not foolish," he went on, "I don't want to die. But it is time some white people died to wake up America. They kill Negroes like flies and, as a white Georgian put it after a lynching in Irwinton: 'It's just another nigger. It didn't stop a checker game.' It's *time* they killed a white federal judge. Let the people of the world see how insane this thing is, then perhaps it will wake up Americans."

I had expected to find hatred; but the Warings have resorted to laughter instead. Laughter at incidents such as the time lightning struck a house next to the Warings' summer cottage on an island near Charleston. The owner, who hated the Judge bitterly, surveyed the damage and put up a sign:

"Dear God, *he* lives next door." Or laughter at the way the story of the stoning of their home spread swiftly across the nation. Almost instantly, calls were coming in from distant cities. A Bostonian got a version that said the Warings were playing canasta when the first rock soared through a window. "Are you people all right?" the caller demanded nervously. When Mrs. Waring told him that they were unhurt, he sighed with relief and demanded hastily: "And for God's sake, are you people still playing canasta? That's out of style." Or laughter at the man who called from California after the stoning and identified himself as a fellow white Southerner. He, too, acted relieved to learn that the Warings hadn't been hurt.

"Inform those damned rebels that they've interrupted a rather important phase of my honeymoon," instructed the caller, "but I just had to find out if y'all were okay."

I did find disappointment. Judge Waring was disappointed in the white minister who "crept into the shadows of my office one dark night to tell me that he was behind me but that his congregation would cut his throat if he spoke out." He was disappointed in the small group of whites who started the movement with him but dropped out when stones started to fly and petitions were put into circulation. The Judge told of a few relatives who "waited until two thirty one morning to call and say hello and tell me that they didn't think it wise to see me any more. Oh, and there was a Jewish fellow who stuck it out longer than the rest. He buckled under to fears of economic pressure."

Judge Waring was disappointed that so few Southern Negroes had spoken out and become militant behind him. He had learned that there is a type of Negro known as an "Uncle Tom," and that Charleston has its share. The Judge told of an attempt by Negroes to gain admittance to Charleston's city college. "In the midst of the battle," related the Judge, "a few Negro Uncle Toms huddled with the mayor. They came out smiling as if they had scored a tremendous victory.

Had they gained entry to Charleston College? No. They had accepted six scholarships to send students to the state college for Negroes at Orangeburg."

"Since my Judge did what he did," interrupted Mrs. Waring, "the whites and Uncle Toms have carried on one of the most sickening little games of appeasement you ever saw. They keep the Uncle Toms quiet by dishing up handouts at troubled intervals—sort of be-kind-to-animals week, you know."

Elizabeth Waring was disgusted. "Why can't there be more Septimah Clarks?" she demanded. "These whites respect her for the way she refused to knuckle under—that is obvious." And it was obvious, for Mrs. Clark so surprised Y.W.C.A. officials by flatly refusing to cancel Mrs. Waring's speech that, in a reaction unexplainable except in terms of new-found respect, they elected Mrs. Clark to their board.

I had done some checking before visiting the Warings. I found that Mrs. Waring is doing more than lecturing in her effort to mobilize Negroes in behalf of their own freedom. You may find her at the Negro Y.W.C.A. any day telling Negro girls how to dress to best advantage in the clothes they have, how to fix their hair attractively and how to walk attractively. "When we hop on these stores for refusing to let you try on dresses," she tells the girls, "we must never be in the position where they can argue that you are too dirty. I know, I know," she adds hastily, "if you're white and dirty you still can try on anything in the store, but you can't afford to have them say that about *you*."

Occasionally a grateful Negro mother will say to Mrs. Waring, or a father will write the Judge: "You're wonderful. God bless you. I'm going to pray for you." Whenever that happens, Mrs. Waring's blood-pressure rises rapidly. "Don't pray for us," she scolds. "We'll make it. They'll never stop me from showing my face. But for heaven's sake, don't pray for me. Get up off your knees and fight."

I also talked with some of the people whom Judge Waring and the more militant Negroes call Uncle Toms. My wife's parents once lived in Charleston, so I arrived with the names of the city's key Negroes. I talked with one who was regarded as influential with white officials—or at least had been until the Warings spoke out and Negroes began to show signs of dissatisfaction with what this Negro could get for them. I told this Negro citizen that I was going to the Warings for dinner. "Humph," he said, then added, after a pause: "Well, that old man is doing a lot of good, but it's that woman. God sent that woman here. But I ain't going over there for dinner. You can't push these things, you know."

"I don't understand," I said. "They invited me to dinner and I accepted. Is that pushing anything on anybody?"

"Well, what I mean is that I can't afford to get on the outs with some of the better white people in town. You see, I been getting things for Negroes in Charleston for years and years. Now, it's all right for the Judge to say that Negroes must be given this and that, but there's got to be some Negroes on speaking terms with the mayor and other officials so they can go in and get these things that the Judge orders up. Now, if I went over there for dinner, I'd be on the outs with the mayor."

Apparently feeling dissatisfied with his own argument, this old Charleston citizen took a new tack. "Anyhow, how come it took Waring so long to get religion? Why, he was corporation counsel of Charleston for about ten years and he didn't do nothing much for Negroes. Why, he used to help manage the campaigns of Senator E. D. "Cotton Ed" Smith (a violent advocate of white supremacy). How come it took the Judge so long to get religion?"

It was not a delightful task, even for a reporter, but I felt that I should ask Judge Waring that question: Why did it take him so long to "get religion"?

"In substance, most of what he said is true," answered the

Judge. "White supremacy is a way of life. You grow up in it and the moss gets in your eyes. You learn to rationalize away the evil and filth and you see magnolias instead."

Then I repeated the charge that all white Charleston was voicing: the Warings simply were getting even because Charleston's top society ostracized them after the Judge was divorced in 1945. I knew that his first wife, the former Miss Annie Gammell, daughter of an old Savannah, Georgia, family, obtained a quiet Florida divorce after thirty-two years of marriage to the Judge. Charleston society, which is traditionally as rigid as any in America, and which then put divorce in the same class as the worst of social diseases, was shocked. A Florida divorce! When South Carolina didn't even have divorce laws! And when Judge Waring married a twice-divorced Northerner and took her to live in the same house his wife of thirty-two years had inhabited, Charleston was atwitter.

"A small group of people tried to turn back the clock," says Mrs. Waring.

"Oh, we had friends after the divorce," recalled the Judge. "We had white friends after my first primary ruling. But when I made it clear that I would tolerate no subterfuge, that I meant to end for all time the Democratic 'white man's club,' that was too much for all of them."

The Judge would not agree, however, that it was simply his wife, with her "damyankee notions," who took the moss and magnolias out of his eyes. He admits that she introduced him to books like W. J. Cash's *The Mind of the South,* and Gunnar Myrdal's *An American Dilemma.* He also says that she was a strong factor in clearing his troubled mind during the months when Cash and Myrdal, projected against his strictly Southern background, left him incredulous and befuddled. In those days they would drive far into the night, sometimes talking, sometimes just thinking. For the dominant factor in his change, however, Judge Waring goes back to the day in 1942 when President Roosevelt appointed him to a federal judgeship.

"All this time I had been a lawyer," he related, again with moist eyes, "and I had felt that it was my job to be narrow, to see only my client's side of a case. After I became a judge, I felt it my duty to see both sides. I began to see the injustices. I saw a lot, and what I saw made me sick. Once I escaped the web of prejudice and hatred, it was absurdly simple: people are people.

"We drive about Charleston and see now that every Negro youngster knows our car. They wave and whisper: 'There goes Judge Waring.' Negro youngsters stand at the post-office steps mornings to wave as I go to work. I see them and know that, though their parents are afraid to cry out, I do not walk alone. Then I realize the gain that I have made. I am not living a phony life. I can look myself in the face, confident that I am meting out justice."

From that Colonial house with the splendidly tiled floors, a house that now is a sort of shrine for thousands of letters and telegrams from well-wishers the world over, and for insult-bearing missives from, chiefly, South Carolina and the District of Columbia, I walked out into the resplendent January night. I told the cab-driver to take me down by the sea, where he could return for me in about twenty minutes.

I stood there at the world-famous Battery, where Fort Sumter was fired upon to begin the Civil War. A cool, invigorating breeze blew off the sea, which lapped gently at the stones below. The quiet peace seemed social ages from the angry Charleston that I had just now vicariously lived through. The solemn tranquillity was a sort of tonic for my troubled mind. I was not sure that I could interpret the Warings accurately to America's Noah Brannons. If I believed any part of white Charleston's charges that the Warings were out for revenge, it would mean that the Judge hadn't "got religion." It would mean that he was a false cry in the wilderness, and in no sense could I call him the voice of the New South. If, as the Judge said, he finally had acquired a passion for justice, I would have to report that the South, almost to a man, had crucified him for it. In that case I would have found only a spark of the New South, a spark that struggled to keep from dying out in the ashes of an old, decadent order.

I stared at the flashing lights along the shore, which seemed to blend into the jeweled sky. It reminded me of a wintry night during World War II when I stood on the bridge of the U.S.S. *Chemung* as she limped toward Charleston harbor with a banged-up turbine. To one inexperienced in navigation, the lights along the shore looked much the same. But an "old salt," wise in the ways of the sea, pointed out the lighthouse that was the "real McCoy" which would guide us into port. I knew then that I would leave Charleston believing that Judge Julius Waties Waring also was the "real McCoy," that he was a beacon that had to start shining in the Southland sooner or later. Even though the Judge was to retire a year later, he had fashioned a glimmering of hope that the ship of freedom also might find its way into Dixie's antebellum ports.

CHAPTER VII

NEVER THE TWAIN SHALL MEET

W HOEVER picked the site for the Atlantic Coast Line Railroad station at Charleston must have had an airport in mind. The station is located miles outside the city, and for that reason, I asked my cab-driver acquaintance to pick me up early enough to get me to the station by two a.m., several minutes before the Miami-bound East Coast Champion was to arrive. On the way, I got the notion that the station might have been put there as a sort of fringe benefit to cab-drivers, who, besides the swollen fare, get an abundance of time in which to tell passengers their troubles or to give their views on matters of the day.

"Man, if it wasn't my turn to meet this train, I'd sure be sleeping it up some," said the driver. "Hell, by the time I get home and in bed my boy is up banging around getting ready to go to school."

"Do you get home that late?" I asked in a tone designed to discourage further discussion of the driver's troubles. I was pretty sleepy myself, not having dared to go to sleep after losing my alarm clock—not with an early-morning train to catch.

"Whatta ya mean, that late?" the driver snapped back. "He's got to be at school by seven thirty, and I think that's too damned early for a kid of six. It's impossible to get him to bed in time for him to get enough sleep."

I had looked into Charleston's school situation, and I knew that because of a shortage of facilities twenty-six classes for Negroes were operating on a double shift. This meant that some six-year-olds started school at seven thirty a.m. and left

101

at twelve thirty p.m. The second group started at twelve thirty and left at five thirty p.m. There were no white classes on double shift.

I decided not to reveal my knowledge, however; I wanted the driver to talk. Cab-drivers often turn up some interesting information about a city, and although their data may be as inaccurate as the next guy's, they at least produce leads. In this case, I was getting a pretty clear indication of what Charleston's average Negro parent was concerned about. I had heard Negro teachers say that, at seven thirty, many pupils were arriving at school hungry, complaining that they hadn't had time to eat breakfast. The teachers felt, also, that five thirty was too late for six-year-olds to be "traipsing home in the dark." I knew, however, that there could be no remedy unless parents themselves complained. Few, if any, teachers would complain outside the security of their own walls.

The school situation had become a mounting issue all over South Carolina, causing upheaval among both whites and Negroes. The whites were concerned with the possibility that separation of the races might be declared unconstitutional in the state's public schools. A group supported by the best legal minds in the National Association for the Advancement of Colored People had sued to abolish segregation in public schools on grounds that it is a denial of equality under the provisions of the Fourteenth Amendment. The suit specifically concerned Clarendon County, South Carolina, a rural area where Negroes outnumber whites, but everyone conceded that if the N.A.A.C.P. won this case the whole segregation system in the South would eventually be abolished.

"Man, I complain about the schools for colored in the city. Every now and then I take somebody out in the country. Holy Jesus, you ought to see some of them shacks," the driver said, when I mentioned the Clarendon case.

I told him that I realized the schools for Negroes could not be very good, since State Representative James A. Spruill admitted publicly that South Carolina still spends only $60 a year per Negro pupil, compared with $191 yearly per white pupil.

"If you ask me, they ain't spending no sixty dollars. If they say sixty in public, they *may* be spending thirty," said the driver.

I added that South Carolina officials admitted that it would take forty million dollars to make Negro schools equal to those for whites, which were considerably below recommended standards themselves. "Has it been Thurmond and other governors who have kept South Carolina the way it is?" I asked.

"Naw, it ain't any one person so much. If you ask me, the worst thing in this state for Negroes is the newspaper here."

"You mean the *News and Courier?*"

"You said it, man."

That was an interesting observation, similar to one I had heard earlier in the day. I had looked through what copies of the *News and Courier* I could dig up without visiting the newspaper's offices. There were days in Tennesseee when I was considerably disturbed by the backhanded, often venomous manner in which the Nashville Banner dealt with Negroes in its news and editorial columns. For bold, out-and-out rancor, the *News and Courier* topped anything that I had ever seen. On June 7, 1949, in an editorial titled "Vishinsky Might Serve," it said:

> *Rather than have the Truman program for "Civil Rights" enacted the* News and Courier *would welcome Andrei Vishinsky to a seat in the United States Senate as a filibusterer against it.*

For a paper with professed anti-Russian views, this seemed to leave little doubt as to how much the *News and Courier* would sacrifice before yielding any new ground to American Negroes. I came to the conclusion that the *News and Courier* is against democracy in general. Almost every edition that

I read carried a brief editorial such as the following, titled "This Democracy," in the November 23, 1950, issue:

> *In the democratic United States a person who is thought unfit to hold any job is nevertheless thought fit to vote and thereby select other men for jobs. Such is democracy.*

On the editorial page of that same issue was an article by "The Bookworm." It dealt with the public-school segregation issue and gave a rather succinct story of things to come in South Carolina. Suggested "The Bookworm":

> *First, we can instruct our legislature to repeal the compulsory school attendance law. This will permit parents to teach their children at home; to protect them from forced contacts of any kind.*

That is what the state's new governor, James Byrnes, a former United States Supreme Court Justice and Secretary of State, threatened that South Carolina would do—abolish public schools if segregation were outlawed. Already knowing that the state would deliver a veiled ultimatum to the federal courts in the segregation case, I could see that South Carolina had not really rejoined the Union. The powers that be consider the state a sovereignty unto itself and not quite bound by the law of the land.

I got my first real idea of Charleston's regard for federal law when I telephoned the train station and asked for a reservation on the East Coast Champion. The man who answered hesitated, then told me that I could get no reservation by phone. When I asked him why, he said that space available wasn't known until shortly before the train arrived. "Don't worry," he added, "we've been getting everybody on."

I learned that, although his reason might have been truthful in my case, there was another reason why I couldn't get a reservation by telephone. My trick of calling for space first was generally known among Negroes, and several colored citizens of Charleston had used it successfully to avoid Jim Crow. Some had had their reservations changed to Jim Crow cars, but Negroes soon avoided this by saying, when they called for space: "I'm gonna send a nigger boy in to pick 'em up." The Negro then picked up the tickets, allegedly to deliver them to some nonexistent white citizen.

The Charleston agent supposedly became suspicious upon seeing Negroes board nonsegregated coaches there. Ticket-sellers began to give telephone callers the old name-rank-and-serial-number-and-indicate-your-race routine. One day they started the routine with Mrs. J. Waties Waring, and were promptly notified that such shenanigans to maintain Jim Crow in interstate travel were in conflict with a recent Supreme Court ruling. When she finished lecturing them, railroad officials decided that it would serve their purpose better to make travelers pick up their reservations in person—unless they could establish their racial heritage rather clearly by phone. I would have to wait until just before train time to learn if I could ride.

I reached the station just before two a.m., and asked the attendant for a reservation. I could see several whites huddled at the window of the white waiting-room, watching the rather fragile attendant fumble nervously with a telephone and a telegraph key. He didn't answer me, but jotted something down. I waited until he got up and conferred with the whites. As he turned back to his seat I repeated my request. He still ignored me. A few minutes later he walked over and said, as if he had done me a tremendous favor: "I got you one. But I got five whites waiting and I didn't git but two of 'em seats."

"How do I happen to be so fortunate?" I demanded.

"Just one of them things," he replied, matter-of-factly.

I looked at my ticket and saw that my seat was in car number one, the first coach behind the engine. I assumed that the railroad still was reserving a coach for colored, despite the court ruling. I was sure of it when I walked out of the waiting-room and saw two steel signs alongside the train ordering colored to board at one door and whites at another. "Heh, heh," I said, "just one of them things."

My first attempt to board and ride a nonsegregated coach in the South had failed completely, although I had learned what Charleston policy was. I had given up the sleep of a Pullman car (I assume I could have secured Pullman space in Charleston) in order to make the coach test. I was determined not to see my sacrifice go in vain. I would go back to the club car, a setting far more "social" than a coach. White reaction in this "social" atmosphere would be more significant, because the setting of liquor, seductive women, and seducing men involves the element of sex; and in this atmosphere, of course, the presence of a Negro among white women is traditionally most taboo. I walked to the club car, only to find it and the diner closed for the night.

One of the white persons who failed to get a reservation in Charleston was a sailor. He was in the diner trying to convince the conductor that there "must be an empty seat somewhere." The conductor shook his head.

"Say, mate, there are fifty-seven empty seats in the car I'm in," I volunteered. I had counted them. The sailor looked at me, and then at the conductor as if to ask what kind of line the conductor was handing him. The conductor's face was beet-red, and he gave me a sinister stare as I walked away hastily. I returned to my near-empty Jim Crow car, observing along the way that Charleston's attempt to preserve segregation aboard the East Coast Champion was a futile one. Negroes who had boarded at Washington or farther North were in every car. Nevertheless, the seatless sailor never showed up to claim one of the fifty-seven vacancies in my coach.

Part Two

It was dawn. The two other Negroes in our "private coach" still slept as I watched the sun climb into the sky like a sluggish rocket. Weeping-willow trees stood like exhausted soldiers, their limbs drooping wearily. Only the roar of steel against steel pierced the morning quiet as the crack train raced toward the playgrounds of Florida.

Soon, I knew, the picture would change. Palm trees, waving a double-dare to the elements like fan-dancers tempting a fraternity smoker, would replace the tired willows. The elongated pines and statuesque cedars would give way to orange groves, stretching inviting beauty before the traveler. The tracks would move closer to the sea, where riders could watch a million little whitecaps polka-dot the ocean's blue.

But part of the panorama—the part controlled more by man than by nature—would remain constant. Unchangeable would be the picture of despair that extends for hundreds of miles down the Atlantic coast, where the shabbiest kind of houses stand alongside the railroad tracks. Their foundations sinking into swampy lowlands, these dilapidated bungalows turn a pitiful face to America riding by. I knew that many, many Americans had traveled that same road without thinking or caring about how many fellow Americans live in those one- and two-room tarpaper shacks. I knew that it didn't have to be that road. Every train-rider, every automobile tourist had seen it somewhere, for it is traditional for railroad tracks and highways to cut through the heart of the Negro's run-down domain.

I sat in the diner, across from a white Army colonel, as we rode through northern Florida. I watched him shake his head as we raced through those wilds of human dejection. Wherever the train stopped for a few minutes, Negroes came out of their hovels to watch. It was not as if they were seeing a train for the first time: children and grownups gazed into the diner, into the club car, into the coaches filled with carefree people with money to spend, and it was as if they had come out to dream.

The colonel stared at a Negro girl, surely not yet sixteen, who walked up to the side of the diner with an infant on each hip. She said nothing, made no motion. I couldn't even detect a wistful look about her, and I sat puzzled. A lad of about eight, using a dead cornstalk as a pony, wielded a capgun near by. Then the colonel realized that I was watching him.

"What would you guess?" he asked me. "Does the boy or the cornstalk have the better prospects for the future?"

"That, sir, depends on how many Americans ride by and look out that window and then ask themselves the same question," I replied.

This made me think of the sailor, who never came to claim a seat. I thought about the sailor because I thought that he, the boy with the capgun, the people in the shacks, and even I, for the time being, had something in common: we all were living under the shadow of what has been, since 1896, the Southland's Great Debate. Each of us, in our individual ways, was living under the shadow of racial segregation, the one thing about which everything in Dixie revolves. Segregation still was the South's god. It had been when I left the South, and I had been across "the line" long enough to see that 1951 had put no other god before segregation.

From what I had seen of Dixie 1951 I was convinced that my destiny, the sailor's destiny, and the destiny of the unknown creatures in the tarpaper hovels all hinged on the outcome of the Great Debate. Every hope for a New South, social or economic, seemed to be linked to the efforts of a few whites, a few militant Negroes, and organizations sympathetic to the Negro's cause of abolishing racial segregation. It is this growing attack on segregation, and the South's counterattack, that produces the real turmoil of Dixieland.

In some areas, I felt, there would be increased turmoil as the white South rises up to defend its most cherished institution. I saw evidence in the willingness of some white Southerners to stand or to go thirsty rather than take a seat or drink water that they had labeled "unclean." I could remember ticket-sellers in Washington and Charleston resorting to subterfuge to circumvent federal law and maintain railroad Jim Crow. I knew how far South Carolina threatened to go in order to keep the children of both races separate in their quest for knowledge. Mile after mile after mile I had seen the signs on toilets and water fountains and waiting-rooms and cafés and taxis and myriad other places and things and facilities, specifying in the unmistakable clarity of black paint and whitewash that blacks are blacks and whites are whites and hardly ever are the twain to meet.

Even the most reactionary citizen would agree that the Civil War failed to free the American Negro completely; but the white sailor and the conductor and the ticket-sellers and Governor Byrnes and the people who put up the Jim Crow signs were living evidence that it also had failed to free the white South. Eighty-six years later the minds and souls of the people were still enslaved to segregation and notions of a superior race. Everything seemed to indicate that Dr. Benjamin Mays, president of Morehouse College in Atlanta, was correct in his appraisal of segregation's effect on the South. He wrote in the November 1950 issue of *Presbyterian Outlook*:

> *What has the worshipping of this god, segregation, done to the South? It has kept the South down. It has stultified the soul of the South. It has circumscribed, twisted and warped the South's mind. It has brutalized the heart of the South. It has perpetuated poverty. It has contributed to the South's illiteracy. It has made us cowards. It has made us "touchy" and sensitive. We are always defending the South, trying to prove we are no*

worse than other people. Defending segregation is our one consuming passion. Segregation is the root of most of the social ills of the South. We are an abnormal people.

Now, because of the federal courts, the Southland's god was in danger of being destroyed. Ironically enough, these federal courts that dyed-in-the-wool Southerners now curse are the same courts that gave the South the right to levy segregation statutes in the first place. Although the colonel who sat across from me, along with most Americans, considered segregation to be merely custom, or localized statutes based on popular opinion, racial segregation has the sanction of the United States Supreme Court. In 1896, in the case of *Plessy vs. Ferguson,* the high court opened a door that Americans thought they had closed forever with the Civil War Amendments, and legislation based on race became legal.

A Negro (seven eights Caucasian and one eighth African descent) railway passenger, traveling between local points in Louisiana, was ejected from a coach reserved for whites, and prosecuted for resistance. A Louisiana statute provided that a railway carrying passengers within the state must provide "equal but separate accomodations for the white and colored races." The court, composed of six Justices appointed by Republican Presidents and three by President Cleveland, voted seven to one that the "separate but equal" statute was constitutional. One Justice did not sit in the case.

The majority opinion, written by Justice Henry B. Brown of Michigan and supported by five Northerners and one Louisianian, held that the statute (1) did not infringe upon the personal liberties of Negroes as guaranteed by the Fourteenth Amendment, (2) was a "reasonable exercise of the state's police powers," and (3) did not "stamp the colored race with a badge of inferiority."

"If one race be inferior to the other socially," the majority continued, "the Constitution of the United States cannot put them on the same plane."

In holding that the statute was not in conflict with the Fourteenth Amendment, the court stated:

> A statute which implies merely a legal distinction between the white and colored races—a distinction which is founded on the color of the two races, and which must always exist so long as white men are distinguished from the other race by color—has no tendency to destroy the legal equality of the two races, or re-establish a state of involuntary servitude. . . . The object of the [Fourteenth] Amendment was undoubtedly to enforce the absolute equality of the two races before the law, but in the nature of things it could not have been intended to abolish distinction based on color, or to enforce social, as distinguished from political equality, or a commingling of the two races upon terms unsatisfactory to either. . . . We cannot say that the act in question is unreasonable or more obnoxious to the Fourteenth Amendment than the Acts of Congress requiring separate schools for colored children in the District of Columbia. . . .

The lone dissenter was Justice John M. Harlan, a Kentuckian and former slaveholder who originally opposed the Civil War Amendments. "If this statute of Louisiana is consistent with the personal liberty of citizens," asked Harlan, "why may not the state require the separation in railroad coaches of native and naturalized citizens or of Protestants and Roman Catholics?" The majority answered that such a statute would not meet with public approval and would therefore be unreasonable.

Justice Harlan, who served thirty-four years on the Supreme Court, went on to write the strongest denunciation of legalized racial segregation ever to come out of the high court. In fact, since 1896, Supreme Court Justices have concerned themselves with whether or not the "separate but equal" provisions were met, and not with the constitutionality of segregation itself. But because of the impending lawsuit in South Carolina, and because of the mounting attack on segregation throughout the South, I knew that the words of Justice Harlan would live again. It was possible, indeed, that out of that half-century-old dissent would spring much of the framework for a New South, and in reality a New America. For that reason, I include in this report the substance of Justice Harlan's dissent. Discussing the three Civil War Amendments, he said:

> These notable additions to the fundamental law were welcomed by the friends of liberty throughout the world. They removed the race line from our governmental systems. They had, as this Court has said, a common purpose, namely, to secure "to a race recently emancipated . . . all the civil rights that the superior race enjoy." They declared, in legal effect, this Court has further said, "that the law in the states shall be the same for the black as for the white; that all persons, whether colored or white, shall stand equal before the laws of the states, and, in regard to the colored race, for whose protection the Amendments are primarily designed, that no discrimination shall be made against them by law because of their color." We also said "The words of the Amendment . . . contain a necessary implication of a . . . right to exemption from unfriendly legislation against them distinctively as colored—exemption from legal discriminations, implying inferiority in civil society, lessening the security of their enjoyment of the rights which others enjoy, and discriminations which are steps toward reducing them to the condition of a subject race . . ." The white race deems itself to be the dominant race in this country. And so it is, in prestige, in achievements, in education, in wealth and in power. So, I doubt not that it will

continue to be for all time, if it remains true to its great heritage and holds fast to the principles of constitutional liberty. But in the view of the Constitution, in the eye of the law, there is in this country no superior, dominant, ruling class of citizens. There is no caste here. Our Constitution is color-blind, and neither knows nor tolerates classes among citizens. In respect of civil rights all citizens are equal before the law. The humblest is the peer of the most powerful. The law regards man as man, and takes no account of his surroundings or his color when his civil rights as guaranteed by the supreme law of the land are involved. It is therefore to be regretted that this high tribunal, the final expositor of the fundamental law of the land, has reached the conclusion that it is competent for a state to regulate the enjoyment by citizens of their civil rights solely upon the basis of race. In my opinion, the judgment this day rendered will, in time, prove to be quite as pernicious as the decision by this tribunal in The Dred Scott Case. . . . The present decision, it may well be apprehended, will not only stimulate aggressions, more or less brutal and irritating, upon the admitted rights of colored citizens, but will encourage the belief that it is possible, by means of state enactments, to defeat the beneficent purposes which the people of the United States had in view when they adopted the recent Amendments of the Constitution. . . . Sixty millions of whites are in no danger from the presence here of eight millions of blacks. The destinies of the two races in this country are indissolubly linked together, and the interests of both require that the common government of all shall not permit the seeds of race hate to be planted under sanction of law. What can more certainly arouse race hate . . . than state enactments which in fact proceed on the ground that colored citizens are so inferior and degraded that they cannot be allowed to sit in public coaches occupied by white citizens? That, as all will ad-

*mit, is the real meaning of such legislation as was en-
acted in Louisiana. . . . It is scarcely just to say that a
colored citizen should not object to occupying a public
coach assigned to his own race. He does not object, nor,
perhaps, would he object to separate coaches for
his race, if his rights under the law were recognized. But
he objects, and ought never to cease objecting, to the
proposition that citizens of the white and black races can
be adjudged criminals because they sit, or claim the right
to sit, in the same public coach, on a public highway.
. . . The thin disguise of "equal" accomodations for passengers in railroad coaches will not mislead anyone, or
atone for the wrong this day done.*

Thus was resolved the Great Debate of 1896, but fifty-five
years later it still raged in the South. Indisputably, the decision shaped the course of race relations in the United States.
Given the green light, the South multiplied its segregation
laws. Cities and villages drew up Jim Crow ordinances and
"by-laws." Negroes rapidly disappeared from municipal, state,
and legislative posts. For years the Negro's role in American
life was a diminishing one.

Although in 1951 I was riding Jim Crow into Florida,
there was evidence in the other coaches that succeeding Supreme Courts had all but gnawed the foundations from under
the 1896 ruling, although no court had seen fit, or shown the
courage, to rule on segregation itself. But within a decade
there has been a tremendous swing in American public opinion. Starting with the rise, and subsequent fall, of Adolf Hitler's regime and its super-race theories, and then with the
rise of Far Eastern nations and the entry of the colored peoples of that area into world affairs, "race" has become an
important word internationally. Former supporters of racial
segregation have become noncommital; once-silent Americans
are beginning to speak out against segregation. The South
found that on May 28, 1951, three of her native sons—Judge

Waring, Judge John J. Parker of Charlotte, North Carolina, and Judge George Bell Timmerman of Columbia, South Carolina—were sitting in Charleston, pondering the question of whether segregation itself should be outlawed. The big, bad wolf that generation after generation of the white South had learned to dread and hate was at the door. Some of the Southerners to whom I talked were glad; others were praying for a reprieve, and striving desperately to find some magic social solution in which to preserve at least some form of racial segregation.

The reprieve came on June 23, when Judges Parker and Timmerman upheld segregation on the basis that the nation's top court still had not declared the separate-but-equal theory unconstitutional, and that South Carolina promised to do something about Clarendon County's schools.

But Dixieland's anxious hours were not ended. In twenty pages of sober dissent, Judge Waring spelled out the issue in words that even the United States Supreme Court would find hard to ignore:

> *If a case of this magnitude can be turned aside and a court refuse to hear these basic issues* [of the legality of segregation itself] *by the mere device of an admission that some buildings, blackboards, lighting fixtures and toilet facilities are unequal but that they may be remedied by the spending of a few dollars, then, indeed people in the plight in which these* [Clarendon County Negroes] *are, have no adequate remedy or forum in which to air their wrongs. . . . If they are entitled to any rights as American citizens, they are entitled to have these rights now and not in the future. And no excuse can be made to deny them these rights which are theirs under the Constitution and laws of America by use of the false doctrine and patter called "separate but equal" and it is the duty of the Court to meet these issues simply and factually and without fear, sophistry and evasion.*

Judge Waring referred to recent court decisions opening graduate schools to Negroes and reasoned:

> *If segregation is wrong then the place to stop it is in the first grade and not in graduate colleges. . . . Segregation in education can never produce equality, and that is an evil that must be eradicated. This case presents the matter clearly for adjudication and I am of the opinion that all of the legal guideposts, expert testimony, common sense and reason point unerringly to the conclusion that the system of segregation in education adopted and practiced in the State of South Carolina must go and must go now.*

The N.A.A.C.P. appealed to the United States Supreme Court, as expected. The Southland could still hold its breath, waiting to see if the last weak pillar would be knocked from under its system of segregation.

I knew that the die-hards would hope and scheme until the last moment. I had a copy of *Pageant* magazine before me as my train sped toward Florida. In it was an article in which Bern Keating, a white Mississippian, asked: "Is Segregation Doomed Down South?" Keating, in the spirit of what must be considered a changing South, was willing to concede something in the hope of salvaging the system of segregation. He was willing to concede, by implication, that discrimination is deplorable; but "segregation and discrimination are two different things," he wrote.

"Discrimination *does* exist in the South," continued Keating, who considers himself something of a liberal. "Taboos against the Negro still *do* flourish. The Negro's life and opportunities are *not* the same as the white man's. But most Southerners of even the most liberal persuasion hold that these discriminations can be relieved *without abolishing segregation.*" The emphasis on certain words is Keating's.

Even the strongest opponents of segregation must agree that Keating's frank admission of the second-class status of the Negro is new and unexpected talk from the Southland. To a man, however, they refuse to concede that segregation itself is not a basic cause of the existing injustices. Said Dr. Mays in *Presbyterian Outlook:*

> *Our god, segregation, breeds inequality and perpetuates brutality. This is because segregation is a badge of inferiority pinned by the strong and mighty on the weak and helpless. And it sets the segregated off so that discrimination and brutality can be easily administered.*

Either Keating or Mays is wrong. If justice is possible under enforced segregation, the burden of proof now is on the South. The South knows it, and the turmoil and social upheaval to which enlightened Southerners point is simply the uneasy, defensive stir created by knowledge of this burden.

CHAPTER VIII

NIGHT TRAIN TO GEORGIA

Miami is a queer city. I knew it the day I arrived, because I remembered the Miami that I had known in 1945. I was even surer when I left Miami that here was a city in which animosities sprang up mysteriously from a source nobody could put his finger on. It was a queer city in that the manifestations of these animosities could be shut off, almost completely, by the faucet of necessity.

In 1945 Miami was a cosmopolitan city. It was virtually a military reservation, with troops of almost all the Allied nations there, including Russian sailors who marched up and down Biscayne Boulevard almost daily. The city had given up Jim Crow to about the same extent that the Armed Forces had given it up, which means that it still could be found rather readily. Yet, segregation was nonexistent in some very surprising places. This served as a lesson of what Miamians could and would do under circumstances that did not encourage folly.

With German U-boats hovering just off the shoreline early in the war, Miami citizens apparently became more concerned with winning the war than with protecting their racial whims. Before the crisis had ended, the military had taken over many of the plush hotels—and there were Negro servicemen moving in with whites. That was how I got to know Biscayne Boulevard and its hotels, Miami Beach and its blue waters and sandy shores. I was Ensign Rowan, in Miami for anti-submarine-warfare training. Even though U-boats no longer were a local menace, I was pretty welcome in Miami.

For my report to America's Noah Brannons, I wanted now to see if victory and the passage of time had made me more or less welcome. My first stop was at the Hotel Villa D'Esta at 8th Street and Biscayne Boulevard. I thought I would be able to walk through the place blindfolded, but I hardly recognized it. It was amazing how plush and costly looking a place civilians could make out of what had been close to a drab barn under the Navy. I had not wired for a reservation; I just walked up to the desk and asked a deeply tanned (or South American) woman for a room.

"Why, you can't stay here," she said, acting as if I had insulted her.

"Is this a joke?" I asked. "Why, I certainly must be able to, and I have stayed here."

"In *this* hotel?"

"Yes, madam. I can show you my room—right at the stairway on the second floor. Have you *anything* available?"

"Er, no, no. We're filled up. When did you say you stayed here?"

"Well, er . . . not since the spring of 1945, I guess."

"Oh! Oh," she said, "the Navy had it then."

"That's right," I said musically, just as if I hadn't the faintest suspicion that I would be marching out of the hotel roomless in a few minutes. I was at my facetious best, and loving it. I looked about the lobby, all decked out in colorful furnishings with a South American motif. "But the Navy never was the kind of host to fix things up like this," I added. "Er, did you say whether you have *anything* available?"

"I am very sorry, but you cannot stay here," she said pointedly.

"Oh, I beg your pardon," I said as I strode out. Somehow, it all had been funny. I didn't have that hot feeling in the pit of my stomach that usually comes when I know that I am being denied something because of my race. This time I was laughing, laughing because the whole thing had been a joke. Here was part of the unexplainable about being an American

Negro: except for the brutal and the really painful aspects of segregation, Negroes have learned to laugh at it, and to view much of its protective pattern as a joke. I had been so amused that I decided not to say, as planned: "Lady, you may need the Navy and me again." That would have been much too serious for the occasion.

I left the Villa D'Esta and walked across the railroad tracks into the Negro section of town. I had had to hold my nose there in 1945, for the slum shacks were the worst that I had seen anywhere in America, with the possible exception of Galveston, Texas. Many of these shacks still existed—in a more dilapidated condition than ever. Some were torn down, presumably to make way for a luxurious, ninety-six-unit apartment hotel for Negroes. This apartment unit would be very close to town. You could get a bet in almost any Negro barbershop that Miami Negroes would see very little new, low-coast housing to replace the slums. The bigots always had found some way to block Negro housing, the pessimists said. Apparently they were right, for less than a year later, a series of nighttime explosions warned that somebody objected to the Negro housing program.

I could see, in 1951, that Miami still was a queer city. It was a peacetime city in which I now rated as nothing. I was ready to leave.

Part Two

If small towns are the backbone of America, they also are, in many cases, the backache of the race problem. Not that any individual Negro is more likely to be exploited or abused in a small town than in a large city; certainly no human being ever lived under more deplorable circumstances than do Negroes in the big-city slums of both the North and South. Often, the slum-dwelling Negro of the big city is

worse off because he has neither the freedom of the North
nor the paternalistic "care" given by white Southerners in a
small town. I knew that small-town paternalism has been a
bigger factor in keeping the Negro "in his place" than all the
Rankins and Bilbos of the last half century. Since I deemed a
report on this phase of Negro life essential to my mission, I
decided to stop in several small towns and villages of the
South.

I realized before I left Minneapolis that this would be the
sticking-point in my problem of finding lodging. It would be
more dangerous than educational—or humorous—for me to
walk into a white hotel in some of these towns and ask for a
room. There would be no Negro hotels to which I could go.
I had reached the point where I would begin calling on doctors, teachers, and preachers. For that reason, I chose towns
where I could approach a family with some sort of reference.
I did not want towns where I was known by any citizen, because friends always feel obliged to give you a guided tour.
And once they learn that you are to write something about
their town they become obsessed with a false pride, and their
town immediately becomes the garden spot of democracy.
On the other hand, it would be an asset to stay with someone
with a degree of interest in my project, for he at least could
tell me who was what in town, and why.

I decided on Milledgeville, Georgia. My wife's brother's
wife's people lived there, and that close a relationship seemed
just the right amount of contact.

The best way to get to Milledgeville, I learned, was to
entrain or fly to Macon, and then take a bus the rest of the
way. I was dissatisfied with the result of my attempt to board
and ride a railroad coach unsegregated in the South. Although it would mean another night without sleep, I decided
to go by train if I succeeded in getting a non-Jim-Crow reservation.

I called the Florida East Coast Line station and asked for
a coach reservation on the New Royal Palm, a streamliner. I

was assigned seat 37, car 4, and was told to pick up my ticket before noon the day of departure. When I reached the station I did not enter the colored waiting-room; I walked to the front of the ticket office, which was in the white waiting-room. The ticket-seller closed his window in my face after telling me to "take the next window." I had stopped at the first window, and he pointed away from the other windows toward the colored waiting-room. I knew then that in Miami a separate window was provided for Negro ticket-buyers. The situation varies from city to city throughout the South.

I pretended not to see where he was pointing, and stepped to the next window in the white waiting-room. "I believe I have seat 37, car 4, on the New Royal Palm tonight," I said. The agent pursed his lips, furrowed his brow and then picked up the phone.

"You got a reservation on the Palm tonight for a Rowan?" he asked loudly, then added softly: "Anything in car 1."

I heard him and challenged: "I don't want car 1; I want car 4, seat 37." I emphasized the 4 and 37 as if to say: ". . . and I mean business."

The agent looked up, surprised. "Okay, okay, okay," he said, "car 4, seat 37, he's got." He gave me my ticket without further ado.

I boarded the train with a bit of uneasiness, but nobody in the coach appeared to resent my presence.

I went into the club car for a sandwich and a can of beer. There was what seemed like a rustle of eyebrows as I entered, but no one said a word. The days of curtains and Jim Crow tables were gone, so I sat at the first available place. I munched on my sandwich, which tasted better than any I had had in weeks; I read my *Time* magazine, making every effort to impress upon the other travelers that this was my normal element, that I had expected nothing less, and that I had not come there to rape anybody. The Negro waiter "sirred" me in a tone that said he was overjoyed to see what was taking place. His home was in Detroit, I learned later.

By the time I finished my sandwich, it was time for the club car to close. "I'd be glad to fix you another sandwich before we close, sir," said the waiter. "You don't have to leave just because we stop serving. I'll take the tablecloth, but you may stay as long as you like to finish your food and beer, and to read. And if you want me to, I'll bring your typewriter in here and you can write if you want to."

I looked up surprised. Word had traveled fast among Negroes on the train that I was "putting one over on Jim Crow." This waiter not only knew that I was in car 4, but he knew that I had a typewriter aboard. "Look, fella," I replied, "I don't intend to wear out my welcome in this car." He assured me that it would not be unusual, that people did it "all the time," so I let him bring my typewriter in.

I don't know how long I sat there, writing part of the report that I would give to America's Noah Brannons. I was alone in the club car except for a young white woman who had a book and four cans of Schlitz that she had bought when warned that the car was to be closed. "Here I sit," I thought, "riding in a 'white' railroad coach across Florida and into Georgia. And here I am alone in a club car with a typewriter, some paper, a white woman, and four cans of beer and a book." She didn't seem the least bit worried—and she read books. Perhaps she also had read Cash's *The Mind of the South*, I thought. In it he said that a white woman has about as much chance of being raped by a Negro in the South as she has of being struck by lightning. If she had read that she obviously saw little reason to worry about me.

I noticed that at intervals the white club-car steward would walk through, ostensibly to look for something in his liquor cabinet. I got the impression that we were keeping him from sleeping, so I gathered up my writing paraphernalia and retired to my coach.

Far into the night I sat awake as the sleek cars pushed across Florida, and then over Georgia's red clay. Neon signs in two-bit hamlets seemed to glow brighter than an August moon in a new bride's eyes. Freedom never tasted so sweet as in Georgia, I thought, and fell asleep.

I awoke, almost with the dawn, to get the only indication that someone resented my being in coach 4. Sometime during the night a white passenger had taken the seat in front of me. He tilted back the chair and fell asleep. When I awoke just before arriving in Macon, I straightened my seat up, and that put my face only a few inches from the white sleeper in front of me. When we passed an Air Force base some youngsters began yelling about the planes and woke him. When he opened his eyes, there he was staring a Negro in the face. I don't know what he thought, but he sprang from his seat, grabbed his pillow, and fairly leaped out of coach 4. He never returned.

This incident did not dim my happiness over the whole trip. I was still jubilant when I left the train at Macon. I had visions of a new day in Georgia, and even the Jim Crow waiting-rooms that stared me in the face could not wipe out the optimism. I walked into the colored waiting-room.

"Taxi?" asked a towering, sleepy-eyed Negro.

"As soon as the redcap brings my bags," I replied.

"Where you goin'?"

"Milledgeville. You can take me to the bus station."

He offered to drive me to Milledgeville for fifteen dollars. When I answered with an are-you-crazy look, he dropped to ten dollars, explaining that he needed the money. "Who doesn't?" I asked, and started to walk away. "I'll tell you what, I'll drive you over there for seven fifty," he said. I wanted to ride the bus for what information I might gain for my report. I told the cab-driver that I was in no hurry, so I would wait for the bus.

I had not seen the afternoon paper of the previous day, nor the paper for that morning. Seeing no daily papers in the colored waiting-room, I walked into the white waiting-room. I walked up to the newsstand and extended my arm, offering a nickel to a woman behind the counter. I was trying to remember if the Atlanta *Journal* or the *Constitution* is the morning paper. The headlines gave no clue. Before I could decide, a voice boomed: "Boy! This ain't the colored waiting-room."

I was startled at first. I looked over my shoulder and saw the station agent walking toward me. "Yes, I know," I answered, trying to be casual.

"Well, what're you doing in here?" he demanded.

"I'm buying a paper," I said, again offering my nickel to the woman, who had her arm extended to reach it.

"Don't take his money! Don't take his money!" the agent ordered.

The woman quickly closed her hand, pointed at me and began to shout almost hysterically: "No, no, no, you got no business in here."

"According to the separate-but-equal theory," I said to the stationmaster, "I should be able to buy anything in there that I can buy in here. There are no morning papers in there. Now, what about that?"

"Well, you'll have to go back and let the redcap come and get a paper," he explained.

"The redcap? He's darker than I am and I've got the nickel —what's the logic there?" I argued.

"He's in uniform."

"Suppose I were in uniform—of the United States Navy?"

"You'd still have to go where niggers belong."

I swallowed hard, but not yet angered, asked: "If your segregation system or democracy had to fall, which would you uphold?"

"Goddamit, I just follow orders here," he snapped. He stared at the camera about my neck and said: "You ain't in New York. You're just another black nigger in Georgia."

Suddenly the rebuffs and humiliations of three weeks in the South began to take their toll. I was angry, damned angry. I stepped toward the agent and said: "Anybody who would cry that he 'just follows orders' and can't explain those orders to his own conscience, and who makes a remark like that, can't be any more than a low, scurrilous sonofabitch."

I realized at once that I had been foolish to argue with him. He looked stunned. No Negro talks to a white man like that in Georgia—unless the Negro is crazy or armed with a gun. Perhaps it was this fear that I was armed that kept the agent from striking me. Instead, he rushed to the phone in the Stationmaster's office. After ordering a Negro redcap: "Follow him, Sam. See where he goes," he started dialing a number.

I knew that if he was calling policemen I probably would get a beating. If he was calling civilians, it might be even worse. I hurried back to the taxi-driver, whose name was Ned Ussrey, I learned from the license in his car. "Buddy, you just made seven fifty," I said. We hopped into his old Ford and I ordered him: "Drive as if you're going to the bus station, but let me out in Milledgeville."

Ussrey drove up the street, and I could see the Negro redcap running behind us, trying to obey his boss's orders. Another Negro, who had had a few drinks, also was in the taxi. "That's old Sam arunning behind us," he half-stuttered, "if-if-if-if a Negro belches in that station he runs and tells the stationmaster."

I discouraged the driver from stopping so the half-drunk Negro could "punch that Uncle Tom redcap in the nose." We ducked the redcap and hit the highway. We bounced along the road in the early morning, and my jubilation had vanished. The clay banks looked as red as the blood of a million Civil War casualties. Stumpy cedar trees looked evil now in their frosty white dress.

I had been too hasty in my jubilation, in my illusions of a New South. I had learned, almost physically, what Senators Pepper of Florida and Graham of North Carolina learned politically: bigotry isn't nearly dead in Dixie. "Georgia still is essentially a police state," I mumbled over the rattle of the car, "and any white man who decides to be is a policeman, where a Negro is involved."

CHAPTER IX

LESSONS IN LEARNING

I stood in the Western Union office at Milledgeville, awaiting payment on a money order that my paper had wired me. I realized that I was wise to have had it sent in care of Dr. J. F. Boddie, the town's most influential Negro, with whom I was staying. He was a source of identification, and I found that I needed plenty of identification. I showed the Western Union agent my press card, my Newspaper Guild card, my driver's license, my Social Security card, two Naval Reserve cards, and a letter of identification that my managing editor had given me. Still she hesitated to pay me the money.

"Who sent you this money?" she asked. I explained to her that any of several people might have, then named all I could think of offhand. The agent gave no hint as to whether I had hit upon the actual sender. "How much did they send?" she asked. I said I was as eager to find that out as she was. She called Dr. Boddie's office, where she had called earlier to locate me, to get assurance that it was all right to give me the money. Although I appreciated her security efforts, I began to feel a bit embarrassed. I asked her to give me the money in traveler's checks if it would make her feel better. Apparently it did, for she decided to pay me.

"Sign here," she ordered, holding the check face-down before me. "You don't mind if I sort of see how much I'm signing for, do you?" I asked in a tone designed to say that two can play the suspicion game as well as one.

While our little quiz-session was going on, a white man had entered the office with a blonde child of about three or four. She looked like a doll in her bright red coat. Suddenly I

128

heard a tiny milk-and-honey voice from behind me, where the girl stood as her father wrote a telegram: "You must be a colored man. Let me see."

The little girl half-skipped around to where she could see my face, and then said with positiveness: "Yes, you are. You're a colored man." I smiled. Her father smiled at me and then added: "Yes, but he's a nice-looking colored man—*he's* probably a *nice* colored man, honey."

The little girl paused, then blurted: "Yes, he's nice, but he's sooooo big. He's a giant!"

The father looked at me and laughed. I thought how familiar the words were, these age-old stereotypes from the mouth of a pretty little girl. I knew of so many ways that she could have learned them. Whenever a Negro is mentioned in the press of the South, and much of the North, in connection with a crime, he usually is described as a "giant" or "big and burly." I remembered, though, that I had gained a few pounds, and thought that perhaps a few excess pounds could make a guy as touchy about his weight as his color.

I counted checks as the two left, turning as I heard the man say: "Tell the man good-bye, honey." The little blonde stuck her hand through the door as her father held it open with his foot. "Good-bye, Mr. Colored Giant, good-bye," she called out, evoking laughter from the office agent and me.

She was a bewitching little girl, but I was not really amused. She reminded me too much of the South of my past. I was too busy studying the relationship between her and her father and between both of them and this past. At so early an age this little girl was being taught, was having it drilled into her at the slightest opportunity, that the people about her are divided into white and colored groups. This much she could learn from sight; more important, she was being taught that there is some significance to this difference in color. I did not think that her father was a bigot and that he was injecting hatred into his child. He seemed far better educated and less hostile than the woman in the battered old Hudson in Columbia, who laughed when her daughter cried: "Mama, mama, looked at the pretty nigger." The little girl's remarks had been too vaguely innocent for me to assume that her father was a bigot. But the fact that she was so occupied with my color was a striking manifestation of the mores of the Old South, which has thrived on father-to-son prejudices and fears and hand-me-down biases.

Perhaps this father was working for a New South and was seeing that his little girl got her lectures about color in a manner favorable to Negroes or other people who might look somewhat different. I would never be sure. But the little girl was a reminder that the people, especially the young, are conditioned to any long-existing way of life, and this compels them to look askance at any other system. I knew to what perfection the guardians of the Old South have learned the processes of conditioning in the realm of racial affairs, for all my own years in the South were years of conditioning. The process started for me—as it starts for any child, black or white—almost with the day I was born, certainly when I learned to speak my first words. A Negro child of three who presses his nose against a fly-swarmed screen-door to watch a passer-by and cries: "'hite man!" with the enthusiasm usually reserved for parades and fire engines is well out into the stream of conditioning, for he has heard his parents use the word "white" as if it were some mystical or godly thing. I recalled my childhood and how I began to sense the special pattern when I heard my father say "sir" to a white youth half his age, although white youngsters addressed him by his first name.

I remembered the day Mrs. Frankie Mae Marberry, a friend of my mother's, took me to work with her. I was to play with the son of the white people for whom Mrs. Marberry cooked. Even in this rare situation it did not take long for me to realize that the relationship was not quite child-to-child. After Mrs. Marberry told me a few times, without explanation, that I had to be the rustler and let the white child be the six-gun-totin' cowboy, unless the white child wanted it the other way, I realized that it was the same superior-to-inferior relationship that held between the white woman and Mrs. Marberry.

As I walked away from the Western Union office, thinking about the little blonde and the role she and other children would have to play in the emergence of a New South, I could concentrate only on the conditioning process, and how it continues and becomes a part, in a thousand little ways, of our everyday living. I remembered a time in McMinnville when I was about eleven. A carpenter named Charley Hill took me to a white family's house so I could watch him build a chicken house. I returned a second day after school and found several boys playing cowboys and Indians. One of the boys, who were all a few years younger than I, shouted: "He can be the Indian, he can be the Indian!" Several boys ran over to get my reaction as one exclaimed: "Yeah, he's just the right color."

But two boys were hesitant. "Aw, he ain't no Indian," one snapped.

"But he's Indian color," retorted another lad.

"Sure, but he's a Nigra, and I ain't never seen no Nigra in a cowboy picture."

"Naw, me neither," mumbled two or three of the boys, almost in unison, and they edged away, again whooping and firing capguns. Over the din I heard the boy who made the original suggestion discussing moving-pictures. "Ain't it funny," he asked, "that there ain't no colored cowboys?" Fourteen years later, in Milledgeville, I knew the answer: it was not funny at all; it was simply that the movie industry had been part of the process during my childhood.

I walked back toward Dr. Boddie's office, and I felt lucky that I finally knew the answer. I looked at the men standing on the street corner, waiting for work, no doubt; others were sitting on the sidewalk on soft-drink cases and packing-crates. I knew that but for the strange faces of both men and buildings I might have called the town McMinnville. I felt that I could see, in these men, the process in its fruition, for these were men who had lived so long among grief, denial, and morbidity that these things seemed natural. They might live all their lives, as I almost did, without ever knowing the reasons for the "little things" that shaped their lachrymose existence. Perhaps there are no reasons, except those which each man creates in his own mind as he yields to the eternal conditioning. It is only after you break away that you see the weblike nature of the conditioning process, the way it becomes day-to-day living, making segregation its own best defender and perpetuator.

I had not seen all these things in the words of the little blonde in the Western Union office; nor had I just broken away from the process. I remembered the night that it happened. It was on a Saturday night in the spring of 1945. The place was McMinnville. I had stopped there en route to Miami, where I was to take anti-submarine-warfare training. With the gold braid of the ensign I had become still gleaming, I felt compelled to spend a few hours in my home town. All went well until I started back to the bus station to continue my trip to Florida. As I walked through the park, which was downtown, three whites picked up a green metal bench and rolled it into my path. "Stand up, sailor boy, and let the nigger admiral sit down," said one of the white men. Then I saw for the first time that one of the whites was a sailor. He was wearing a white uniform that was unbelievably filthy, and he appeared to be just emerging from a drunken stupor. He stood in mock salute, his thumb in his nose. "Hell yeah," he said. "There oughta be a seat fer the nigger admiral."

I ignored the three and walked around the bench. But the impact of their remarks had been enough: there really was no seat in that park for a "nigger admiral." That night I realized that I had walked through the park thousands of time with the subconscious realization that I was forbidden to sit down there. My sister had sat there with the town's approval while she was playing nursemaid to a white child. Other than that, the green iron benches were not meant for us, and I had accepted this without conscious questioning until a war came along; then I could see the drunken whites, and the women known to be prostitutes, and jailbirds, and mountaineer yokels spitting tobacco juice recklessly, and a sailor saluting contemptuously—all free to use the park. It seemed as if my head were being inflated, because my jaws bulged with helpless anger. But I walked on, and when the sensation wore away I was free of the web. The reconditioning process was under way.

I returned to Dr. Boddie's home, a large brick structure near the edge of the Negro section, but definitely inside the "line." It was an aged home, but well kept and by no means a poor man's home. The furnishings were not pretentious, but they spoke of security and comfort, almost wealth. There were old pictures, some on tin, and antique pieces of furniture that looked as if they had been handed down from generation to generation since before the Civil War.

Economically, Milledgeville had not been unkind to Dr. Boddie. But he had worked hard. Every so often he would mention that he soon would retire, that he had overworked. After all, he pointed out, there are 7,500 Negroes in Georgia for every Negro doctor. This is ten times the national ratio of population to physicians. I watched Dr. Boddie move about the house, almost never still, always reminding himself out loud that he had to do something for one person, and something else for another. He obviously had worked too hard, and too long; his nervousness indicated as much. After all, his job had been bigger than the bare statistics indicated. I knew that one third of Georgia's Negro doctors were practicing in Atlanta, with another third in such larger cities as Macon, Savannah, Columbus, Augusta, and Athens. That left a frightful job for all Negro physicians who decided to give their talents and learning to the scores of thousands of rural dwellers.

We sat down to a lunch that had been waiting for the hour or more that Dr. Boddie and I were late. Mrs. Boddie, a strikingly charming woman, proved to be a motherly, down-to-earth person. "I hope you don't mind just an ordinary meal," she said. I answered, truthfully, that nothing would please me more at that stage of my travels, and I dove lustily into what turned out to be far from an ordinary repast.

Much later, I leaned back, overstuffed and ready to do the rest of the day's research with my head on a pillow, when Dr. Boddie got a call. He hurried from the phone toward the door, turning to me to say: "Let's go." I grabbed my coat and hat and followed. I had no idea where we were going, but I sensed an emergency call. We jumped into his 1946 Oldsmobile and whisked out of town. He drove swiftly and nervously along a gravel road on which he weaved back and forth to dodge large potholes. I tried to keep down nervousness by telling myself that a doctor who had spent better than three decades wading streams, climbing fences, and driving helter-skelter over treacherous country roads ought to have some idea about where danger lies. He took the bumps in stride, zigzagging in an effort to miss as many as possible. During all this he talked about something else.

"How do you plan to get to Atlanta?" he asked.

I said by bus, and he replied that it was possible his wife would drive into Atlanta the next day.

"Oh, does she go to Atlanta often?" I asked.

"Oh, quite frequently. We buy most of our clothes, do most of our shopping in Atlanta. I don't go often, though. Never have time. You know how women are; they go in to Rich's and make a day of it. Get better shopping service in Atlanta, though."

I knew that this was to avoid a situation that I had found to exist in another small town, where the better stores refuse to sell clothing to Negroes except for items that need not be tried on. As a concession to the Negro "leader," who has considerable wealth, the stores mail dresses to his wife at her request—but on the basis that once the package is opened no dress can be returned to the store. A drive to a big city to shop precludes any such situations, as the Boddies must have learned many years before. I did not comment on this.

Soon we came to a stretch of lumpy earth, far worse for driving than the road on which we started. At one point I thought the car would stall when we drove across a swollen creek. Then we were in a field where there was no path, but from the way that Dr. Boddie drove I knew—or hoped—that he was sure of the route. Saplings and wild-berry bushes seemed to mark the way as we bounced across the muddy fields that the doctor had driven by night as well as day.

"I've put a lot of miles on this car—a lot of rough miles," he said, as if he were psychic. "They've promised me the first new Oldsmobile that hits town. They can be pretty decent at times . . . but they make my boy mad. He says they'll call him doctor or anything, but never mister. Not even the telephone operators."

"I tried to drive out here yesterday," he continued before I could get in a remark, "but I got bogged down in mud. I got an old man across the way to pull me out with his team of mules. The bad spot is right up here."

As the muddy area, with the deep tire ruts, came into view I felt the car lunge forward with extra speed. From the way we bounced along, more in the air than on the ground, I knew that the mud would have a difficult time getting a second grasp on the vehicle. Finally I sighted a rickety frame house behind piles of uncut firewood. The doctor drove around the largest pile, right up to the house. He braked sharply: the front bumper almost touched the wooden steps as the car's body rocked forward. He cut off the motor, opened the door, picked up his bag, and took a step toward the door in what seemed like one motion. Seeing that I was doubtful as to whether I should enter the house, he said: "Let's go."

By now a short, dark man in a gray jacket with sham-patched elbows, the jacket tucked into his wash-faded overalls, held the door open. We walked into the dark, dusky front room of the house, where a gaunt-faced boy of about six lay moaning, breathing in short, heavy gasps and turning weakly in agony.

"Thank God, you got here, Dr. Boddie," said the boy's mother. The doctor gave only a passing greeting, going directly to the bed. He pulled back the quilt: I could see the boy's chest bulge with each heartbeat. The lad's moaning ceased. His eyes open wide, his lips closed and ash-gray, he just stared at the doctor. The father, mother, and an older girl stood in the middle of the room, imposing a wistful sort of silence.

"He's intolerable hot, Dr. Boddie," the mother whispered. The doctor shook his head. The father pulled the door open to let in light from outdoors, and then the doleful silence returned. I made a few cheerful remarks to the father, who seemed little consoled by my efforts. By now the doctor had taken a syringe from his bag and was making soothing remarks to the boy. He turned the youngster's fanny ceilingward, and the mother's face wrinkled in anticipated vicarious pain. "Ma'am, are there any black-walnut trees near here?" I asked, using the first words I thought of to draw her attention from the boy. She looked at me, but before she answered a little cry from the boy indicated that the needle had pierced his skin and another dose of wonder drug was on its way to help save a life.

"Your boy's going to be all right, ma'am," said Dr. Boddie. He waited a few seconds to add: "He's got pneumonia. But your boy will be okay soon." The last sentence all but drowned out the words of the father: ". . . pay you, doctor, when my government check comes." He repeated the remark, indicating that he was a disabled veteran. Dr. Boddie lifted his hand as a gesture that the promise was good. He left some medicine that, thanks to science, made it almost a sure thing that the boy would soon be well. This was a double miracle—the miracle of the antibiotics and that of a doctor who could, and would, journey to the backwoods shack.

There are hundreds of small Negro communities and rural areas of the South that have no Dr. Boddie to brave weather and wilds to keep them healthy. McMinnville is one such community, having had no Negro doctor for about fifteen years. Of course, from the ideal standpoint, there is no reason why a community of Negroes should need a Negro doctor. But the fact is that the vast majority of Southern Negroes must depend on Negro doctors for their medical care. In McMinnville, as elsewhere in the South, there have been cases of white doctors doing notable service among Negroes, without regard for pay. But a Negro is never sure that some noble doctor can be reached in time of crisis. The winter of 1938 was a cold, tough one for McMinnville—especially for Negro McMinnville. My father, like most men with outdoor jobs, found himself without work. One night during this winter he got a terrible nosebleed. We put the keys down his back, brown sack-paper under his tongue, the scissors down his back, applied cold, wet towels to his forehead and the back of his neck, trying the practical, the superstitious, and even the ridiculous. Nothing worked. I ran four blocks to a telephone, only to find that the kindly old doctor who had delivered one of my sisters and who had given my family our occasional medical care could not be reached. I called another doctor.

"Does Tom have the money now?" he asked.

"I don't know, sir, but I 'spect he ain't. He ain't worked much. But he's bleeding awfully bad."

"Well, I got a woman due with a baby any time. You better call somebody else."

I called another doctor, dramatizing the occasion to the utmost of my ability before letting the physician reply.

"Where's Tom living now?" he asked, the question being legitimate because we did move rather frequently in those days.

The city officials hadn't thought of Congo Street at that time, and the best answer I could think of was that we lived in "the second house from Hughes' pasture, in front of Cope's junkyard."

"Tom works for Smith and Walker, doesn't he?"

"Yes, sir, but the weather's been kinda bad."

"Well, you tell Tom to go to bed. His nose will stop bleeding."

I took the bad news home. My mother cut open the end of a mattress to get cotton with which to pack my father's nose. He turned on his stomach so the blood wouldn't back down his throat and would get a chance to clot. Eventually it did, but my father had lost a lot of blood. Subsequently, he spent close to a week's pay for pills that the doctor said would "build him back up."

The situation had changed little, if any, in 1951. I found that one Negro who had been laid off his job just before his wife was to deliver a baby could get no doctor to accept his promise to pay. One finally delivered the child when the school principal signed a note guaranteeing payment.

"I wouldn'ta felt so bad about it," this Negro told me, "if it hadn't a been that I was one of this doctor's steady patients when he got out of school and came here to start a practice. He had mostly Negro trade. More Negro trade than you could shake a stick at. You could tell when he started picking up white trade, 'cause he started playing hard t' git. He started asking for money right away. He been knowing all along that we don't make that kind of money to where we can save for doctor's bills. He started talking about not liking to come into the colored section at night. Everybody knows McMinnville colored folks ain't never bothered no doctor at night, or no other white person 'cept maybe some crackers asking about colored girls. But them doctors are jes like store owners: they give you credit, even if they overcharge you, 'til they get fat, and then, man, they're gone."

I thought about all this as I stood in the shack, looking at the little black boy whose difficult breathing spelled agony, and at his parents who must have prayed that Dr. Boddie would be able to overcome the barriers of streams, muddy fields, chewed-up roads, and too many calls from too many

places. I thought how incongruous it seemed to regard as lucky
a kid of six with penumonia—but he was, in a way. He was on
the lucky side of another problem that leads back to the Southland's great debate—racial segregation. The shortage of Negro
medical men has some Northern implications, for it is no
secret that for years medical schools of the North all but closed
their doors to Negroes. Some still do, and Meharry Medical
College in Nashville and the Howard University medical
school in Washington, D.C., still produce the vast majority of
the nation's Negro doctors. Under pressure of public opinion,
many Northern medical schools have at least partly lowered
racial barriers, and Negroes now study in some fifty unsegregated medical schools. The number of their Negro students
still is inordinately small, although Negroes await admission
to medical colleges all over the country. The schools attribute
this to "the inability of Negroes to pass the stiff entrance-
examinations." Since the majority of would-be Negro doctors
get their basic training in the South, the blame falls on the
South and its inadequate Jim Crow schools.

So this little boy was "lucky," in that there were so many
not fortunate enough to have a doctor on call. These were *les
miserables*, I thought.

For a few thoughtful moments I felt as if I were not a Negro
at all: then I was fully aware that I was. A great weariness
had fallen over me, and I wanted to end my journey. I longed
for an escape from reporting; from worrying about tiny varia-
tions in the Jim Crow structure; from trying to analyze segregation and its effects upon the lives of the people involved. I
had begun my journey feeling that, as a reporter, I could live
a black life and write about it as a black man, and then wipe
away the effects with a smug shake of the head. I found that
it was not that easy, because the mind is human, and it tried
to make human things make sense. Confronted with things that
I considered both inhuman and insensible, I began to live the
experiences and try to make personal sense out of them, more
for the human being—the Negro—that I am than for the

reporter I was trying to be. Then I realized that it had to be that way, for the whole story of the South is a human story of living, primarily in conflict, and since I was again part of the South I was bound to feel the conflict. As I wished for an escape I felt unjustly fortunate, in that all I wearied of was temporary: I could dodge the rebuffs by refusing to put myself in contact with whites, and before too long I would again be out of the South.

I decided to take the temporary remedy of dodging rebuffs for the remainder of the day. When we passed a sign advertising a drive-in theater, I said to Dr. Boddie: "That ought to be rather relaxing. I haven't seen a movie in ages. Or isn't the drive-in open this time of year?"

"You can't go there anyhow," he replied. "They don't allow colored in the drive-in." Already I had expressed unwillingness to go into a Jim Crow balcony of a downtown theater, so the subject was closed. Still, I satisfied my wish to get away from being a reporter. I joined a few colored citizens, primarily the younger Boddies, at a bridge party, where I got just enough tasty steak, hot rolls, and beverage of the evening to sleep soundly and to dream of something other than magnolias, run-down schools, and sick little black boys, grimacing but not quite forgotten in a tumbledown back-country shack.

CHAPTER X

NEW TALMADGE, OLD TRICKS

For a while I thought that I would never get out of Milledgeville. I crawled out of bed early on a frosty morning, expecting to catch a bus for Atlanta. After I packed and dressed, my host casually mentioned the bus's arrival time in Macon.

"Did you say Macon?" I inquired with alarm, only to be told that the standard bus-route to Atlanta is through Macon. There is an alternate route, but I could get no bus that way until early afternoon. I decided to wait, for I had no intention of returning to Macon.

"You've got a lot of time to kill," said my host.

"You know what some of those highway signs say: 'It's better to kill time than people.' That holds especially true when I'm the 'people' involved."

Perhaps it was just as well that I did not leave until early afternoon, or a police alarm might have gone out over the state for me. A few hours before my departure I got a call from the drugstore, which was run by Dr. Boddie's son. The Western Union office had called there for me, "and she sounded as if it was kind of urgent." I figured that my wife or the paper had sent me a message, since no one else knew of my whereabouts. Still, I could not imagine either of them wiring instead of telephoning. I rushed over to the Western Union office.

The agent was poring over some traveler's checks when I entered. "I can't figure this out," she said. "I'm missing a book of traveler's checks or something. I don't see how anybody could have got in here. You were the last one to buy any,

141

and . . . I thought you might be able to help me figure out what happened."

She was straining to be polite. The implication was clear, however: she was afraid that I had cheated her out of some checks. Fortunately, I had the answer—unless someone really had stolen a book of checks, in which case I probably would never convince her that I was not the thief.

"Once I got back to the Boddies'," I explained to the agent, "I had a terrible time recording the serial numbers of my checks. It finally dawned on me that you gave them to me out of sequence. I believe if you check you'll find that that's what throws your records out of kilter."

I took out my book of checks and showed her what I meant. She got her record and in a few minutes the whole thing was straightened out, to the embarrassment of the agent, who apologized for calling me in. I told her that it was no trouble, that I had to pick up a bus ticket anyhow.

When I started into the bus station to get the ticket and check my bus's departure time, I paid little attention to the entrance arrangements. I saw only one door. A Negro who sat in a parked car made sure that I would violate no customs, however, by shouting to me that I was about to enter the front —the wrong door. "Hey you. You go 'roun' to the side," he advised. I stared at him for a few seconds, using my eyes to ask who requested his advice. Then I did as he suggested: I entered a waiting-room for Negroes and bought a ticket for a Negro seat at a window for Negroes.

I returned to the bus station several minutes before departure time. There is no more miserable way to travel, I feel, than standing on a bus. I arrived early because I wanted to be sure of a seat. When the driver pulled out his ticket puncher and went to the bus, that was my cue to move toward the door of the bus. My Negro companion thought otherwise. "Colored can't board until all the whites are on," I was told. "Are you kiddin'?" I asked in faked surprise. I did not know that such was the case in Milledgeville, but I knew that it was customary in much of the area. During World War II, in most of the Deep South, protocol for travelers was that white service-men lined up first, followed by white civilians, Negro service-men, and Negro civilians, in that order.

I didn't want to embarrass my companion, so I waited un-easily. I thought that the whole student body of the Georgia State College for Women was about to board the bus. When it appeared that all the women were on, I offered my ticket to the driver. He paused for a few seconds. I was not sure whether he hesitated to let me board, or whether he was trying to decide what I was doing with a portable typewriter. He took my ticket and I walked to the Jim Crow seat, thankful that it still was empty.

A few minutes later about a dozen white girls ran up, half out of breath. One thanked the driver for waiting, indicating that he knew they were coming. Evidently he had hesitated to let me board for this reason. There were seats for only five of the women, not counting the four spaces beside me, which I knew they would not take. I felt uneasy, not because I feared that one of these white girls might sit down, but because some white man might get on and resent my sitting while white wo-men stood. Just before the bus pulled out a Negro woman with a blue, Aunt-Jemima-type bandanna on her head got on with a little boy. This lessened the possibility of any "incident," and gave me considerable relief.

A few grunts from the big engine and we were out of Milledgeville. There were no blossoms, and the only greenness was an occasional pine tree. Farmland, enclosed in barbed-wire fences, lay flat and brown, peaceful and overworked. Occasion-ally a Negro stood in a field with a horse and a crude plow. Watching these Negroes plod along in the brilliant sunshine, I all but forgot that it was winter. Nature had provided for me all the signs of those summers, more than a decade ago, when I visited my grandmother's farm at Yager, Tennessee, and lived in virtual paradise.

It might have been easy to dream my way back to Yager

and a peach orchard where I could take my pocket knife and eat off the trees, or where grapevines, an apple orchard, a watermelon patch, or vines loaded with wild muskedimes surpassed all the storybook wonders of the world. But this was not Yager; this was Talmadge Territory. This was the backbone of the dynasty of Georgia's Governor "Hummon" Talmadge, rabble-rousing master at the kind of harangue that tickles the livers of the wool-hat, pineywoods folk. This was the Old South at its oldest, where with one wrong move a Negro may be in for a fate worse than that of a hound caught sucking eggs. I did not intend to make any wrong moves. After all, it was not too far away, in Walton County, that four Negroes were slain in 1946 in the Monroe Massacre, perhaps the most publicized lynching in United States history. My camera was pushed deep into my topcoat sleeve, and the strap was secured by a large safety pin. My ties were where I felt a Negro's ties might best be in Talmadge Territory—in my suitcase, where I also crammed my briefcase. I covered the typewriter with my topcoat. Wearing trousers that needed pressing, and with my shirt open at the neck, I knew that there was little danger of anyone accusing me of acting "biggety—like white folks." I was just an ordinary Negro exhibiting what I hoped appeared to be normal curiosity in goings-on aboard the bus and in the small towns where it stopped. The less contact with Mr. Talmadge's friends, the better, as far as I was concerned. I had hopes of seeing Talmadge in Atlanta.

The landscape rolled by with amazing uniformity. Frame farmhouses sat back off the road, helping silos and barns fill the space between small towns and villages. The thing most apparent to me was that anybody who was anybody had a statue of a Negro in his yard. Between Milledgeville and Atlanta I counted ninety-six yards in which there stood a coal-black image of a Negro eating watermelon, kneeling in a crap-shooting position, holding a fishing pole or simply showing a monstrous set of pearly white teeth to travelers. This apparently is part of the culture—if the word itself does not create paradox; also, it is part of the eternal conditoning, an effort to portray the Negro as the backwoods whites want and believe him to be.

But these images are not based on African myths. The South still produces real-life Negroes cast from these front-yard stereotypes. The bandanna-clad woman beside me didn't laugh with the faked, nauseating jolliness of the television Aunt Jemima, but she was sickening enough to give some basis to the Aunt Jemima legend. Her little boy fidgeted like a wiggleworm in hot ashes all during the trip. His squirming evoked a volley of shouted threats to "whip yo' behind till it ropes like taffy," to "beat some uv that dirt offa you," to "paddle a mudhole in yo' fanny," and a flock of similar punishments—all unless the boy, Ajax, remained still.

Neither time, new scenery, nor blunt threats stopped Ajax from fidgeting. He managed to work up a hunger, of which he gave notice just outside the little town of Covington. "Mama, I want a biscuit," he bellowed with persistence.

"Dern it, Ajax, shet up. Do I look like any dern biscuit t'you?" This brought quite a laugh from white passengers, which inspired my bandanna-clad seat-companion to repeat the question several times. Soon the laughter wore so thin that passengers had no difficulty hearing a coed exclaim to her companion: "Ain't these colored folks a mess?"

I was pretending to sleep, but I suppose I flinched noticeably. At any rate, the Negro woman became indignant. The coed had offended her sense of pride, and she had to let it be known—with me doing the listening, of course. She kicked my foot and mumbled: "These stringy-haired crackers give me a pain in the you know what, always trying to make like us cullud folks ain't got no sense."

"Ma'am," I said in the most overdone of dialects, "they sho do. And this cullud boy ain't gonna open his mouf 'n' say nuthin' to lead 'em t' be'lieve they's right. I is goin' t'sleep." I turned my head back to the window, partly from fear that she would spit in my face. I didnt go to sleep, however; I thought about the girl's declaration about colored people and how it jibed with what Judge Waring told me. "The white-supremacists think of the Negro only as an inferior, incapable animal made to be kicked around. Any Negro who fails to fit the pattern is regarded as a freak. Bunche is a freak, Jackie Robinson is a freak—any dignified, competent Negro is a freak to them."

I stared at farm wives, children, sharecroppers, work crews, and at the Negroes and whites who loafed on their separate corners in Covington. Each town was like the last one—just another stopping-point along a human frontier. There was meaning in the whole area only if you could look at one of the Negroes on the corner and realize that, ignorant from lack of schooling or contact with other broadening aspects of life, he counted for absolutely nothing, politically or socially. On the other hand, the tobacco-chewing, red-necked, fellow citizens across the street, while equally ignorant, meant everything politically, if nothing socially. Because of Georgia's unique vote-counting system, each of Talmadge's back-country friends exerts, on the average, twelve times as much voting power as a voter in Atlanta. This is because Georgia assigns the least-populated county a minimum of two unit votes and the most-populated county a maximum of six votes. The candidate who gets the most votes in a given county wins that county's entire unit vote. Thus more than 600,000 people in Fulton County (Atlanta) exert no more political control than 145,000 in Troup County.

Although these country people control Georgia politically, the story of race relations in the state is not theirs. Rather, it is the story of the man who knows the makings of their minds. It is the story of a demagogue who has mastered the art of playing the peckerwood, of exploiting the credulity, prejudice, and ignorance of these people. The story of Georgia is the story of Herman Talmadge, repeating the shrill cry for white supremacy made famous by his race-baiting father, Eugene.

Young Talmadge became Mister Georgia in January 1947,

when the General Assembly illegally named him governor to fill the vacancy left by his father's death, which came just before "Ole Gene's" fourth inaugural. "Hummon" ruled for only two months, however, until the State Supreme Court deposed him in favor of Lieutenant Governor M. E. Thompson, generally considered weak and inept, and whose only claim to fame was that he had been secretary to Ellis Arnall, one of the most progressive and respected governors Georgia ever had.

"Hummon," a University of Georgia law-school graduate and a Navy veteran of thirty-two months in the Pacific, vowed, however, that "the court of last resort is the people of Georgia. This case will be taken to the court of last resort."

This was the ace up young Talmadge's sleeve—his ability to sway "the people," meaning the backwoods yokels. Like Louisiana's Huey Long, he kept aglow the illusion that he stands for "the people." In the masthead of his weekly *Statesman*, a small newspaper in which he makes scurrilous attacks on his critics, he lists: "The People—Editor; Herman E. Talmadge—Associate Editor."

In 1948 Hummon kept his promise. With a stray black lock tumbling down on his forehead, and sporting the same red galluses and big black cigars that were the political trademarks of "Ole Gene," young Talmadge went out into the sticks crying for white supremacy and states' rights. Even an automobile accident could not stop him. Sporting a black eye and bright yellow crutches, he hobbled to the farthest crossroads to scream: "Let's keep the nigger in his place." Rural Georgians, the very people whom I observed as my bus rolled through land still smarting from the touch of William Tecumseh Sherman, ruled in favor of Hummon and white supremacy. Using President Truman's civil-rights program as a ready-made, bitter issue, Talmadge had won in the "court of last resort," and was elected to serve the remaining two years of his father's term.

Once in office, crafty, cocky Herman Eugene Talmadge became quite reserved—for a Talmadge. The snap of the red galluses was gone; Hummon began to say "Nigra," a word

usually used by whites too proud to say Negro, not crude
enough to say nigger; Ole Gene's son even saw a Northern
Negro journalist now and then, much to the consternation of a
lot of people.

Talmadge's first legislature recognized the principle of the
secret ballot (leaving only South Carolina to discover it). It
passed a law requiring blood tests before marriage, and approved a program to raise the rather subhuman level of education in the state. As it turned out, this was window-dressing
behind which it killed a bill to unmask the Ku Klux Klan,
which had endorsed Hummon in 1948. It also rammed through
a re-registration bill, designed to disenfranchise more Negroes
and slash the voting lists so as to make elections easier to swing.
More important, the legislature passed two measures making it
legal for Talmadge to succeed himself, something no other
Georgia governor had been able to do. Obviously, Hummon
still was cracking the whip.

Despite this, there were Southern journalists who called
Talmadge the nation's unhappiest governor. He really wasn't
like Ole Gene, they said, but simply longed to get back down
on the farm. Being governor got on his nerves, said one writer,
who called him a "fugitive from a psychiatrist's couch." But
in 1950 Hummon was back, running for re-election as governor instead of for the seat of Georgia's senior Senator Walter George, as many thought he might do. This took organized
labor out of the sad position of having to vote for Talmadge,
which it threatened to do if Talmadge opposed George, "because Talmadge is more liberal."

Hummon went back to his white-supremacy routine. He
convinced poor whites that "there are not enough good jobs
in the South to go around," and that unless the people re-
elected him Negroes would take the good jobs through federal
enactment of a Fair Employment Practices Act.

Analyzing Talmadge's rise to power, *U.S. News and World
Report* magazine said: "White supremacy is more than just a
phrase. It is more than a hold upon self-respect. It means

food and clothes. It gives [the poor white] an edge over the Negro in a fight for a living." Talmadge, according to the magazine, simply was reminding these people that they were warding off empty bellies by electing him.

If the U.S. *News and World Report* writer is convinced that white supremacy means these things to rural whites, I am not. The back-country people who vote Talmadge into power never get the good jobs. Those I saw were ignorant and impoverished, by any normal standard. To save his own empire, Talmadge is seeing to it that the rural folk never learn that "good jobs" are products of a progressive, co-operative economy, and that with the racial bickering prevalent in their society there can never be enough "good jobs" to go around, not even among the whites.

The pineywoods Talmadge stalwarts reminded me that Booker T. Washington once said you can't keep a man in the gutter unless you stay there to hold him. Ole Gene's son had found that to be only half true: he was keeping the Negro in the gutter by duping the poor white into staying there and holding him.

That, I knew, was the story of Georgia, of how a man who counts for little, by the least noble of measuring-sticks, can take a false idea and poison the minds of men and stop the clocks of human progress. Hitler had done it in Germany; Stalin is doing it in the Soviet empire; and Malan does it in South Africa. That was the story, and it was as clear as the crisp blue Georgia sky above State Highway 12.

The bus stopped for several minutes at Hub Junction, forty-one miles from Atlanta. I got off to relax. I walked into the station and picked up a candy bar. The man behind the counter refused to take my money: "We don't serve no colored in here."

"Not even to take out?"

"I said we don't serve no colored in here."

"Okay, okay." I put the candy bar down. "Where is the colored restroom?"

"The what?"

"The lavatory . . . the toilet."

"Out there," he replied, pointing across a field to a crude wooden shack. On it, in huge whitewashed letters, was the word COLORED. I walked out to the privy and looked in from a nose-holding distance. The sawdust floor was wet with urine. The seat was covered with clay and human feces. I walked (with apologies to Hemingway) across the field and into the trees.

I strode back to the junction and saw that another bus had stopped. A rather obese Negro, whose shirt collar was ringed with sweat, stood in the shade of the bus. He was an over-friendly soul who identified himself as a religious lecturer. He gave me a card and started talking about the heat. I remarked that it was pretty warm on busses. He said that he wasn't riding a bus, but the blue Buick parked near by.

"I'm gonna be riding this bus, though, if they catch my cousin," he said with laughter that made his stomach shake so that I feared his pants would fall off. "I swear I won't know him."

"What do you mean, 'if they catch' your cousin?"

"That fool's in there a-passing. I tell him he's sho got nerve. He's got nerve enough to slap a white woman in Mississippi."

"Passing?" I asked, laughing at what I thought to be just a joke in which, the last time I heard it, the white woman being slapped was in Georgia.

"Yeah, he's passing. And he ain't much lighter'n you 'n' me. When we get hungry in these country places he walks right in and orders some sandwiches. If they tell him they don't serve colored, he says: 'I don't blame you; I wouldn't serve no damn niggers, neither.' Them crackers get so flabbergasted they don't know what he is, and they serve him. They figure that anybody who don't like niggers is on their side."

I looked around the bus to see a light-skinned, but to me obviously Negro, man come out the front door with a sackful of sandwiches and two Coca-Colas. After he started the Buick, my fat friend walked from behind the bus, which I realized he was using as a shield, and jumped in. They sped down the highway as I stood there wide-eyed. I had heard that old "I hate niggers, too" gag told in a lot of ways, but I didn't think anyone was foolish enough actually to try it—at least, not in Talmadge Territory.

Part Two

The governor would not be able to see me, Talmadge's secretary informed me. He had gone hunting with some members of the legislature. This did not surprise me, although I was a little disappointed. I had wanted to interview Talmadge to get his side of today's South, to let Americans see the tremendous range of thinking between a Georgia governor and a South Carolina federal judge. Somewhere between them was the real South of 1951—just where, I had not decided.

I left my hotel and walked out on Auburn Avenue, the city's main Negro street, the business center of what actually is a black island in a sea of whites.

The story of Atlanta is a tale of two cities—two Negro cities. I stood in one of those cities, in the community of slums and degradation that revolve around Auburn Avenue. Almost everything that met the eye was Negro—of, for, or about Negroes. These were sights I might have seen in many cities. I could have been on Baltimore's Pennsylvania Avenue, Nashville's Fourth Avenue, Memphis's Beale Street, Minneapolis's Olson Highway, or St. Paul's lower Rondo Street. I looked at the hotel from which I had just stepped. Not bad, as Negro hotels of the South go. Still, it was no palace. There was the way the door to your room shook open even when it was supposed to be locked, and it made you fearful of leaving your luggage in the room, or of sleeping there. There were other circumstances that almost forbade sleep. You could see that the bedspread was not clean, so you knew to pull it back before sitting down; you simply hoped that the sheets were cleaner. You watched the bugs in the bathroom, the streaked yellow of the bathtub, the floor that obviously hadn't been scrubbed since the termites moved in. A roach had dropped off the sink when you turned on the light, and you crushed it with your foot; but you still couldn't fight off the feeling that bugs were crawling down your neck and digging down into your hair, trying to find a warm nestling-place on your scalp; and you scratched. You feared you might have caught lice. And then you began to itch all over. And the more you scratched, the more you itched, and the torment mounted until you ran out of the room, glad to walk on Auburn Avenue, away from the hotel in which you stayed because there was nothing better available.

I walked for blocks and blocks, and everything that met the eye was Negro. There were Negro beauty parlors, and a Negro liquor store, Negro taverns, bookstores, cafés, barbershops, and myriad other things Negro; and a Negro drugstore at which I stopped to buy a Negro newspaper. I looked at the fountain. Not bad at all. I sat down and ordered doughnuts and milk. It had been a long time since Milledgeville and my last meal. I had planned to eat much earlier, but the grease-splattered counter in the musty Jim Crow corner of the Atlanta bus station had killed my appetite. And I had walked past the other places that stank of smoke and wet grease, and some of them of human beings. The sidewalks and the curbs had helped to ward off hunger, for I saw the paper wrappers and brown sacks and chewing gum and snuff spit and phlegm that littered the thoroughfare. I walked until I tired, and then I stopped in a shoe-repair shop. A boy of about twelve started shining my shoes.

"These stitches on the sole are pretty dirty, mister," he said. I agreed. He vowed that he would change that. He worked for what seemed like ages, and when he finished the stitches were white again, and my shoes had been cleared of the scuffs and friction marks of weeks of travel. The youngster gave a wide, proud grin, and I could see that he had worked up a bit of perspiration. His pride elated me: I gave him a dollar—even before I remembered happily that the *Tribune* was paying the bill.

I walked out and saw a pickup truck with two white and two Negro military policemen sitting in the rear. It was the first interracial scene that I had come across in Atlanta. It didn't last long, for the Negroes jumped out on Auburn Avenue, waving good-bye to their white buddies. The Negroes would patrol Negroes, in line with the policy for civilian policemen.

I walked off Auburn Avenue, past houses whose shabbiness no longer moved me. They were houses that spoke of a queasy life at the nadir of human existence, but I had seen worse in so many places. I walked back to Auburn Avenue and caught a cab; I was going to the "other" Atlanta.

I went out northwest, to the Hunter Road area, where fine homes and fine cars lined the streets. There were sidewalks, and houses painted in pastel colors, with gay green shutters, red-shingled roofs, and attached garages. Stone houses with arched façades had lawns and stone-lined driveways. All this belonged to Negroes. This was what Senator Lister Hill meant. This was what he referred to when he declared over a national radio network that the Negro of the South is not mistreated or denied opportunity today. This was where he meant when he said: "You all come on down South and see how our Negroes really live." Here were homes with carpets on the floor and running water in the kitchen and Scotch in the den. Here one could find three-speed phonographs and a tuxedo or two. Negroes had a separate country club and a nine-hole golf course all their own.

I stopped at one of these homes, on the recommendation of

a Minneapolis friend. I heard how Negroes "really are going to town in Atlanta," and I got an account of how Jim Crow was on the run.

"The old South ain't what she used to be," said my host as he poured some water into a third of a glass of Scotch and handed it to me. "Take that Klan. We ran it right through the ground. Not underground, through the ground." I remembered that it was Atlanta where the Ku Klux Klan sprang into ignoble being in 1915, spreading terror across the Southland and into the Midwest. Then it faded into bankruptcy, its office building becoming a rectory for Catholics, whom Klansmen were dedicated to hate. But the Klan did not die, as my host indicated, for the Klan program survived and sprang up in organizations of new names. These hate groups did not thrive because a few diligent and decent citizens stamped at their vitals by seeing that they were continually plagued by legal troubles.

The woman of the house was persistent. "Atlanta is not a Southern city at all, much less a Georgia city," she offered, in a quote that I recognized as one I had just read in *Holiday* magazine. She talked on, extolling a new "citadel of democracy," and I listened. But less than an hour before I had listened to the cab-driver gripe. "Atlanta is jes like the rest of the South," he exclaimed. "I seen it all. A nigger's a nigger in all uv it, even if he can say his A-B-C's backwards and turn white as pigeon droppings."

I wondered if both he and the people I was visiting had not overstated each theory. Atlanta seemed considerably removed, in racial policy, from the backwoods hamlets through which I had just passed. However, despite her gaudy streets and splendid mansions, her churning factories and filthy alleys of warehouses and slums, all lending the air of a Northern metropolis, I knew that Atlanta was a Southern city. Atlanta is racially segregated by law and custom, and the human straitjacket that this imposes was as evident in Atlanta as elsewhere. Negroes ride in cabs driven by Negroes; they sit in Jim Crow seats in public vehicles; they sit in bleachers to watch a baseball game; and in many buildings they are expected to take the freight elevator up, although they may descend on the first elevator to come along.

I saw some justification for Negro Atlanta's heralding the fall of Jim Crow. Atlanta is a big university center, and the students and educators have done much to improve race relations. On the Negro side there are Atlanta University, the school of social work (drawing Negroes from all over the nation), Morehouse College, Spelman College, and Clark University. And on the white side there is Emery University, where a few professors have spoken out boldly, proving again and again the value of educational institutions unfettered by legislative strings; and to a lesser degree, there is Georgia Tech. These, with the Negro's political and economic strength, have made Atlanta flexible enough to adjust its racial policy in a trying situation without creating a crisis. This was shown in 1951 when the N.A.A.C.P. held its national convention in Atlanta—the first time it had convened in any Southern city in twenty years. The delegates were greeted by the mayor; segregation rules were relaxed so a mixed group could hear Dr. Ralph Bunche speak in the city auditorium; policemen were instructed, as were bus drivers, to leave delegates alone, even if a racially mixed group sat together. The city even turned its head while the N.A.A.C.P. gave a dance in which white and Negro delegates danced together.

"You can talk about your colleges and your votes, but Negro business did it," said my host, himself the operator of one of the Auburn Avenue establishments. "Money talks!" he added for emphasis. There was the schism—the breach between the two Negro Atlantas: a moneyed class had sprung up and with it had come class conflict. Once I knew that it existed it became evident everywhere, even when I took another walk the next day down Auburn Avenue.

I talked with C. A. Scott, publisher of the Atlanta *Daily World*, primary member of what actually is a chain of newspapers. Scott's paper, usually consisting of six to eight pages, is a typical Negro newspaper in that it denounces race prejudice and discrimination in big, bold words and bigger, bolder type. It is unique in that it thrives as a daily primarily on advertising from Negro businesses. Scott, a pleasant, well-educated man, surprised me when he said he opposed "fighting segregation, *per se*." His theory was that Negroes must build up more businesses. I asked if he did not think segregation itself was a barrier to building up Negro business. "In a way," he conceded, "but let them fight segregation on a higher level. Let them fight segregation in Maryland and Kentucky. We have a two-way fight down here—a fight to survive and a fight in which we strike out strategically against segregation."

I left a little confused, wondering just what is a strategic strike against segregation by one who does not oppose it, *per se*. I wanted to find out what other Atlanta businessmen thought about segregation. Almost to a man, they argued that money talks.

"Will money talk a bus driver into letting you select your seat?" I asked one.

"Money enables me to own a car so I can tell the transit company to go to hell," he replied.

"Does money soothe your pride when they Jim Crow you at an opera performance?" I asked another.

To keep his dignity intact, he said, he stays away from the opera.

I asked another man if his money could get his son into the University of Georgia or into Georgia Tech. He informed me that he could send his son to Harvard. He admitted that this offered no solution to the thousands of Negro parents who couldn't send their sons to Harvard, but he blamed this on the fact that "they haven't built up enough Negro business."

It was hard to separate honest theory from mouthings inspired by vested interests, the latter being one of the strongest allies of the South's dual system. Each of these Negroes profited from segregation. It appeared that Atlanta was simply a blown-up, more complicated laboratory for the "soft-soap" technique that I had seen so much of in small towns. In the latter communities Negro leaders always are jockeyed into a position where they must defend segregation because it favors them.

The two Atlantas that I saw were indications of what is happening to some degree throughout the South. The Negro has adapted himself to the "system," which businessmen are afraid to attack because of fear—and many will admit this— that the end of segregation will mean the end of Negro drugstores, barbershops, beauty parlors, theaters, restaurants, and the like. They do not choose to gamble, and the fear springs from the logic of inferiority; they assume that the Negro businessman cannot survive except among his own, except when protected by the tariff of racial seclusion. I found this dilemma most evident where the fight for Negro equality stood greatest chance of succeeding and the danger to vested interests appeared most real. The confusion among Negroes was simply a sign that the vast conditioning-program had worked well. In Atlanta, where a convention of outsiders could crack what once was a rigid pattern of life, the New South seemed so near. It seemed to be rapping on the door. But the Negro hands that hold the latchkey also hold the purse strings, and the fear is that to turn the key is to lose the purse; so in the world of vested interests the purse-holder thinks Old South.

CHAPTER XI

APOLOGIES TO SOUTH AFRICA

Birmingham, Alabama, is the capital of Jim Crowism in America. Birmingham, industry's Pittsburgh of the South, is Jim Crow in birth, life, and death. It is, with apologies to Johannesburg and Capetown, South Africa, the world's most race-conscious city. Birmingham is a city of gross tensions, a city where the color line has been drawn in every conceivable place; Eugene "Bull" Connor, white-supremacist police commissioner, sees that no man, white or black, crosses the line.

I visited Birmingham because of its industry, its labor unions, and my knowledge of the racial friction that manifested itself at intervals in house bombings and police brutality. I wanted to see if Birmingham's industry meant the same thing to the Negro as did Alcoa's industry in Tennessee or if the labor movement in Birmingham meant to the Negro what some Americans predicted it would.

I arrived in Birmingham by Jim Crow train (I had failed in my argument with Southern Railroad officials in Atlanta) on a Sunday afternoon. I spent a little more than two days in the city. During those hours I tried desperately to escape the feeling that I had been swept out of the mainstream of American life. I tried to find just one aspect of Birmingham life not dominated by a segregation decree. I failed. I found only countless examples of the inconsistency, the irony, the pathos, and accompanying evil that is segregation. Here is Birmingham as I met and lived it:

For about half a block after leaving the train I walked toward the station among white passengers. Then it ended. We came to steps of which one set was for Negroes, one for whites.

Any notion of ignoring the distinction faded quickly, for there was a policeman standing at the steel gate for whites, seeing to it that Negroes went through the other gate, which led into the Negro waiting-room. It was like a stockyard loading: once in the enclosure, the animals can go but to one place.

I had no idea where I would stay in Birmingham. I asked the woman at the Traveler's Aid desk (a Negro "branch" was set up in the Negro waiting-room) what hotel she recommended. She named the Rush. Then I called the parents of an Oberlin classmate to get their opinion as to whether it was a place infested with thieves, prostitutes, and bedbugs. They, too, said the Rush is as good as anything available to Negroes in Birmingham. I had double-checked because I knew enough about Negro so-called hotels that are no more than "love pads," operating under the eye of the police so long as the proprietor deals out the customary "cut" and so long as no Negro takes a white woman in.

I found that I would have to ride a cab driven by a Negro. I looked out for one and saw a sign, WHITE CABS ONLY. Even a segregated parking-place is set aside for Negro cabs. I hailed a driver who took me to the Rush, where a huge, red-lettered sign hung over the sidewalk, leaving no doubt that the hotel was FOR COLORED. I got a clean room, although it was without bath or telephone. Despite the apparent cleanliness, I was cautious not to make the mistake that I made in Atlanta. There I left my toothbrush out of its plastic container, and when I returned to my room roaches and waterbugs were having a jolly time nibbling on the toothpaste-sweetened bristles.

I edged into the teeming streets of Birmingham's Negro business-section, and my immediate feeling was that I never had seen so many Negroes in my life. I had, of course, but not crowded into so small an area. The street scene made it evident that housing and other facilities are far inadequate for Birmingham's Negro population. The junkiest little sweets shop was crowded. All along the streets, dumpy little places, many of them operated by whites, were reaping a bonanza.

I ran into food trouble for the first time on my journey. Either Birmingham has no eating-places comparable to those for Negroes in Atlanta, Miami, and Washington, or I asked the wrong people for recommendations. The place labeled "tops" by three people had been closed by policemen, I found upon arrival. I went to a place described as second best. It was so small and crowded that it was almost impossible to walk between the tables. I was hungry, so I ordered fried chicken, an old Southern stand-by. To my woe, the chicken was tough, the rolls were baked hard and crumbly, and the sweet potatoes must have been three-day leftovers, the syrup having thickened and become white. In general, the food was lousy, I informed the proprietor, who sat behind the cash register.

She took my money with nonchalance and told me: "In Birmingham, particular people eats at home." When I stepped back on the street I knew what she meant. You could poison all the "particular" people in overcrowded Birmingham and she still would have enough customers to do a profitable business. I ate sandwiches at a little ice-cream parlor until I left Birmingham.

I looked for Sunday-afternoon entertainment and ended up heading for a movie. I found three all-Negro (owned by whites) movies, two of which were showing third-run, third-rate features. A first-rate film was showing at the third theater, but I had seen it four months before in Minneapolis. One white theater in Birmingham admits Negroes, but only to the balcony. I got a wry chuckle from the sign at the side door of this theater: "Balcony kept open continually for your convenience and entertainment."

I decided against the movies, and walked on down the streets, watching the many faces that mirrored joy and sadness, hope and resignation. For blocks I just looked and listened. At one corner I saw a policeman, one hand on his hip, the other on his gun holster, giving an aged Negro peanut-vender a tongue-lashing. A few Negroes leaned against the aged buildings and watched silently. Others paraded by as if nothing out of the ordinary was taking place.

I tired of walking and decided to ride a city bus downtown. I found that both races enter through the front door, as is customary in most cities of the South. I did not read fast enough, however, and had to be told by a gruff motorman that "Nigras step up on the left side, white people on the right side" of the steps. Sure enough, painted side-by-side on the single set of steps were the words COLORED and WHITE. There was only one money box; the fares were the same for both races.

I sat behind a wooden bar near the rear of the bus. The bar is the official "segregator," and a sign on it warned both whites and Negros not to move it. Although it was not the case on my bus, I saw others on which Negroes stood packed in behind the segregator although there were many empty seats in front of the bar. This can work the other way, of course, but drivers usually see that the bar is where no whites will be inconvenienced.

Instead of riding downtown, I got off at the street where my hotel was. Again I erred by starting out the front door—down the colored side of the steps. The motorman closed the door in my face and ordered me to go to the back door. Only whites could exit at the front. I followed his instructions, and then went to my room.

Monday was a busier day, but it was the same Birmingham. And I was the same Negro, fenced in by law and custom, confused by paradox, left aghast by obvious fear in the eyes of innocent people. All this at one time. I stopped to take a picture of a uniquely Jim Crowed restaurant called George's. This place, in the Negro section but run by a white man whom I assumed to be Greek, lived up to the letter of the law by having whites eat on one side of a horseshoelike counter and Negroes on the other, but in full view and chatting range of each other. The same Negro waitresses served them all. I noticed that a white and a Negro man were conferring across the few feet of space that performed the imaginary segregation. They said that although they worked side by side in Fairfield, a Birmingham suburb and steel-mill center, they could not eat together. I wanted to take their picture but found the room too small to get the shot I wanted, so I stepped outside, planning to take my picture through the window. As I adjusted my camera an old Negro woman caught my arm. "Don't let 'em see you, don't let 'em see you," she cautioned.

"Don't let whom see what?" I demanded hastily.

She nodded her head toward town, where I saw two policemen approaching. I mustered up a "policemen-be-damned" look and snapped the picture. The policemen looked at the camera but said nothing. Later I found that the trembling old woman's fear and excitement *had* affected me. I had forgotten to take the cover off my lens.

I called a taxi to take me to a few places I wanted to see. I carried a bundle of shirts along in hopes of finding a one-day laundry. The first laundry to catch my eye was the Imperial. A sign painted high on the building proclaimed proudly: WE WASH FOR WHITE PEOPLE ONLY.

"Nothing working in there but colored, neither," said my taxi driver, Samuel Clemens, who knew by my exclamation that I had seen the laundry sign.

"I'd sure like a word with one of the workers," I said. Clemens said he knew a girl in there and would take me in the back way. "I'm Army bound, what the hell have I got to lose?" he philosophized.

Clemens parked and we walked into the laundry. "Why do you work in a joint like this?" I said boldly, trying to catch a worker off guard. The perspiring washerwoman was not surprised, however. She knew to what I referred and acted as if she had been criticized before. "Shucks, the joke's on the owner," she countered. "They do wash *some* Negroes' clothes here, 'cause mine's in one of them tubs there."

Clemens and I returned to the taxi and he drove me to

Birmingham's monument to bigotry—a home shattered by dynamite set off by hoodlums in the struggle to maintain strict residential segregation. It was the night of December 21, 1950, that the blast shattered the eighteen-thousand-dollar home of Mrs. Mary Leans Monk. The explosion, which came less than thirty-six hours after the United States Court of Appeals ruled unconstitutional the city's racial zoning law, injured a sleeping child who was hit by falling plaster.

The house had been unoccupied for several months while the issue was argued in court. When the verdict came, on December 20, Mrs. Monk, her son, William, and Mr. and Mrs. C. W. Askew and their two children moved in. Mrs. Leans was walking into her bedroom the night of the 21st when she heard a thud on the porch outside her bedroom. She ran out just in time to escape the blast, which tore half her bedroom wall away, wrecked the living-room, and damaged other rooms of the brick structure.

When detective G. L. Patty went out to investigate the bombing, he cracked: "The [court] decision must have been what she was waiting for, because she moved right in." Police found no witnesses. Nobody had seen "strangers" in the neighborhood, which is just outside the prescribed "Negro" section.

It was the fifth bombing of Negro homes in a short span of time. The city commission used this flareup of anti-Negro activity as an excuse for approving the segregation ordinance— an assumption that the solution was to keep Negroes out of "white" neighborhoods.

As I stood before the ripped building, an unoccupied, spoiled concession to intimidation and violence, I realized that it had been eight months since Dr. John Buchanan, a white Baptist pastor and head of a committee of five hundred Birmingham citizens, had demanded that "if the local police authorities are not able to find the violators, they should call upon the state forces, and if necessary the federal forces, to apprehend these law violators." A Birmingham paper joined the group in offering one thousand dollars for information leading to the arrest and conviction of the home-blasters. Apparently money must play second string to segregation in Birmingham: nobody knew a thing. Policemen, to whose diligence in enforcing segregation former Senator Glen Taylor can attest, were still following leads up blind alleys.

I went downtown and strolled past restaurants I would have been arrested for trying to enter. Yet the waiters, waitresses, cooks, and dishwashers—all the help except the person behind the cash register—were Negroes in practically every café. I found a cook plucking feathers off a chicken behind one place. I asked what he thought about his boss's racial-seclusion policy.

"Ain't it silly?" he ventured. "I make the biscuits with my black hands. Colored waitresses drag their sleeves in the gravy and stick their fingers in the coffee. That's just mellow fine. But any one of us is too dirty or too something to sit out front and eat."

I walked on, thinking of that famous dissent by Justice Harlan in opposing the "separate but equal" theory in 1896. "If a state can prescribe as a rule of civil conduct, that whites and blacks shall not travel as passengers in the same railroad coach, why may it not also regulate the use of the streets of its cities and towns to compel white citizens to keep to one side of a street and black citizens to keep to the other?" asked the jurist. "Why may it not, upon like grounds, punish whites and blacks who ride together in streetcars or in vehicles on a public road or street? Why may it not require sheriffs to assign whites to one side of a courtroom and blacks to another? And why may it not also prohibit the commingling of the two races in the galleries of legislative halls or in public assemblages convened for the consideration of the political questions of the day?"

Why not? I found that Birmingham has done these things; she has more than fulfilled the fears of Justice Harlan. Although I could choose my side of the street, there are many streets in Birmingham on which a Negro dares not be seen on any side after sundown. Whites and blacks *may* be punished for riding together on the public street, even in a private vehicle, unless the relationship is obviously that of master and servant. Birmingham *does* restrict whites to one part of the courtroom and Negroes to the other. I found that in the courthouse, where the words "Justice to every man . . ." are inscribed above the elevators, a Negro can ride to his justice only in a Jim Crow elevator. Birmingham *does* prohibit the commingling of the two races, either in public or private hall, to discuss the political questions of the day.

Former United States Senator Glen Taylor, Idaho Democrat, has experience of this. He was arrested in 1948, not for commingling, but for entering the wrong door of a little Negro church—a door that policemen had labeled COLORED instead of the one they had labeled WHITE.

Taylor, then a somewhat unpopular candidate for Vice President on the somewhat unpopular Progressive Party ticket, found that very few people cared. There was silence all the way up to the United States Supreme Court, which dodged the issue, as expected, because it was an outright challenge to the legality of segregation. A nation that had learned to say: "What the hell, they're only Negroes," was saying: "What the hell, it's only Glen Taylor."

I thought the case was forgotten, but I found that Negro Birmingham remembers. They tell, with a wry chuckle, about how "Bull" said that, come hell, high taxes, or Henry Wallace, Birmingham was going to have segregation. Then he dispatched the bulk of his police force to the Negro church to see that there was no hand-holding across the aisle during the Progressive Party rally. Gangsters promptly showed an academic interest in Connor's deployment of policemen by staging a robbery in the cop-shy downtown area.

"Everybody, including his fellow Senators, put the screws on old Taylor in that deal," said the proprietor of my hotel.

"But just wait, the President of the United States will take an unsegregated step here one day. Then Americans will see that it can happen to anybody."

I disagreed, for Presidents are politicians and politicians "do as the Romans do." I thought about how lost I was—lost as any Negro is lost in a city like Birmingham, where his every step is controlled and where he has no passport to that self-made world that Negroes flock to in order to dodge the rigors of a segregated society. I knew that many thousands of Negroes in Birmingham also are lost, in the sense that they are not part of that Negro group able to turn isolation into contentment. I feel that these thousands are lost in the paradox of the rules that circumscribe their lives. Certainly, they must realize that, despite the city ordinance governing public-bus segregation, a Negro woman may ride anywhere up front— so long as she is escorting a white child. State legislatures of the South have made such provisions in their segregation statutes. These Negroes must be aware, too, that I, or any Negro man, can enter the swankiest hotel in Birmingham, walk through the lobby and roam upstairs unquestioned—if I wear a white coat and black bowtie. With that same coat and tie I can enter the front door of the most exclusive country club. Under these circumstances, no white bus-passenger, hotel guest or country-club socialite will cry "contaminated!" Why? Because, in the South, a Negro woman with a white child or a Negro man in a white coat and black bowtie means: IN SERVITUDE.

Birmingham had doubly convinced me that segregation is not based on cleanliness, education, body odors, or economic status. It is the symbol of—it is synonymous with—white supremacy.

I found that a tremendous number of Negroes of the South are aware of this. The white South also is aware of this new feeling, and in a lot of cities the system is preserved by giving a little at the edges. Birmingham has served notice more than once that she will give no ground. Perhaps that accounts for the brooding tensions that hang over the city, tensions as obvious as an elephant in a bird's nest.

That is why I disagreed with the hotel proprietor. I feared that long before Presidents start making unsegregated moves in segregated places, some of Birmingham's lost thousands will act boldly. The tiniest stroke against an immovable city regime will be the spark to send the tensions exploding. As usual, a shocked, embarrassed America will wonder how it happened.

Part Two

You ramble through a city like Birmingham, where the Negro's lot is lowest, where little or no progress has been made, and you ask yourself why. Why is it that, although Negroes represent close to half the city's population, they are as subservient, on the whole, as prisoners of war? Why is it that Atlantans can demand and get an end to Jim Crowism in City Hall elevators and Birmingham Negroes cannot? Why is it that Josephine Baker can demand that a top night-club let Negroes attend her performances unsegregated in Miami, whereas she would be run out of Birmingham for the suggesion? In search of the answer to these questions, I spent hours talking with Negro "leaders," with Negro politicians, with officials of the N.A.A.C.P. branch, with Negro ministers, with a Negro editor, and with ordinary Negroes in dismal little taverns.

Was it the answer that I found so many of Birmingham's Negroes in greasy, smoky taverns, ready to shout: "Down the hatch with the beer; down to hell with the N.A.A.C.P.," as one man did when I told him that I was soliciting memberships for the N.A.A.C.P.? Nobody, not even the N.A.A.C.P., had ever done anything for him, he said, and he visited the tavern to "drown my blues with a bottle of beer." He considered it the purest drivel for anyone to tell him that by wasting his time and money in such joints he simply was dooming himself to "the blues" for another generation. His argument, however, was that he first had to lose "the blues I've already got." Perhaps it was drivel, I thought; at least, it was not the answer that I sought, for the man and his beer simply were another example of the old argument about whether apathy leads to squalor, or squalor produces apathy.

Was the answer behind the bridge hands, where highfalutin Negroes sipped highballs made with liquor that they had to buy at a Jim Crow store? (Birmingham has one state-run liquor store for whites, one for Negroes, with both run by white personnel.) An inevitable concomitant of Negro withdrawal into a close-knit upper clique of those able to dodge most of segregation is the development of "I've got mine" attitudes. This was evident in the words of a Negro doctor, who said to me after I mentioned that Miami and Galveston had some of the worst slums that I had ever seen: "Well, I can't complain. The syphilis victims are paying for my house." From what I saw and heard, Birmingham has its share of greedy Negroes, lining their pockets with dollars through political graft, racketeering, overcharges, and somewhat more legal means of exploiting segregation, which keeps the less fortunate of their race where exploitation comes easily.

It was obvious that the illiterate, clowning Negro, caught in a vicious circle where he is an enemy to himself, is one of the reasons why Birmingham is the human sinkhole of race relations; it was equally obvious that "big shot" racial leeches are sucking at the bloodstream of progress. But in the end I concluded that Birmingham does not have surplus enough of either of these to account for the social stagnation that was so evident. The basic factor seemed to be that the city's Negroes are stripped of any effective political power. This, I found, can be attributed to two things: deceptive skulduggery on the part of election officials and, perhaps more important, apathy on the part of Negroes.

Some forty per cent of the Negro teachers in the public

schools of Birmingham never have tried to vote. Of the
108,000 Negroes of voting age in the county (Jefferson), less
than 5,000 were qualified to vote when I was there. One reason, of course, is the poll tax of $1.50 yearly. It is cumulative
up to $36, and must be paid in a lump sum. It prevents many
Negroes as well as whites from voting (Alabama is one of five
Southern states with a poll tax in effect. Tennessee recently
repealed its law.)

Even more effective in preventing a buildup of Negro political strength is the registration system, under which regis-
trars defy the law and continue to use what is, in effect, the
Boswell Amendment, already declared unconstitutional. Under
this amendment the registrar could ask an applicant to "interpret the Constitution." If the applicant failed to answer
"satisfactorily" he was declared ineligible to vote. The amendment was applied almost exclusively to Negroes, who represent
a third of the Alabama population.

That the amendment still is being used is also much the
fault of Negroes. "We brief Negroes for weeks, telling them that
they can refuse to answer the questions. Still they try to answer them and fail," said Emery O. Jackson, head of the local
chapter of the N.A.A.C.P.

I went from Jackson's office to the street corner, where I
stopped Negroes at random. I asked them if they were registered voters. If they said no, I asked if they had tried to register. Many had not, and their standard alibi was: "Ain't no use
beating your head 'gainst a brick wall." I found several who
had tried and were turned down. One man admitted that he
was one of those counseled by the N.A.A.C.P. I asked him
what happened when he asked to be registered.

"First she asked me who was the first President of the United
States," he said. "I knew I didn't have to answer, but the
question seemed so easy. I answered that one and three more
questions. Then she asked me how representatives are apported
(apportioned) or something, and I couldn't tell her. She says
to me: 'Now, don't you think we've been fair, but you just

failed?' I had to admit that she was just as nice as she could be."

I recounted the interview to Jackson, a fire-and-tongs, quick-tongued Negro who, in the words of "Bull" Connor, "ought to be run out of town." Jackson tossed a copy of the Birmingham *World*, a weekly that he edits in the Scott chain, into the air and pounded the desk. "Holy Jesus. If I hear that again. They come back saying: 'Them white folks was as nice as they could be,' and I ask: 'But did they register you?' and they say: 'Well, no, but they sho treated me nice.' Then I feel like murdering somebody—myself, even." Another copy of the *World* flew ceilingward.

Ebb Cox, field representative for the CIO United Steelworkers Union, sat shaking his head. I had put Cox on the defensive over the telephone by asking him about some Jim Crow union-meetings that I had seen. He decided to meet me for a face-to-face chat on the subject.

"The CIO has schooled Negro members for three years on voting rights," added Cox, a Negro who looked as if he were of Puerto Rican descent. "We used sample ballots and everything. The union even 'loaned' them money to pay their poll taxes (according to that Taft-Hartley law, it's got to be a 'loan,' you know), and then we hired cars and taxis to take them to register. Because they tried to pass the Boswell test, or because of some trickery by the registrar, we got less than four per cent of our pupils qualified."

Jackson, who is so high up on Connor's blacklist that none of his reporters can get a police press-card, becomes furious when the voting subject is raised—furious at a lot of people. "I'm in the Omega fraternity," he snorted, "and I know that our members will pay thirty dollars for one dance with a little free whisky thrown in. Yet, they won't pay their poll taxes. I tell them that to get rid of the poll tax they have to help vote it out. I keep telling them that they are the people who have sense enough to refuse to try the Boswell test—and they could answer the questions if they did try."

"What do your frat brothers say?"

"Some of the fat boys—fat because their bellies are full of crow: you know, Jim Crow—act as if I'm a crackpot. That's why you see me walking. That's why I'm not driving a Cadillac."

"What about World War II veterans? They've been pretty militant in many of the places I've visited so far."

"Listen, mister, listen," zealot Jackson said in a soft scream, "there are twenty thousand veterans in this county, and they don't have to pay a poll tax. But they can't get registered. You see, you can pay a poll tax almost anywhere in Birmingham, but you can register at only one place. Everybody has to pass before God—that's the registrar—and the registrar sees that the 'quota' for Negroes isn't exceeded. Those vets go in to register and are refused for almost any reason. They come in here complaining that their rights have been denied, and ask for N.A.A.C.P. help. I ask them to sign a complaint and they say: 'Okay. Okay, I'll be back.' I catch them on the street corner a week or two later and they explain that they 'didn't want to get into a mess and lose my job.' That's a dad-blamed twenty-dollar-a-week busboy or pick-and-shovel job he's worrying about."

I found that the voting situation is more acute in rural Alabama, where artifice is ignored for the less troublesome method of physical threat in preventing the Negro from voting. In Wilcox, Russell, Henry, and Lowndes counties, no Negro has been known to vote in more than fifty years. Eight of every ten Lowndes Countians are Negroes. More than half the population is Negro in Henry County, where the N.A.A.C.P. filed a suit to re-enfranchise Negroes in 1951. In all Alabama, where there are as many Negro citizens as there are people im Utah, Nevada, and Wyoming combined, there are fewer than fifty thousand Negroes qualified to vote.

This brought me back to Cox. I reminded him that the labor movement once was heralded as the great force that would crush segregation. Although I had seen examples—Alcoa, for instance—of its pushing toward that end by giving Negroes equality of economic opportunity, from what I had seen in Birmingham the optimism was unwarranted.

"A few months back the CIO announced nationally that it would disregard Jim Crow laws wherever they existed," I said. "I see that Jim Crow union-meetings still are being held here. What happened to the CIO resolution?"

"That referred to meetings on CIO property," he said.

"Does the CIO consider local union-halls CIO property? Segregation still is practiced in some of them." By this time I had to explain that I was grinding no personal axe against the CIO, that I was very much aware that the AFL has some lily-white unions, and that I, a CIO member myself, simply was asking the questions that I felt the readers ought to have answered. "Take Connor," I went on. "Everybody knows where he stands. But didn't the Birmingham CIO Council endorse him for police commissioner in every election but the last one? How does this square with the CIO's national proclamation against bigotry?"

Cox admitted that the Council publicly endorsed Connor in elections other than the one just past. "The proclamation was a success in the last election in a sense," he explained, "because it prevented them from endorsing him openly. Still the Council supported Connor under cover in the last election."

"Isn't it true that the CIO has been looking at a politician's attitude toward organized labor and closing its eyes to all else?" broke in Jackson. "The CIO boys here will tell you: 'Connor is a good union man; he leaves our picket lines alone.' So the CIO backs him, period. Nothing, I mean *nothing*, else matters."

Cox admitted that Connor has built a reputation of being a good labor-union man. "But confidentially," he continued, "we have a great deal of internal strife on the race question. We show them the economic value of solidarity, of rising above race hatred to push together for something more than starvation wages. Brother, that fatter pay check impresses 'em. Then some crummy sonofabitch tells 'em that, first thing they know, some Negro will be crawling in bed with their wives and daughters and we have to start all over again. Oh, we got a lotta internal strife on the race question."

"As I remember it, there was considerable internal strife over communism, and the national body kicked the Reds out. Do you think there ever will be a time when the unions will kick the bigots out?"

"Not in the South—at least, not for a hell of a long time. Not as long as we all are fighting to keep a management that is both anti-labor and anti-Negro from kicking the whole CIO out. Remember, too, that the Commies were booted out because a large portion of the anti-Red membership was stirred up over the issue. That just ain't the case over segregation. Most of the whites just don't give a damn. It's hard even to get Negroes stirred up to the point of action. Of 38,000 steel-worker members in District 36 (Alabama, Mississippi, Louisiana, and Florida), 42 per cent are colored. In one local at Fairfield near here, I have 5,000 colored. I called one meeting and found two men there. You call a political rally and almost nobody shows up; mention a barbecue and they curse you forever if they don't get that free thirty-five-cent sandwich. You plead with them to show a little spunk, to come out and help fight for their freedom, but they never quite make it. What do you do, get a shotgun?"

CHAPTER XII

RUN! THE RED VAMPIRE!

WILLIE MCGEE was born a nobody. He lived a nobody. And had it not been for an international war of ideologies and a decades-old racial-sexual taboo, he might have died a nobody. Just an obscure, ignorant, scarcely reliable Negro grocery-boy in Laurel, Mississippi. But the war of ideas and the sexual taboo do exist, and because of them Willie McGee died May 8, 1951, not quite a "somebody" in the ordinary American sense of the word, but a martyr and a symbol the world over of a lot of things to a lot of people.

Willie McGee, thirty-seven-year-old World War II veteran and father of four, was very much alive the February morning that I walked off a bus, uneasy, my bones aching from a long, uncomfortable ride. As I got off in Laurel, a town not originally on my itinerary, my reasons for being there became clearer. I remembered that, throughout my journey, self-styled fighters for freedom asked me so many times: "You don't have anything to do with Communism, do you?" And before the trip, scores of whites had asked me: "What do you think of Paul Robeson?" which really was asking what I thought of the American Negro and the lure of Communism. As I observed what the Communist press the world over was doing with Willie McGee, and what the equally bold reactionary portion of the American press was saying, with all but a tiny element of the non-Communist, left-of-center American press paralyzed with timidity, I knew that the whole, ugly issue of Communism as it affects the Negro's fight for full equality was on review in Laurel.

Laurel had another lure for me: the overtones of sex in its

role as the dominant factor in Dixie Negro-white relations were spelled out clearly in the case of Willie McGee. Some of the things filtering out of Mississippi read like an episode from my youth in Tennessee.

I knew the background of the case, as does almost every Negro boy and girl in America; as do far more citizens of Calcutta, Paris, or Shanghai than of Chattanooga, Pittsburgh, or St. Paul. In the early morning of November 2, 1945, according to prosecution, Mrs. Troy Hawkins lay in bed in her Laurel home with an ill child beside her. Her husband and two other children were sleeping in the adjoining room. A man, who Mrs. Hawkins testified was a Negro but whom she could not identify because her room was pitch dark, crept into her bed and raped her. She said she did not cry out because she did not want to wake the children. The next morning police rounded up five suspects.

Meanwhile, the head of a company for which McGee drove a truck called the police and said McGee did not return the previous evening with $15.85 of the company's money. He asked that McGee be picked up. This was done and McGee returned the money, declaring that he had not intended to keep it. The larceny charge was dropped.

A neighbor of Mrs. Hawkins reported, however, that a grocery truck was parked near by at 4.30 a.m. on the 2nd, when the alleged crime occurred. Police reportedly found McGee's fingerprints in the Hawkins house. On the strength of this evidence, although the defense charged that Mrs. Hawkins never had a medical examination to establish rape, McGee was charged with the crime. A deputy sheriff later contended that McGee had confessed, although McGee repudiated the confession, contending that policemen tore off his clothes, beat him with blackjacks, and kept him on bread and water in a sweatbox until he cried guilty.

Willie McGee got a one-day trial in a courtroom surrounded by bayoneted guardsmen who held back an angry mob. A jury deliberated two and one-half minutes and found McGee guilty. He was sentenced to die. But because of the atmosphere under which the trial was conducted, the Mississippi Supreme Court ordered a new trial.

Wiry-haired Willie McGee got a new trial at Hattiesburg, thirty miles away. Another all-white jury hastily found him guilty and he was again sentenced to die. A national storm of protest began to mount. People who had no feeling that McGee might be innocent denounced brutal police tactics; even if McGee were guilty, they cried, the case showed unequal application of the law at best, for never in the history of the state had a white man been sentenced to die for rape. McGee's supporters argued that Negroes had been kept off the jury panels, and asked for a new trial. Because of several United States Supreme Court decisions holding that Negroes cannot legally be excluded from such jury panels, the new trial was granted.

By this time Willie McGee was losing much of his normal support, simply to the wear of time. More important, the Communist vultures were moving in. The Civil Rights Congress, labeled as a Communist-front organization by the United States Attorney General, was running the show. The Reds, shedding crocodile tears, put a fatal "curse" on McGee, for non-Communist liberals began to shy away. A Negro leader explained that the "case would warrant the support of the general public, but because the Communists are connected with it, the people are afraid to say anything."

In July of 1948, Negroes were sworn in as jury-panel members for the first time in the history of Jones County. Three Negroes were selected as jurors, and McGee again was convicted. Despite the cry of "unequal application" of the law, Circuit Court Judge F. Burkitt Collins sentenced McGee to death for the third time. All this time Willie McGee had been silent on the advice of his attorneys.

The execution was delayed as the case was appealed to the Mississippi Supreme Court, which upheld the verdict. The case then was taken to the United States Supreme Court, which refused to review it. The Mississippi courts then set Willie McGee's death date as July 27, 1950.

A delegation organized by the Civil Rights Congress went to Jackson to plead with Governor Fielding Wright, Dixiecrat candidate for Vice President in 1948, and to ask him to grant clemency to McGee. Aware that the delegation was coming, the Jackson *Daily News* played hard on the angle that the Congress is labeled as a Communist-front group. In a fire-eating, front-page editorial, the *Daily News* shouted: "Why the hell go to Korea to shoot Communists when the hunting is good on home grounds?" Hoodlums were quick to get the idea, and a crowd was at the state capital to jeer as the delegation arrived. Police went on a "twenty-four-hour alert."

The pleading was futile. A Chicago member of the Congress and a white Mississippian who served as one of McGee's attorneys decided to rush to Washington to plead with Justice Harold Burton. They were set upon by a mob at the Jackson airport. Aubrey Grossman, organizational secretary for the Congress, returned to his Jackson hotel room and found six men waiting for him. They beat him. Stephen Fischer, reporter for the New York *Daily Compass*, which had run a series of articles on the affair, as told by Mrs. Rosalie McGee, the doomed man's wife, "got slugged pretty hard" at the train station when twenty men attacked him. Police rushed Fischer out of town.

Twelve hours before McGee was to die, Burton granted a stay until the whole court could meet in the fall and decide whether to review the case. His action met with considerable disapproval in Mississippi, where Wright saw it as assisting a "Communist plot to destroy our judicial system." Judge Collins screamed that there was "no precedent whatsoever" for this "outside meddling" by Burton.

McGee's attorney's talked of new evidence, of which they had more than broadly hinted during the third trial. It was my curiosity about this "new evidence" that really lured me to

Laurel. After checking my luggage on to New Orleans so I would have nothing to prevent a hasty departure, I set off through the town, trying to find out what the ordinary Negro knew and believed about the Willie McGee case.

For the afternoon, I was a "respectable" Negro. I cleaned up in the rear of a little café, where I put on the tie that I was carrying in my pocket. I found a barbershop and had my shoes shined. Then I rambled through the Negro section of Laurel, a town of about twenty-five thousand persons, of whom nearly one third are Negroes.

I showed a Negro teacher a card identifying me as an N.A.A.C.P. official. I said that, as a member of the Minneapolis branch and Minnesota Conference of the N.A.A.C.P., I was personally interested in the McGee case and rumors that it was a frame-up.

"Well, it was pretty much whispered around among Negroes since 1942 that McGee was going to get in trouble with that woman," said the teacher.

"You say 'whispered around'; who knew about it for sure?"

"Well, I suppose that gang McGee ran around with. But their word ain't worth a damn. There was so much talk among other people that I figure where there's smoke there's a little fire."

"When did you first hear talk of this?"

"Most of the colored folks were talking about it the day this McGee was locked up—that was in 1945."

"Isn't it possible that this rumor was started by Communists?"

"These people they're calling Communists hadn't even heard of the case then. These were local Negroes talking. And listen, it's tough enough being a Negro in Mississippi without being a Red. I don't think you'll find any Negro Communists here."

I asked a Negro professional man if he had heard anything about supposed illicit relations between McGee and the alleged rape-victim.

"When this fellow was first locked up there was talk about

a note she gave him asking for a date when McGee worked at a filling station. That was before McGee was in the army."

"Did anybody else know about this note?"

"Several men claimed they did. And then, after McGee came back this woman was supposed to be giving notes to the colored gal that worked next door—notes for McGee."

"Who lives next door, and who is the colored woman who carried the notes?"

"I believe it is a Miss Jansen who lives next door. I don't know a thing about this colored girl."

"If there was such general knowledge among you and other Negroes, why wasn't it brought out in the first trial?"

"Listen, mister, I been in Laurel a long time. I can tell you that with that howling mob outside, no Negro was going to get up in court and swear that he knew of any Negro sleeping with a white woman. That mob would have ripped McGee to pieces and done the same for any Negro who claimed to know of such goings-on without tipping off the white folks. You know, it's kinda like admitting to being an accessory before the fact, or something."

"It seems to me that if it was such general knowledge among Negroes, some of the whites would have known it."

"Yeah, it does. But you see, these white folks don't believe anything like that goes on. They just refuse to believe that any white woman would *want* to lay with a Negro. And if she does, it ain't voluntary. It's rape. If you'd ever lived any time in the South, you'd know what I mean."

"Yeah . . . yeah. Perhaps I would," I replied. "By the way, what about this confession that McGee is supposed to have made? I get damned sick of having to defend every Negro, guilty or innocent. What about this confession?"

"Well," he said, "McGee said they beat him to get it. Frankly, I don't see how anybody can doubt that."

This Negro's inclination to believe that McGee was beaten was based on his knowledge of police tactics in Mississippi, where it is not uncommon for "a little pressure" to be applied to Negro suspects. On July 24, 1951, the nation learned from Sheriff George Marshall at Indianola, Mississippi, that a private detective and a deputy sheriff beat three Negroes until they confessed to a murder that never occurred. Marshall said he assumed that Detective Charles Underwood and Deputy C. H. Sheffield "used a leather strap" to work out the "confession," in which one of the Negroes said they killed a man, missing at the time, by hitting him in the head. As it turned out, the missing man was in East St. Louis, Illinois.

"One more question," I continued. "It seems that McGee is certain to die unless someone believes that story. Do you think you or any of the other colored would tell the court what you've told me—to save McGee's life?"

"Well, I hate to see a man die for nothing, if McGee is innocent. But any way you look at it, he was a fool. As for me, I've got to live here. I can't afford to be accused of playing ball with the Commies. I say that no colored person in town is going to open his mouth in public."

"Suppose some paper wrote up what you've told me—would you back it up?"

"What do you mean, some paper?"

"Oh, some non-Communist daily newspaper."

"Well, as I said, I've got to live here. No daily newspaper is gonna feed my family. Nobody can quote me on nothing."

I walked away from him into the growing darkness. It was much colder than I had anticipated. The air smelled of an odor that I had not known since those autumns in Tennessee when everything smelled of football. I could breathe and trace the air to what I thought was the bottom of my stomach. It was so empty that I swore I could feel the cool atmosphere bounce around in it. That was the way I used to feel after football practice in McMinnville. In those days I had to race my brother, Charles, home, for he watched until the final play of practice and then dashed for the lion's share of the supper my mother had saved for us.

But there was no supper to rush to in Laurel. I went into

a junky café in which I filled up on cheese crackers, on pea-
nuts that must have been delivered the day the ancient structure was built, and on two bottles of orange pop.

I had sacrificed the warmth of a tie and buttoned shirt-collar
in order to look like the wandering, jobless scalawag that I
would pretend to be that night until my train left for New
Orleans. I wanted to see what some of Laurel's "nobodies"
knew about Willie McGee, with whom they supposedly were
on rather close terms. I sat munching on the crackers and
feeding coins into a jukebox that was loaded with blues and
a few religious songs. I played a number by Leadbelly until
I thought that "lonesome train" would sweep right through the
joint and take my weary soul away. I pretended to enjoy the
record, however, and tried to act the part of the most casual
hobo ever weaved into musical legend by Leadbelly. I rubbed
my face and felt the black sharp stubble. It felt the same as on
a lazy day off in Minneapolis, so I could say to myself confi-
dently: "Brother, you must look like hell."

I watched each person enter the café. All the time I was
"casing" the joint, trying to determine where the doors were
and what took place behind them. The wall was lined with
cards advertising soft drinks. Just over me was a make of calendar that I hadn't seen since I left the South. Advertised on it
were Cardui, something supposedly of interest to women, and
Black Draught, a concoction I once sampled out of youthful
curiosity and ended up missing a baseball game because of temporary residence in the privy. For a few moments I was caught
in the nostalgia generated by the calendar's little flags, whose
colors indicated the weather for the particular date. It had
always fascinated me that the calendarmaker would predict the
weather for more than a year ahead, not even bothering to
make geographical allowances.

The place was getting noisy now. Cigarette smoke began to
swirl around the yellow, flyspecked light bulb; it half hid the
cobwebs that draped from the wall to the soft-drink cards,
giving the illusion that they supported the placards. Between

records on the over-loud jukebox the splatter of grease sounded over the hubbub of human chit-chat. A stubnosed woman was frying bologna. I noticed that a heavyset woman with short, nappy hair and very bad skin was eying me as I pumped another quarter into the jukebox. I realized that I was showing too much disregard for money to be a bounder looking for a job. I jabbed one hand down deep into one pocket as if to say that I had come to money's end. She sidled over to where I stood reading song titles.

"You're new around here, ain't you, pretty boy?" she asked, her foul breath almost flooring me.

"Naw, this is home," I replied. "Anywhere a freight train slows down enough for me to get one foot on earth is home to me." I walked away, hoping that she was easily offended. With the pockmarked face, the bulging belly, and breasts that sagged down to her waist, she was miserable just to observe, let alone converse with.

"Whatcha know, Joe?" I snapped recklessly as I paused at a table where two men in their early thirties sat, drinking what I thought were Cokes. One replied in tones that didn't exactly lay out the welcome mat. I sat down anyhow and asked them how easy it was to get a job in Laurel. "They told me up yonder no'th uv here that Laurel's got more plants'n' any town in Mississippi," I added.

"Yeah, they got a few jobs here. Where you from?"

"I came down from Meridian. Say, uh . . ."

"Meridian? I got people there. Do you know . . . ?"

"Naw, I'm sure I don't. I just stopped over in Meridian from Nashville," I interrupted. "I skipped out of Nashville when a white chippy threatened to make it hot for me."

"You and Willie, huh?" said the thin, brown-skinned Negro, whose artificially straightened hair hung down on the collar of his leather jacket. He pulled an Old Granddad bottle from under the table and poured a slug of whisky into his Coke bottle.

"Willie who? What do you mean, me and Willie?" I asked.

"You and Willie McGee. Say, get yo'self a Coke and take some of this."

"Man, Old Granddad is a little rich for my blood. I been drunk three days of plain old rotgut. Say, who's this Willie McGee?"

"Granddad, hell. This ain't nothin' but rotgut liquor—just plain old Jo Splo," said this taller Negro, who seemed to do most of the talking. I looked at his long hand with the oversized finger-joints and assumed that the work he did wasn't brainwork. His incessant drumming on the table drew my attention to his filthy nails; his chatter about the liquor, using the terminology for bootleg booze that I had not heard for years, turned something over inside me.

"Who's this Willie McGee?" I repeated.

"Ain't you heard of Willie McGee?" asked the heavyset, darker Negro, who wore a cotton, sweater-type jacket tucked into his overalls. He kept fumbling with a pencil in the bib pocket of the overalls. "He's the guy that fooled around and got accused of raping some white woman. Man, ain't you never heard of Willie McGee?"

"Seems to me as I read a little or sumpin' in the Pittsburgh *Courier*," I replied. "I don't read nothin' much. You say he got messed up with some white woman?"

"Yeah, and he's sho gonna get burnt fo' it," broke in the tall man. "Just tough titty, I say. Just tough titty. Oughta had more damn sense. Now take me. I was down by Masonite the other day and one of the white girls—I come in contact with a lot of 'em down by Masonite—asked me if it's true that cullod men are hell on wheels 'tween sheets, like they say. That's how she put it, 'hell on wheels 'tween the sheets,' just as bold and unconcerned as anything. I told her that being a man I ain't got no way of knowing 'bout cullod men. I don't know what she's got in mind, but I ain't fo' it. These crackers'll never git to make no light bulb out of my ass."

"Where'd ya say this all happened?" I asked.

"Down by Masonite."

"What the hell's Masonite?"

"Masonite Corporation—that's a great big old plant."

"Oh, I see. And some babe was giving you the old come-on?"

"I reckon so. But, man, I'm too smart for that mess. I wouldn't say boo to 'er, least not around Masonite. Say, don't you want a slug of this stuff?"

"Naw, man, I been sick as a pup all day," I lied. "I wanta be sober and try to get a job tomorrow. I'd be much obliged fo' a little help. By the way, any of you guys know this McGee?"

"Yeah, we knowed 'im pretty well," said the overall-clad Negro.

"Did you know that he was getting into any trouble?"

"Yeah, I knowed what was going on. I knowed that McGee told his wife he been doing 'er wrong. He said the only way fo' him to straighten up was to leave. So he went out west, supposedly to get away from this woman."

"From this Hawkins woman?" I asked. I realized immediately that neither of them had mentioned the woman's name. I was supposed to know nothing about the case. I thought for cover-up words but decided I didn't need them when the short man nodded his head to say yes. I thought the tall one, who had seemed suspicious all along, gave a curious look when I mentioned the woman's name, but he said nothing. I was sure they didn't catch on.

"Man, I'll bet that jury had contuption fits when y'all told what you jest told me," I jabbed.

"Jury hell. We ain't told no jury nothing," said the tall man, "and we ain't 'bout t' tell no jury nothing. No use making bad matters worse. Go to court and say what we just said, we wouldn't have no job. Might even wake up some night with the house afire."

"Well, I'm gonna make a little run," I said. "In case I need some help landing a job, what's you fellow's names?"

"I'm Bill Mason and this is Sammy Johnson," said the tall Negro hastily, at the same time rolling his reddening eyes at his stumpy buddy. "What's yours?" he demanded.

"Charles Newton," I snapped, plucking a name from a short story with which I was tinkering before I started my journey. I walked to the door, cognizant that the two men were mumbling behind me. I stood outside for a few minutes, trying to appear nonchalant and also waiting to see if the two Negroes would follow me. There was no cab in sight, anyhow. Soon a squeaky-voiced little man with very gray hair asked if I was looking for a taxi. He offered to take me where I wanted to go. I accepted hesitantly, checking his license number and making sure no one hid in the back seat before I got up front with the driver. He took me to the Southern Railroad station. En route I asked if he knew what sort of guys Bill Mason and Sammy Johnson were. He said he didn't know any Bill Mason and Sammy Johnson.

"I meant them two guys I was sittin' with," I explained.

"I don't know 'em very well," said the driver, "but they call the light one Long Bob. I can't call the short one's name at all—don't get out that much these days. But they ain't no Bill Mason and Sammy Johnson. Did they say that's what their names is?"

"No, no," I said snappily, "I thought I heard a woman refer to them by names sorta like that."

I put my tie back on and boarded a train for New Orleans. I was confused and no little disgusted by the Willie McGee case. How could I write a newspaper report if nobody would stand behind his story, if fearful men gave false names?

A great fear, either of the tinge of Communism or of physical harm, had made clams out of people who swore they knew the Gospel truth so long as the swearing wasn't public. Even were they to speak out I was not sure a jury would believe them, for evidence of this so-called clandestine romance was no more ironbound than was the evidence to the contrary. But to me the story, the real lesson, was that these people were afraid. Theirs was not an incredible story, not to a Negro who lived in the South for eighteen years and knows that almost daily some sordid manifestation of humanity's sexual lust spreads itself across dogged racial taboos. Theirs was not an incredible story, not to a Negro who had come so close to tragedy in McMinnville one summer night in a baptismal area on the Barren Forks River.

I left Laurel disgusted and unhappy. Amid such evident timidity, I felt, only the craziest Negro would walk into a white man's house and rape his wife while the white man slept in the next room—unless he knew his way around in the pitch-black house, and unless he had reason to believe that the woman wouldn't cry out. And the one thing nobody had accused Willie McGee of was insanity. The creeping fear that I found still evident in Laurel made one other thing evident to me: it meant absolutely nothing to put Negroes on a jury panel for the third trial. No Negro juror would dare hold out against the majority of whites favoring conviction—not after whites had twice found McGee guilty; not in the face of public yearning to see McGee singed out of existence.

But there were other disgusting things about the McGee case. The defense was wishy-washy. The story of long-standing illicit relations between McGee and the alleged victim appeared to be an admission that the defendant might have been in bed with the woman, but at her invitation. How did this square with Communist contention that McGee was driving his truck in Hattiesburg, thirty miles away, at the time of the attack? And how did either of these stories jibe with testimony of a woman defense-witness that McGee was with her at the time of the alleged attack? And why was McGee silent all this time; why didn't he tell his own story?

It was a tiring, weird befuddlement that I carried out of the little southeastern Mississippi community—all because of a "nobody" who was close to death in a case surrounded by enough doubt for it to drag out in the courts for more than five years. There seemed so much unsaid, too little known truth, for a man's life to be taken, even when the man was a "nobody." It seemed, also, that I had turned up too little *known* truth to write a newspaper article: nobody would be quoted, for nobody wanted to get his fingers burned. Even I took the cowardly way out by sheltering my own fingers and proceeding to forget that I ever visited Laurel.

A few weeks later, I read Mrs. McGee's story. It was the same story that Laurel Negroes told me. She said she had been advised to keep quiet about the alleged illicit relations. But with McGee on the brink of death, she cried, she had decided to "tell everything. . . . I don't want my husband to die. . . . If Willie goes, he will be the third man in our family to get killed by the lynchers."

The Mississippi Supreme Court rejected the story of illicit relations as a "revolting insinuation and plainly not supported," and the Communist press let all barrels fly. The March 15, 1951, *Daily Worker* printed, little more than a month after my Laurel visit, almost everything that I had been told in Laurel. It was practically a special edition devoted to Willie McGee. Elizabeth Gurley Flynn, later seized in the round-up of second-string Reds charged with plotting overthrow of the United States government, detailed the alleged romance in her column. John Pittman took the "text" of his column from the thirty-ninth chapter of Genesis, likening the case of Willie McGee to that of Joseph and the wife of Potiphar, captain of Pharaoh's guard. In the biblical story, Potiphar's wife asked Joseph to lie with her, and when Joseph refused she ripped off his garment. She then accused Joseph of trying to force her to lie with him, contending that when she cried out Joseph fled, leaving his garment. The Communists were telling the world what had been whispered in Laurel: Willie McGee was a twentieth-century Joseph.

Out of the misty half-truths of the Willie McGee case, one thing emerged crystal clear: the Communists were reaping a propaganda bonanza and American democracy was suffering in the court of world opinion. The United States Embassy in Great Britain asked the State Department to send information on the case with which it could counter "propaganda in the London press." The Embassy still was smarting under the applause that went up in Parliament a few days before, when a Member read a letter denouncing the execution, in Martinsville, Virginia, of seven Negroes charged with raping a white woman while, at the same time, the United States was freeing Nazi war-criminals.

Telegrams and letters poured into President Truman's office. Included were appeals from eight Chinese Communist organizations. Mr. Truman also got appeals from labor unions, N.A.A.C.P. branches, groups in many non-Communist foreign countries, and from plain citizens the world over. Mississippi's Governor Wright said he, too, received more than fifteen thousand letters and telegrams from all over the world. "A lot of them are Communist-inspired," he shouted.

Willie McGee did not die March 20. Again he was spared, and it began to appear that this bushy-haired Negro who had been granted six reprieves—three on his "last" day—might escape the destiny of a date with the electric chair.

But the United States Supreme Court again rejected the case. The candle was burning shorter for Willie McGee. The Mississippi court again set his execution date—May 8, 1951.

It seemed that I could remember the day, even in my short lifetime, when the march of students on campuses far and near, the cry of pickets in the nation's capital, and fifteen thousand appeals from neighbors and strange people in far-off lands would bring certain clemency for a doomed man. But not for Willie McGee; not for this wiry-haired grocery-boy who lived in an age when the word "Communism" is anathema; not for this man who had been sucked up by the red vampire of Communism, which flapped its verminous wings and blinded Americans to everything but the fact that "the Communists are supporting Willie McGee." This was the red vampire from which everybody ran. A white editor echoed the thoughts of a great many Americans when he wrote: "Anyone who helps McGee helps the Communists."

May 8 drew nearer. The Communists were far bolder and more ingenious in their efforts to bleed the last drop of propaganda from McGee's doomed body than American "patriots" were in their efforts to counter this propaganda. These "patriots" apparently never stopped to think of how the Reds got their "symbol," and that Americans aided the Politburo far more by cursing victim McGee and letting him die than by trying to see that he got a punishment comparable to those given to whites guilty of the same crime. Instead, Americans had worked themselves into such a lather swatting at the red vampire that McGee was doomed, not so much for his guilt, questionable as it was, but because he had Communist support and had become the center of an obvious campaign to injure the United States politically in foreign lands.

The telegrams and letters continued to pour in to Governor Wright, who declared himself "sick and tired" of "outside interference." He was the last man between McGee and death, now, although a few people who were convinced that McGee was innocent—and the Communists, of course—pleaded in the final hours for a stay from District Judge Sidney Mize at Jackson; Judge Wayne G. Borah of the Fifth Circuit Court of Appeals in New Orleans; Associate Supreme Court Justice Hugo Black; and Supreme Court Chief Justice Vinson.

That the Communists were the kiss of death to McGee was best explained in the words of a white journalist: "Communist support has just about sent McGee to the chair. Governor Wright is a very stubborn man, and now he is determined to see McGee burn." Whether Wright would have granted McGee clemency had the Negro's sole support come from the Campfire Girls is doubtful, but the governor turned his back on all pleas with Communists figuring in the appeals.

So the string ran out after five and one-half years. Late in the afternoon of May 7, authorities took Willie McGee out of the lynch-proof Hinds County jail at Jackson, where he had been kept for safety, and drove him the ninety miles to Laurel, scene of the alleged crime. When police reached the Laurel courthouse with McGee, a crowd of about three hundred surged forward.

"McGee is going to die; let's everybody be nice," shouted a patrolman, and a reverberating shriek went up from the throng.

The crowd continued to grow as night fell. Men in work clothes sauntered down to the courthouse on leaving their jobs. Women left the supper dishes unwashed and joined the throng.

The bushy hair that gave McGee the look of a wild man— a look exploited by photographers—was shaved off. At about eleven p.m. the husband, brother, and two brothers-in-law of Mrs. Hawkins filed into the courtroom where, with eighty-one others, they would observe the proceedings.

Outside, the mob had swollen to about seven hundred persons. Amid the bloodthirsty tumult there was the sardonic chatter of a woman inmate joking with the mob from her cell. Laurel's streets were bare of Negroes, with McGee's spiritual adviser perhaps the only black man not locked within his home so as not to get mixed up in any post-execution celebration. Occasionally a policeman would remind the crowd: "We don't want any demonstrations."

Near midnight they began to strap McGee into the portable chair. He watched with the interest of a man about to learn something, but it was knowledge he would find little use for in this world. At 12.07 a.m. on May 8, 1951, Willie McGee was dead. The word passed along a human chain and out the window to the waiting throng. "McGee is dead." Triumphant yells pierced the otherwise somber night. It was the end of a vain struggle.

I rolled over in my bed later on the morning of May 8, some one thousand miles away and three months after my visit to Laurel, and saw a short page-one story in the Minneapolis *Tribune* stating that McGee had lost his fight. I got the funny feeling of guilt, the feeling that I had failed . . . not McGee, who wasn't worth all the fuss for himself, but the cause of free, honest conviction. I found a bit of consolation in my knowledge that, although McGee was dead, the things men attached to his fight were still very much alive. The name of McGee would live a long time—in the minds and consciences of honest people who feel that, guilty or not, he paid too much; and wherever a Communist could wave the memory of him to decry American democracy among the colored peoples of the world.

McGee's death made page 29 of the *New York Times*. In Paris, where the Assembly of the French Union halted activities for a minute of silence in his honor, all the afternoon papers headlined the execution. Said the leftist, non-Communist paper *Combat*, "The Mississippi executioner has won out over the world conscience. . . . Yesterday morning a little of the liberty of all men and a little of the solidarity between the peoples died with Willie McGee."

The American press was neither so sentimental nor so philosophical. *Time* magazine, its vision still partly obscured by the flapping of the red vampire, cried: "The Communists, as usual, had managed to distort the case." It went on to give what it called "the facts," a list of evidence that left not a shadow of doubt but that McGee was guilty of a heinous crime.

John Herling, a Washington writer and radio commentator, noted that from the moment of execution the Communists were through with Willie McGee and his family. French entertainer Josephine Baker, on tour of her native United States, had to supply funds to prevent a potter's-field burial for McGee, whom she too had tried to save. Miss Baker said some scathing things about the Communist rats who ran out with their propaganda prize and the balance of money they collected for "the cause." To many Americans—honest people who have spoken out for full equality for Negroes—this was the total lesson of *l'affaire* McGee: stay away from things backed by Communists. Said the Minneapolis *Star*, which ran Herling's piece on its editorial page:

It seemed to the Star there was a solid lesson for good-hearted people in John Herling's story about how the Communist party in America exploited the Willie McGee case to fill its coffers, then left others the expense of burying him. Dollars have power, and to give them carelessly to unexamined causes may put power into dangerous hands. It's a sad commentary of the state of the world, but care must go along with charity if good-hearted people aren't to help pay to get their own brains beaten out.

As I remembered that day in Laurel, when nobody dared give his name, and as I thought of the shabby strings of doubt that enshrouded the case, it appeared to me that there must be a deeper and ultimately more important lesson than the old and fairly obvious one of Communist exploitation. Nobody seemed to remember that the Communists magnified an issue because a onesided application of the law gave them an issue to magnify. This onesided judicial practice did not originate with the Reds. Had Willie McGee been given a "white man's sentence," the case might have died in the same obscurity that once engulfed McGee, and the Communists would have had to work much harder for their symbol. To me, the great tragedy is that enemies of liberty must be laughing at American "patriots" who tie themselves into mental and physical knots berating Communist exploiters. The Reds will find another Willie McGee tomorrow and the next day so long as Americans fight over who "uses" these McGees rather than fight to make the McGees hard to find.

CHAPTER XIII

AN AMERICAN IN NEW ORLEANS

It was with a great deal of hope and expectation that I rode into Louisiana. There was a delightfulness about the rolling pine hills and the vast marshlands, spawning-place of gigantic sugar crops, breeding place of myriad muskrats. This was bayou country, home of sugar plantations, strawberry crops, sweet potatoes, cane syrup, and rice. This was where bluffs overhanging the Mississippi River gave way to a lush delta region and a vast alluvial plain. This was the Pelican State, rich in pirate lore and Spanish-French background. I knew that it was a strange state, a state in which New Orleans, long touted as one of the best cities in the South for the Negro, is perhaps as much an anomaly as is Atlanta to Georgia. New Orleans is a new world compared with the northwestern part of the state, where some of the most backward, bigoted people of anywhere in the world live.

But I was not yet concerned with these people. I was concerned with the Gulf metropolis, where the fetus of human freedom supposedly lay in the womb of enlightened politics. I was concerned with a city famous for its Negro jazz-players—jazz born in the sad, dirgelike rhythms of the levee. This was a city that had shown in 1950, I thought, that it preferred an honorable man to a bigot when it elected de Lesseps S. Morrison as mayor and rejected Alvin A. Cobb.

Cobb had made every known appeal to racial hatreds; he tried every trick in the demagogue's book, and yet he lost. Morrison had succeeded where liberal candidates in North Carolina and Florida failed, in the face of such appeals, and I wanted to find out what Morrison thought it meant. Did it mean that the people of the South were tiring of the race issue? Did it mean that it no longer was political suicide to appear friendly to the Negro? Morrison had given Dr. Ralph Bunche the key to the city, and as a result was called a "nigger lover" at election time. Morrison stood by his action and still was elected by a great margin. I had heard many politicians say that they refused to speak out for fear of becoming lost in the labyrinth of voter prejudices. I hoped what Morrison would say would give them courage.

I was disappointed, as I feared I might be. Morrison did not answer my request for an appointment. David McGuire, Morrison's public-relations director, wrote that I should telephone him upon reaching New Orleans. I did. The mayor was very busy, McGuire said, conferring with a "big manufacturer who plans to move a plant here." Mardi Gras time also was at hand, he said. Another important reason why Morrison was not particularly eager to see me, McGuire said, was that "the racial issue is too risky. We've got a fellow named Cobb here, you know."

"Yes," I replied, "but I thought the last election took care of Cobb."

"Oh, that wasn't a fair test," countered McGuire. "A great mass of people may be swayed by Cobb. He has a lot of money behind him. We feel that the mayor won last time because there were other issues. Next time there may not be those other issues and the bigots could win—strictly on the race question."

"I see—thanks," I said. My bubble of hope had burst. So even the winner felt that victory had not come because the people saw right on his side, and preferred right. Here, from McGuire, was an admission of fear that next time Morrison might go the way of Frank Graham and Claude Pepper if he spoke too freely about the Negro question. This meant that there had been no great awakening, no spark of humane wisdom on the part of the general public.

I still doubted that this fear was completely justified. I could not believe that the people had changed so little. I thought of the towns where baseball teams did their spring training, towns where Negroes once were forbidden to appear on the same field with whites, and realized that the great mass of baseball fans, certainly no intellectuals, were rising almost to the man to cheer the diamond exploits of the Robinsons, Dobys, Campanellas and Newcombes.

I could pick up a paper of any day and read a news item about some tiny indication of change. Even in New Orleans, a Negro had run for the board of education and carried more white precincts than colored. But the mayor, who had become ensnarled in the issue of white supremacy, apparently saw in his victory nothing new about the hearts and minds and souls of the people of New Orleans.

Had this been the only instance of a white liberal expressing doubt that the South had changed significantly, I might have ignored it. But I had heard it before. I had heard it in a little Alabama town, where I huddled in the office of a white man known throughout the nation as a liberal. He prefaced our conversation by swearing me to secrecy about the meeting, by making me promise never to reveal his name in my writings. So worried was he that I might break my promise that he wrote letters following me throughout my journey, reminding me to remember.

This Alabama liberal told me that he did not believe in racial segregation and a lot of other things about the South. He simply was afraid to speak out, he confided.

"When you go back, Rowan," he said, "you've got to tell the side of us fellows in the middle. You've got to tell them what we're up against. Look at old Judge Waring out there in Charleston—he's doing a wonderful job, a magnificent job. But they crucified him. We all can't be Judge Warings. We all can't be crucified or we will have defeated ourselves. Look at what happened to Charlie Dobbins in Montgomery."

I remembered the Dobbins affair. Governor Gordon Persons had appointed Dobbins, known as a Southern liberal, to the state board of education. Before the Alabama senate would confirm the appointment, a few die-hard reactionary members called him on the carpet for an investigation of charges that he is a "nigger lover." First they made Dobbins swear that he would never try to change the teaching or textbooks of the state; they made him swear that he would oppose integration of the two races in the public schools of the state. Then one senator pointed out that the motto of Alabama, under the sign of the rooster, is white supremacy.

"Do you believe in white supremacy?" a senator asked Dobbins.

This Southern liberal, flabbergasted and already having compromised his soul, appealed to the chairman on grounds that the question was improper. The chairman ruled the question out of order. Then Dobbins decided to answer it anyhow: "I believe in *right* supremacy." His appointment was confirmed.

"I know Charlie Dobbins," the small-town liberal told me. "He doesn't believe in racial segregation. Why, he hates the ground the white-supremacists walk on. But he can't speak out. It would mean the end of his weekly paper in Montgomery, and that would wipe him out as an effective fighter for Negro rights in the South. Remember, Rowan," he repeated, "tell them about the problem of us in-the-middle liberals when you get back."

I thought about this as I walked about New Orleans. This fear of public scorn bothered me, coming from politician and ordinary citizen alike. I had heard so many whites say that they had no feeling about segregation, or wanted to see the end of it, that I felt the New South would soon exist were they to join together. But I knew that another fear helped to prevent this: the fear of being labeled a Red because of supporting something that the Communists also are smart enough to espouse, although this something be a basic American principle.

I thought about this as I sat on a stool in the Jackson Brewing Company, amazed at how such items as a bottle of beer are symbolical of the edging and nudging and constant rooting by

which Negroes are moving into the business world, closer to
the almighty dollar. I was staying at the home of Mr. and Mrs.
Solomon Borikins, New Orleans hotels being strictly Jim Crow.
Mrs. Borikins is a public-relations specialist for the Jackson
Brewing Company, manufacturers of Jax beer. She convinced
the firm that if Negroes spend their money on Jax beer, Jax
beer ought to spend some money on Negroes by hiring them.
Once she got the job, she set out to convince Negroes that Jax
was the beer that would give Negroes an equal break, therefore
they ought to drink Jax.

I made the round of stores, restaurants, and honky-tonks
with Mrs. Borikins as she gave out menus, mirrors, and assorted
placards, all advertising Jax. She chatted with proprietors about
beer, and what Jax meant in the Negro's fight for equality.

As we went about I expected to see Negroes in revelry, get
the feel of jazz, feel the mirth of the Mardi Gras. But nature
had given New Orleans its coldest weather in more than a
quarter century. None of the city's houses was built for below-
freezing temperatures, least of all any of the drafty shacks in
which thousands of Negroes dwell. Nor did Negro families
have warm clothing and bedding. It seems we went through all
the miserable streets where shivering urchins ran hasty errands
and trembling men and women went about life's necessities. I
had caught New Orleans at what must have been its worst in
light of the praise I previously had heard.

I talked to a lot of Negroes that day, in taverns, on the
streets and in overventilated houses. We talked about the
changing times—about how "everything's gittin' better but the
weather." We talked about politics, and the way Negroes
are voting in large numbers in and around New Orleans, and
about how it is not unusual now for Negroes to go right into
the mayor's office to complain about something.

I caught an aged Negro carrying an armful of stovewood,
which he piled on the rear porch of what appeared to be a
duplex. A little restaurant sat so its front was almost facing the
rear of the house.

I introduced myself to the man, who said he was George Andrews Baumann, and that he once taught school in Arkansas. I told him that I was a Minneapolis newspaperman and asked what he thought of Morrison.

"Pretty good, so far as he goes," he said, adding: "He's nigh well the best one we've had—that is for *our* people."

The old man, who said he was seventy-three, began to list the advances made in Louisiana since days of his childhood. He gave Morrison and present-generation workers of both races most of the credit.

"But listen, son," he warned me. "Don't go back and write that we've reached heaven already. 'Tain't so. Don't give anybody the idea we can't use some help."

"But from what you say," I protested, "you're doing all right without help. Wouldn't Northern helpers just be meddlers who would gum up the works?"

"Tell you, son," he replied, "I'm getting along in years. I ain't gonna see the solution to this thing. 'Tain't gonna come in my time. But we're moving along. It may come in my children's time. Ain't but two things can stop it, and that's fake liberals crying "let us alone" and Negroes fighting their own people. So don't go telling nobody we're in heaven, son. We still need all the help we can git."

This old man had touched on something that I had been asked scores of times. I knew that, once I made my report, I would be asked by hundreds of Noah Brannons of the North about Southern liberals and their contention that the race issue is their problem and that they ought to be left alone to solve it as they see fit. Also, I had been asked, and undoubtedly would be asked many times in the future, whether Negroes are happy now, whether they don't prefer things the way they are.

As I stood there in freezing New Orleans, in an abyss of human wretchedness, I knew what the old man meant. Baumann was resigned to dying without knowing absolute freedom, but he knew it was coming. He did not express worry about the Talmadges, Cobbs, or Rankins. He was worried about two types of men who pose as the Negro's friends: white pseudoliberals and Negro renegades who attempt to soothe white America's conscience by asserting that the American Negro no longer is oppressed, denied opportunity, or exploited. Former teacher Baumann was worried by the "I hate sin" patriots who always are turning up a rosy end of Jim Crow.

I knew that the old man had a point. He referred to Negroes like Davis Lee, of Newark, New Jersey. Lee is the publisher of a scandal sheet known as the Newark *Telegram;* neither the paper nor publisher is recognized by Negro news-gathering organizations. Lee makes regular tours of the South, pretending that his paper has a circulation of one hundred thousand, although there aren't that many Negroes in the nation who ever heard of it. Yet Southern editors fall for his line on each trip because Lee says things they want to hear. In Columbus, Georgia, in March 1951, he was quoted as saying:

1. The Negro is treated better in the South because the whites realize his shortcomings and go out of their way to help him. "Up North," he said, "you're strictly on your own."

2. In Columbus the Negro is sitting pretty. His homes are equal in some cases to anything the whites have, and there are good schools and adequate business opportunities, and relationships between the races are excellent.

3. The Negro has nothing to fear from the Georgia white man. Under new Georgia bills, better schools and housing facilities are on the way. "If they will only be patient," he said.

4. If segregation is wiped out, Southern Negroes lack the capital and training to compete successfully in the white man's world. Nonsegregation would mean that all Negro businesses would be wiped out. Within the framework of segregation, he stated, the Negro can build an empire.

Wherever Lee went in the South, editors jumped gleefully at his statements that Negroes should push, not oppose, segregation. Doubtlessly, a few whites who are immovable in their belief that, because of the Negro's "shortcomings," paternalism is best for him, got encouragement for a new stand behind segregation. Other than that, Davis Lee's remarks are not too important. The few people who have heard of Davis Lee attach little importance to his opinions—not even the editors who run his remarks to such length.

But there are Negroes of greater fame and respectability who apparently have neither heart nor soul when it comes to feeling the plight of less-well-off Negroes. Eccentric George Schuyler, associate editor of the Pittsburgh *Courier,* the nation's largest Negro weekly, is perhaps the most eminent example. For more than a decade, Schuyler has confused white America by writing that the Negro is, or ought to be, contented with the gains he has made and the rate at which he continues to gain. In the April 23, 1951, issue of *The Freeman* magazine, for example, Schuyler put into succinct words the type of thinking that has made him hated by thousands of American Negroes, many of whom consider him a racial traitor, and some of whom have dubbed him "the Westbrook Pegler of Negro journalism." Decrying news stories, books, and movies that are concerned with America's ill-treatment of her Negro citizens, Schuyler wrote for *The Freeman:*

> *There exist a few books presenting a genuine picture of Negro-White relations in the United States, but these are not the books which have been displayed, read and discussed by literate foreigners. What they have read are* Kingsblood Royal, Freedom Road, Strange Fruit, Native Son *and others ringing the same charges, all by American writers, and all stressing the hatred of whites for blacks, and vice versa.*
>
> *The news services send abroad mostly the sensational and discreditable, salted with occasional mention of Marian Anderson, Jackie Robinson or Ralph Bunche. On the screen, foreigners see such rot as* Home of the Brave, Pinky *and* No Way Out. *Small wonder they believe in this* [oppressed] *Negro.*

Mr. Schuyler continued:

*Paradoxically, the average white American is as misin-
formed as the average European. He is helpless in the face
of this effective anti-American propaganda abroad because
of his ignorance. In a vague way he senses that there is
something wrong about the picture presented, suspects
that this American Negro assailing his guilt complexes is
a phantom, but he is tongue-tied by lack of information. Indeed, his information is almost identical with that
which has corrupted the European, for has he not read
the same books, the same magazines, the same newspapers,
and seen the same movies? He knows little more about the
Negro than he does about the Navajo. Since the Comintern
started its drive to foster racial conflict around 1928,
the American's source of information have fallen increasingly into the hands and under the direction of Communists, fellow-travelers and self-seeking race hustlers. In
their various ways, these have constantly held up the treatment of Negroes here as a horrible illustration of the fail-
ure of American Democracy!*

*Actually, the progressive improvement of interracial
relations in the United States is the most flattering of all
the many examples of the superiority of the free American
civilization over the soul-shackling reactionism of totalitarian regimes and the tradition-bound old class societies. It
is to this capacity for change and adjustment inherent in
the system of individual initiative and decentralized authority (which has reached its highest development in this
country) that we must attribute the unprecedented economic, social and educational progress of the American
Negroes. The history of capitalism having been one of
continuous mass improvement, it is not surprising that
this has also benefited the colored people here. The most
"exploited" Negroes in Mississippi are better off than
the citizens of Russia and her satellites.*

The saddest part of Schuyler's article is that he correctly stated that the average white American knows next to nothing about the Negro. If the white man knew a little more, he would know that, basically, Schuyler is a show-off, and that almost all Negro America knows it. He would know, also, that throughout the years Schuyler has exhibited a passion next to crankiness for "being different." In this instance he also has exhibited his shrewdness by saying, as is usually the case, what he thinks white America wants to hear. In a warped sort of way, he has used the Negro question in an effort to show that democracy is better than totalitarian regimes—something Americans of all races like to be reminded of these days. Schuyler has tried to portray himself as the "grand American patriot," defender of democracy—which even honest American critics of bigotry agree does not need defending. To say that Americans fall short of the democratic ideal does not attribute weakness to democracy, but to the humans who fail to reach the democratic goal. And all manner of arguments about the relative merits of democracy and "old-class societies" are irrelevant in the face of human weaknesses.

In his narrow thinking, Schuyler has classified as an anti-American propagandist every American who dares say that the Negro still is being denied freedom; he has labeled these same Americans, as well as the custodians of the fourth estate, "Communists, fellow-travelers and self-seeking race hustlers." When, after decades of depicting Negroes as shiftless, spineless, irresponsible buffoons, the film industry finally mustered up enough courage to make movies portraying Negroes as human beings, and racial hatred as the cancerous evil that it is, almost all America applauded. That the film industry could do such a turnabout was the *real* proof of the American capacity for change. But Schuyler, being "different," characterized these antibigotry movies as "rot" and called them part of a vast, Comintern-directed campaign to make democracy look bad in the eyes of the world. According to Schuyler, one has to be anti-American to speak against the imperfections in her social and economic framework, and appeal to the basic decency of Americans themselves to join hands and right the wrongs.

And in accusing the American press of promoting a sinister Communist plot by spotlighting racial injustices in the United States, Schuyler has exceeded himself in ludicrous absurdity. Anyone familiar with the record of the daily American press on racial matters knows that it long has given great play to Negro gains and minimized incidents of bigotry. The press has, to a large extent, been guilty of doing the Negro a disservice by portraying him, as did the movies, as an irresponsible half-human with monstrous criminal tendencies.

It cannot be denied that the press of foreign nations gives what Schuyler and many Americans less "patriotic" consider undue prominence to stories of racial inequality and conflict in America. But it is grossly unfair to the American Negro, to democracy, or to American critics of bigotry in America to say that American critics work with the desire of such disproportionate publicity in the foreign press.

Schuyler deplores the critics, rather than the conditions that make such criticism possible and necessary. He would put the Negro in the position of a stepchild, being lashed by his stepfather and warned at the same time not to cry out because doing so would jeopardize the stepfather's reputation as a kind, lovable parent.

But most damaging of all, Schuyler has indulged in the kind of mental gymnastics that at best impede racial progress. "Admittedly we have a long way to go . . ." he writes, "but considering all the factors involved . . . where can the record be equalled? Certainly not in India, China, Russia or the British French and Belgian empires." This line is damaging because it is one easily gobbled up by the Americans who can be content with the smug belief that whatever America has or does is better than the comparable thing for any other nation.

But that essentially is a silly, un-American argument, because it is an undemocratic argument. Is it an American test by which we decide that what the American Negro gets is satisfactory because Negroes in South Africa get something worse? Americans can only judge America by the American standard, and that is the standard of democracy. If Americans are short of their own democratic standard in the treatment of Negroes, their actions become no more laudable because Hitler massacred Jews, the Soviet empire is enslaving millions, or the Malan regime is an evil, monstrous thing spreading hate throughout South Africa. Nor does it make sense for Americans to decide that Negroes are doing all right because they own more automobiles and lawnmowers than all the people of Uruguay. The American ideal says that the worth of a human soul is not measurable in automobiles and lawnmowers. Negroes are human beings with souls, and the Negro soul measures its dignity by the standards of the total American dignity, not by any Uruguayan standard. The Negro, according to democracy's own standard, would rather be a pauper and free than have a Cadillac and an enslaved soul.

But white America believes Schuyler, primarily because his articles soothe their conscience. Schuyler sugar-talks away their guilt complexes by asserting that such guilty feelings ought not to exist, that they are products of Communist skulduggery and treachery. White America also believes because it considers Schuyler sincere, intelligent, and learned on the subject.

It is for the latter reason that they also listen to the Southern liberals, the "freedom-for-you-sometime-soon" gradualists. I met scores of Negroes and a few whites in the South who were greatly concerned with a few haloed liberals who impede progress with the cries: "We can't solve this problem overnight"; "let us alone, this is our problem"; "this would do more harm than good"; and so on.

Baumann, the aged former schoolteacher, who had brought up the issue of fake liberals, reminded me of Judge Waring. The Warings expressed much distrust and considerable disgust with men such as Hodding Carter, Greenville, Mississippi, publisher, and Ralph McGill, Atlanta editor, who rocketed to national prominence chiefly on their reputations as liberals in a land where the word had long been out of style.

Judge Waring reminded me of how the circle of Southern liberals came to be: "They all start out by deploring lynchings, for which it takes no courage, not even in darkest Mississippi or South Carolina." He went on to tell how they spoke out against robbing Negro sharecroppers in a manner that approached legalized slavery. They cried aloud that the Ku Klux Klan ought to be destroyed, that wearing of masks in public should be banned. Even in the South it was becoming popular to denounce hoodlums who ride by night, cowardly cloaked in sheets and the security of numbers. Almost all the budding liberals said a Negro ought not to die on a sidewalk because a white hospital will not admit him; so they urged building a Negro hospital, and not that the white hospital should change its policy.

At this point, the entire field of Southerners surveyed the scene. By symbolizing what to most of them seemed to be a world of courage and humanitarianism, they had become leaders. And leadership was more than most of them could stand. They had become enemies of the acknowledged bigots, thus gaining the respect of "the good people of the South" and a majority of white Northerners. Most decided to rest there—on their laurels. Only the Warings, Lillian Smith, Aubrey Williams, Myles Horton, and a few others were willing to go further, to say that racial segregation is the root and perpetrator of all the evils previously denounced. And because they were small in number, like Christians in the Catacombs, they were crucified.

The others became "spokesmen for the New South," whose self-appointed task it is to convince the world that (1) every place else is the kettle, and the kettle can't call the pot black when it comes to racial bigotry; (2) the South is solving its own problems; and (3) any help will not be appreciated and is likely to bring on tragedy.

I left Baumann, thinking about his worries, which I knew

were my worries. I left Mrs. Borikins and walked on alone through chilly New Orleans, past men huddled in jackets and houses closed as tight as could be against wintry winds that blew misery off the sea and the boggy land.

Gradualism is so popular, I thought; especially in these tense times when Americans seem to think that the only alternative is revolution—and revolution carries a foreign connotation. It would be so simple to write a report embracing the popular theory of gradualism. The theory finds easy acceptance when it is someone else's freedom that is to come later. The theory finds easy acceptance with a Negro who has broken within the confines of opportunity, who has found a job with a decent salary, who has a degree of certainty as to where the next meal will come from, and where his family will find clothing and shelter.

I walked on, as I had done in a dozen communities, past shacks and railroad tracks, through rubble and the gloom of human dereliction. I knew that I could not join the cry for gradualism. Not after walking through misery in a score of miserable places. Not after returning to McMinnville and seeing friends who had walked the streets with me day after day, now worrying about their children, who went about in the same kind of shabby clothing that I had worn, carrying the same hunger-borne stomachaches that I had carried. I knew that I was not the one to tell such parents: "Be patient, democracy will come to you later."

Democracy and Christianity have set up a simple test for judging circumstances involving humans. The Christian or democrat puts himself in the other person's place. I knew that I could not put myself in the place of Joe Doaks, Negro, Slums, U.S.A., and say: "Be patient, democracy will come to you later." Those are *his* children with holes in their shoes, no underwear, and no winter coats. It is *his* family that leaves the dinner table with stomachs not yet full. The millennium could arrive too late for Joe Doaks; it conceivably could arrive too late for democracy.

In a world that rolls on the brink of disaster, it is easy to say that the Negro should subordinate his fate to that of his country and democracy, as Schuyler seems to imply. But there are no separate fates. Negroes are Americans; they are fused into the country's hillsides by the sweat of generations, by ages of toil and bloodshed. The destiny of the American Negro is also the destiny of America and democracy. To protect its own permanent fate, freedom must cease to be a sometimey, color-conscious thing.

Part Two

I was ready to leave New Orleans, even with the taste of disappointment in my mouth. I planned to stop in Monroe, a town of about twenty-five thousand in the northwest portion of the state. Monroe and the surrounding area had been in the news quite consistently because of acts involving racial violence.

I phoned the city ticket-office of the Missouri Pacific Railroad and asked for a berth from New Orleans to Monroe. I was assigned to lower berth 8, car 1162. About noon I took a taxi downtown and walked into the ticket office.

"I came to pay for Rowan's ticket and reservation to Monroe," I said.

"Is it for you?" the ticket agent asked. I sensed what was coming. I could have said: "No, I'm the boy Mr. Rowan sent after it." They would have given it to me, probably without further questioning, for the "Mr." would have indicated that Rowan was a white man. But I remembered that I would have to pay with traveler's checks and my signing them would reveal me as Rowan.

"Does it make any difference?" I asked.

"Well, if you're colored I can't sell you a Pullman ticket to Monroe—that ain't across no state line. Are you colored?"

"What do you mean, 'am I colored'? Am I?"

"You know what I mean: are you colored? I have to know that."

"You see what color I am," I snapped. "Why don't you ask what you want to ask: am I American? Well, I am!"

"Then I can't sell you a Pullman ticket to Monroe."

"Then give me one to Little Rock—you'll sell one interstate or someone will pay through the courts," I retorted.

"I can do that, but I'll have to put you in the car that goes through to Little Rock. The train arrives at Monroe about three a.m. We leave the Monroe car there, but you can't sleep in it. To get off in Monroe you'd have to get up before three."

I didn't want that, so I decided to bluff.

"Somebody's going to sell me a Pullman ticket to Monroe or the whole United States government will know about it. I've ridden Pullman intrastate in the South before."

"You must have had a government order," he replied.

"I'll get a government order now, if that's what it takes," I said angrily.

"Oh, are you a government man?" he questioned.

"I'm not at liberty to disclose what I do," I said suggestively. "But here's my name," I added, tossing him my naval-reserve card.

The agent looked wide-eyed at the card (which meant absolutely nothing) and picked up the phone to call someone in another office.

"There's a colored guy here who wants a ticket, Pullman, to Monroe, which ain't across no state line. I told him I couldn't sell him one. But he's got some navy credentials and acts like some kind of government man. What should I do?"

"I don't intend to bicker here all day," I said. "I'm going into this Western Union office next door. When I return I want to know what the story is."

When I returned there were signs that my visit to the Western Union office was considered something official, involving the government. Of course it was not. But my Pullman ticket was ready. I was assigned "lower berth 11, car 1162."

"What do you mean, 'lower berth 11'?" I demanded. "According to my timetable, car 1162 has only ten sections. There isn't any 'lower 11.'"

The agent's lean face became crimson. "Well, actually that's compartment 'C' we're giving you," he explained.

A compartment at lower-berth cost?" I replied.

"That's correct," he said.

"So the stockholders take a licking in this deal?" I needled him.

"Heh, heh," he laughed, "I guess they can afford it."

CHAPTER XIV

THE LAST FRONTIER

I sat in compartment C that night, having what I thought was the last laugh on the Missouri Pacific Railroad. Something for nothing: a compartment at lower-berth fare. I knew that the compartment was meant to be my private domain, to keep me "out of the traffic," so to speak. But I was too obstinate to co-operate. I had learned the wonderful taste of a ham sandwich and beer when served with a dash of that erstwhile elusive freedom to eat it wherever a first-class ticket entitled a passenger to entry. I went to the club car and ate my sandwich. White passengers showed so little concern that the ticket agent's fuss seemed senseless. Then I returned to my compartment and wrote until a wind that knifed under the window raised goose-pimples and sent me to bed shivering. I lay for a few minutes and stared out at trees casting trembling shadows on the snow-crusted earth. Then I pulled up the extra blanket and fell asleep.

A few hours later I was awakened by the backward movement of the train. I thought we had reached Monroe and that car 1162 was being removed from the train. I grumbled drowsily at its being moved so roughly, and resumed sleep.

I awoke later with a start. I had asked the porter to wake me at seven a.m. Already it was 8.20. The train still was moving. I jumped into some clothing, already organizing a bitter protest at being carried past my destination. I opened the door and saw smoke coming from the next compartment. The porter was in it.

"Why didn't you wake me at seven? Where are we?" I demanded.

"Oh, we're still a long piece from Monroe. Thought you might as well sleep," he replied.

"Long way from Monroe?"

"Yeah. Ran into a freight wreck down the line. Had to back up and use another railroad's tracks."

"How far to Monroe?"

" 'Bout a couple hours out, I guess."

This news made me unhappy. According to my timetable, I could get only two trains daily from Monroe to Little Rock— the one that I was on and one due out in the early evening. The lateness of my train would leave me only a few hours in which to see Monroe, for I wanted to catch the evening train out. Stories of racial strife had come out of Monroe at regular intervals, and a majority of reports had shown law-enforcement officials in a somewhat unsavory light. I wanted to see just what role law-enforcement officials do play in a community with a reputation for racial beatings and bloodshed. I wondered if I would have time to get this information.

I got my answer at about ten a.m. when the train crunched to an irregular halt. While I sat wondering what was happening, I heard a lot of commotion. Passengers were running off the train. I jumped up and got off too, to find that our engine was off the track. Because we were hours late, our train had had to yield the right-of-way to another one. In pulling onto a snow-covered side track the engine ran off the rails and onto a snowbank.

"Might as well go git y'all's coats and go on down and git some grub," shouted the engineer. "We gonna be heah awhile."

There no longer was food on the train, the snack car having been left at a junction point. I went back to my compartment to get a coat.

I walked back toward a path that led down a hill toward town. I asked a Negro what town it was. He pointed to a frame building with COLUMBIA painted on it.

"You live here?" I asked.

"Naw. I'm on the train," said the Negro, who identified himself as Amos Smith.

"Then you don't know what kind of town it is," I said.

"The hell I don't!" he snapped. "I work at Sterlington, about twenty miles from here. Drove through here twice last summer and got arrested both times. Cop told me to stop. I did. 'Boy, you ain't got no brakes,' he tells me. He hauls me off to the judge and I gets fined fifty dollars. I didn't argue; I was glad t' git away. I comes back four weeks later and this same cop wheels up 'side me. 'Boy, you ain't got no brakes,' he says to me. I says: 'I stopped when you said stop, didn't I?' Well, he hauls me in to the judge and says: 'Judge, this boy ain't got no full pedal of brakes.' The judge takes his word and fines me a hundred dollars."

"Did you happen to have all that money handy?" I asked.

"Naw, not the second time. But I managed to git it. Man, this is a rugged place. But a man's gotta eat no matter what town it is. If you're going down, me too."

We started down the hill with Smith still chattering about the town. I began to wonder about the clothes I had on. I looked rather hoboish in the clothes that I had jumped into so hastily when I thought we had passed Monroe. I had no tie on, and I looked singularly unimportant.

"Why don't you fellows give a lady some help?" said a feminine voice behind us. I turned to see a shapely young colored woman struggling down the hill in high-heeled shoes. We waited until she caught up.

"They run Honey Washington out of this durn place, but I gotta find me somewhere to make a phone call. That man's gonna be mad as all getout when I don't get to Little Rock on time," said the woman.

"Who's Honey Washington?" I asked.

"He's a colored guy who's s'posed to be with the agriculture department. They didn't want nothing to do with him 'round here, though. Run him outta town. But I gotta find me someplace to make a phone call. My man's sho gonna be hot."

I looked at her puffed right eye. She was nursing a shiner. Perhaps that explained her concern about some man being angry, I thought. I was more concerned with our reception in the little Northwestern Louisiana town of two thousand, however. Several townspeople already were flocking up the hill toward the derailment. We met a white man at the foot of the hill. He indicated that a restaurant was to our right about a hundred yards down the road. It was the Trailways bus depot, he said.

We walked to the bus depot. A weather-worn, almost illegible sign indicated that the place also was known as "Ilah's Cafe." People stood in the front door and at the windows watching the black smoke billow through the snow-laden trees and into a brilliant blue sky.

"What in the world's done happened?" asked a white woman in a red, two-piece suit. She looked about thirty and appeared to be the boss of the café.

"Train 116 ran off the track," I said, adding a bit of Southern drawl to what I actually had retained.

"Ma'am, y'all got a phone I can make a important call on?" asked the Negro woman.

"Well, er, yeah. I guess so," said the white woman. "Right over there in the corner. Better tell the operator it's emergency 'cause this snow's got lotsa lines down. Ain't been able to make no long distance calls atall lately."

When the Negro woman walked in the front door, so did I. I noticed that Smith went around the building, looking for a back door. The Negro woman went to the phone and the white woman began quizzing me about the train. I noticed that she kept walking toward the kitchen, obviously leading me to "where I belonged."

"Y'all got any sandwiches a fellow could take out?" I asked her.

"Yeah," she said, and began to list the kinds available.

"How much are two cheeseburgers?" I asked.

"Cost *you* fifty cents apiece."

"Why the emphasis on the you?" I demanded, unwittingly dropping my faked accent.

She ignored me and told a tall, white-haired white woman: "Fix this boy two cheeseburgers." She walked back into the front, where white passengers now were arriving from the train. Seeing that she was out of sight, Smith kicked my foot. "No cheeseburgers," he mumbled twice, nodding at an enameled pan that was half covered with a dish towel. I saw that the hamburger in it was covered with a layer of cankerous green.

"Two ham-cheeses, she should have ordered," I said to the old woman.

"Two ham-cheeses" she repeated unconcernedly. She was dumping two fried eggs into a platter. She broke the egg yellows with a butcher knife, then sopped bread into the running egg. After each bite she licked her fingers. She pinched off a corner of one piece of cheese after cutting two slices with the unwashed butcher knife, and put the nibble of cheese in her mouth. Again she licked her fingers.

By this time a man about the cook's age came out of the front of the café. "Whatcha fixin'?" he asked the cook. Upon being told he picked up two pieces of ham with hands of unknown cleanliness and dropped them into the skillet in which the eggs had been cooked. I watched in silence as the old woman continued to sop up the egg and lick her fingers. When the cheese had melted on the bread she took it out of the stove. She lifted the ham from the skillet with the tip of the butcher knife and dropped it on the cheese-covered bread. After a few more swipes at her eggs, she pressed the ham down with her fingers, pinching off an occasional bite. She put the two sandwiches in a paper bag and sat them on the side of the stove. About five minutes later the woman in red returned and picked them up.

"That'll be a dollar," she said.

I handed her the dollar, seething inside but afraid to complain. I was happy for once in my life that I waited in the kitchen to see my sandwiches prepared. I opened the back door and hurled the sandwiches into the bushes, letting this act disclose my disgust. Then I walked away hastily toward downtown, unsure if I was being "taught a lesson" or if the cook made the sandwiches in her usual, unbiased way. I went into a grocery store and bought a quart of milk, some bananas, some rolls, and cold cuts. Then I started back to the train.

By this time the whole town knew that a train was stuck at the top of the hill. Several spectators already had reached the derailment scene. Taxis were making a beeline up the narrow road with offers to drive passengers to Monroe. Halfway up the hill a man was stuck in a Henry J.

"Boy, gimme a shove," he said as I came alongside.

I looked at his spinning wheels. "Push won't help a bit if you ain't used to snow," I said. "I can't push but I'll try to drive it out for you. I'm used to snow."

"Reckon you can, boy?" he asked, giving me a queer look.

I offered to take the wheel and he moved over. I rocked the car a bit and got going. Another taxi sped down the narrow slope and in dodging him I got stuck again. I rocked the Henry J. again, thinking how nervy I was to say I couldn't push, but that I probably could beat the taxi-driver at getting the car out of the rut. He could have resented my "superior driver" attitude, but I had been correct in presuming that he was more eager to get to the train and get a load than he was to start a ruckus with me. I got the car moving again.

"You gonna get a Monroe load?" I said.

"Hope so. If they all ain't gone."

"I'm going to Monroe, if you're short on a load," I said.

"Boy, you can't ride with me. You hafta get one of these colored boys with cars to drive some of you boys up t' Monroe."

"I'm probably the only colored guy that wants a taxi," I argued.

"But you can't ride with me, boy. I'll probably have some white folks in here anyhow."

"Okay," I said as I pulled the Henry J. on a little rise alongside the tracks. I got out and walked over to the engine. Someone had rounded up several Negro men, who were digging and shoveling under it. I walked up to see what was going on, easing among the many white persons who watched.

A bony, thin-faced white man who apparently bossed the work crew sighted me. "Boy, why'n't you pitch in and give 'em a lift?" he asked. I knew he referred to me, but I looked around as if I expected to see some other Negro to whom he could be speaking.

"I'm sorry, mister, but I came along for the ride." Before he could close his sagging mouth I had taken several steps toward my Pullman car. I decided that I had on the wrong clothes. I looked too much like a defenseless hourly laborer. I dressed in a suit that I felt assured me I would receive no further invitations to dig under the engine. I got my camera, deciding that I wanted to get pictures of what I considered a personification of the lyrics by Oscar Hammerstein II in Old Man River: "colored folks work while the white folks play." Every Negro who had appeared on the scene was put to work, while scores of whites swarmed the area.

I drew a few curious stares when I appeared with my camera. I snapped one picture and a Negro workman gave me a contemptuous gaze. I ignored him and snapped a picture from another angle. Then I paused to take down a few notes.

"Say, fellow, you better be careful wid that camera. This ain't New York, you know. This is Loos-ana." I turned slowly. It was R. L. Pettis, the porter, whispering to me.

"I'm not worried," I replied. "Nobody knows why I'm taking the pictures. They are curious and don't feel that the pictures will hurt or embarrass them, so they don't know what to do. If anybody protests, I'll stop, of course."

"Man, I don't know 'bout these people," retorted Pettis. "This is a rough little town. People talking 'bout going downtown. I went right over that barbed-wire fence and got some coffee from that colored family."

A white man, short and very chubby, waddled up as Pettis

was ending the sentence. He asked Pettis where he got his coffee. Pettis told him.

"My god," said the white man, whom Pettis knew as Herman Lovett. "I live closer than that family. Hell, the damn train is in my front yard. Why'ncha come over to my house for your coffee?"

"Well, er, you know how it is," stumbled Pettis.

"Hell, fellow," said Lovett, "I been meeting these trains for nigh on to twelve years. You know damn well you can come to my house to get some coffee."

I listened with interest, for here was an example of something that I needed to remember. I thought of the scores of times after I first left the South that I was to have some dealings with a white person, only to learn beforehand that he was a native of the South. I remembered the funny feeling that learning this evoked, as if my informant had said: "He's your mortal enemy, you know. The guy is a bigoted bastard." It had been a task in a number of cases to remember that a white man wasn't necessarily anti-Negro because he was a native of the South. In his simple, ordinary way Lovett illustrated that point. He showed no signs of having read books, heard sermons, or known people who gave do-good lectures, in order to get the idea that he ought to be willing to give a Negro some coffee. In twelve years of meeting trains he simply had come to know Pettis as a decent enough guy to enter his house for coffee in such out-of-the-ordinary circumstances.

Perhaps, by 1951, the number of Southern whites like Lovett was larger, but I knew that his kind were not new. I remembered that they always existed, even in my home town, but in miserably small and ineffective numbers.

I walked back to my Pullman car. Nestled in a thicket of trees was the two-room shack, enclosed in barbed wire, where Pettis had got the coffee. Leaning against the fence, gazing at the train and all the commotion surrounding it, were three poorly-dressed Negro youngsters. I walked over to chat with them. When I asked if I could take their picture the boys expressed eager approval; but the little girl's pride bristled. "Mama would die if I had a picture took in this," she said, referring to a large, rather deteriorated felt hat that covered her multibraided hair. She took the hat off, then put it back on after deciding she preferred it to braids.

As I took their picture I noticed someone opening the door of their house. A woman and five more children came out on the porch. I walked down to talk with the woman, Mrs. Almeda Wooten. Yes, all nine of them lived in the two rooms, she said. Soon the oldest boy, who stood at the fence, began to talk:

"I'll sure be glad when this snow gets gone. I gotta get back to school and learn sumpin. I'm gonna be engineer of old 116 some day."

There was hope in the most hopeless of situations. This boy, not quite free, could dream. And the way he told it gave you the feeling that his daydreaming was something more than a waste of time.

"I'll bet you will be an engineer—of a long, sleek streamliner," I said. "I wouldn't be at all surprised."

Part Two

About an hour later two engines from Monroe reached the derailment scene. One was to try to free the stuck engine, while the other took the passenger cars on to Monroe and Little Rock. By that time we were more than eleven hours behind schedule, so I decided to pass up Monroe. I told the porter that I would go directly to Little Rock, and asked him to transfer my bags from car 1162 to 1161.

"There's no empty compartment in 1161," he said.

"I don't want a compartment. All I want is a seat."

"Well, suh, I'll talk to the conductor," he said, "but there's mostly white women in that car. They ain't too happy around here about colored men riding where white women are. Fact is, that's the main thing they's against."

"Never mind, never mind," I said brusquely, "I think I'd better talk to the conductor myself." I did, and I got a seat in car 1161 with no difficulty. Still, I knew that the porter's words generally were true. Any way you turned the issue of race, the ultimate question would be sex. I knew that. I had seen the taboo rise up in a score of cities in a score of ways. I sat there, the only Negro in the Pullman car, staring out at the bleak, wooded land, thinking of another Texan and another day during World War II. Ensign Dunaway and I had been roommates aboard the U.S.S. *Chemung* for a while, and when a stateroom became vacant we had individual rooms, but shared a bathroom. That hardly was unusual except that Dunaway had declared, upon learning that I was to join the crew, that he would "refuse to eat in the same wardroom with a Goddam nigger." Lieutenant Frank Wehking, the assistant engineering officer, was still laughing, when I left the ship months later, at the poetic justice of me getting for a roommate the officer who swore he wouldn't eat in the same room with me.

Like another Texan, Noah Brannon, Dunaway simply "didn't know" some things about Negroes. His contacts with Negroes had been extremely limited and not of the sort to produce either friendliness or broadmindedness. Although we never became chums, I know that I gained his respect as a naval officer and as a human being; also, I whetted his appetite for discussion of the "problem." Many were the hours that he came into my stateroom and talked, trying to find a subtle entry into the discussion of race prejudice.

One night in the South Atlantic I sat alone on the deck, moody and lonely, listening to Frank Sinatra sing: "I Fall in Love Too Easily." The yeoman played it at dusk every day as a special favor to me. Dunaway pulled a chair up and sat beside me.

"You know, I'm convinced by now that a lot of things are wrong with the South," he said without bothering to ease into a discussion of the subject.

"There's a lot wrong with all of us, or we wouldn't be sailing these miserable damned seas like vultures, looking for somebody to kill," I said.

"But I mean the South, my South," he persisted. "I'm ready to admit that plenty is separate there but very little is equal for the two races—and something ought to be done about it. But there is one thing that's been bothering me. What about interracial marriage?"

"Okay, what about it?" I asked, willing to stop there. Dunaway had launched a discussion that I felt could get nowhere. I knew that he wasn't ready, or sufficiently "prepared," for such a discussion, although he asked for it. In that respect he was like most Americans, who are tremendously worried, or curious, about mixed marriages, but any discussion of the subject finds them entering with their minds made up. I knew that I had been sticking my head in the sand by dodging that phase of the subject, for it is the crux of the whole question. Yet, all the groups fighting for equality for Negroes have dodged the marriage issue deliberately and skillfully because of a feeling that it is the most explosive phase of the problem and that the public has not been carried along far enough for organized defense of mixed marriages.

I tried to tell Dunaway that the right to vote, to freedom from fear, to a decent job or decent housing, has nothing to do with intermarriage. I said, as writer Langston Hughes once pointed out, that in the North millions of Negroes manage to go to the polls without cohabiting with white women. "To ask an industrialist for a job isn't to ask him for his daughter's hand," I argued. Yet, this was skirting the "but what if" issue. Dunaway knew this, and said so. He knew that the dynamics of human association and behavior are much more complex than my argument would indicate, so we talked on.

As I sat in the Pullman car, surrounded by white women

and thinking of the porter's remarks, I knew that the issue of mixed marriages still was the crux of the problem, both to the Southerner and the Northerner.

"People who go to church and school together and work side by side where they associate freely, begin to see good qualities in each other," a New Orleans white woman had told me. "Now, take our Epworth League. If we mixed the races there it is certain that some white and Negro youngsters would fall in love. Now, I am not so sure that that is good. Now, isn't segregation justified in that it prevents youngsters of different races from falling in love?"

Here, I knew, was topsoil—hard, crusty soil of the mind that was impervious to the seed of a New South. There could be no growth until this soil was softened. Here was the "question of our time."

The key to the question, and perhaps to the whole problem, lay in the way this woman had put her question: Is it, or is it not, good for two youngsters of different races to fall in love? About this question the most violent opinions emerge. There has been no answer because there are too few facts on which to base one. And the few facts that exist have been like corn-flakes in a whirlwind, because they have been disguised and hidden in the opinions and prejudices of whoever happened to be speaking.

By 1951, I felt, something was happening to the South, even on the issue of mixed marriages. When I left in 1943 such marriages simply were not discussed, except by men who sought to stir the passions and hatreds of the people by forecasting the "mongrelization" of the human race unless the people voted for him. Interracial marriage simply was so much out of the question that respectable Southerners dared not bring it up. Southerners were discussing it in 1951, and from what they said it still is out of the question. But significance lay in the fact that it no longer was a terrible crime to talk about it. In that respect, the South and the rest of the nation are alike. Everywhere there have been signs of Americans juggling about in their minds their beliefs about mixed marriages, trying to arrive at some view consonant with their belief in democracy. Perhaps no body has discussed the issue so sanely and so thoroughly, giving consideration to all the major theories and beliefs that have motivated American policy on the subject, as did the California Supreme Court in 1948 in the case of *Perez vs. Sharp*. Sharp had, on behalf of the state, refused to issue a marriage license to Andrea Perez, a white woman, and Sylvester Davis, a Negro.

Attorneys for the mixed couple seemed to have only one positive argument: the white woman and Negro man loved each other and wanted to marry. They felt that they had a constitutional right to do so, having satisfied all state requirements except that involving race. For this reason, much of the time of attorneys for the plaintiff was spent refuting arguments of the state, which cited a list of opinions, popular among both jurists and ordinary citizens, in an effort to show that a state has a constitutional right to prohibit such marriages. The most commonly heard and judicially important of these arguments are allegations that (1) without a legal ban there would be a rapid increase in the number of interracial marriages; (2) mixed marriages should be prohibited because the offspring of such unions generally are inferior; (3) interracial marriages should be outlawed because "Negroes, mulattoes, Mongolians and Malayans" are physically inferior to Caucasians and more "subject to certain diseases"; (4) colored people (primarily referring to Negroes) are mentally inferior to Caucasians and "continued intermarriage would cause retrogression of the human race"; (5) social tension and unrest are caused by mixed marriages, the participants bring public scorn upon themselves and their families, and this is a threat to the general peace; and (6) only the "dregs of society" in both races want to intermarry, and such unions of "dregs" are "publicly obnoxious" and must be forbidden for "the public welfare."

All these arguments represented an attempt by the state to

prove that mixed marriages are detrimental to society. Thus, the state contended, it had a right to regulate marriage for the good of society—as in the case of bigamy.

The court took up the arguments, one by one. The charge that a flurry of mixed marriages would follow removal of the ban was quickly rejected by a majority of the jurists hearing the case. It was a legally immaterial argument, they held, for if one couple has a constitutional right to marry, that right is not nullified because fifty or one hundred or ten thousand other couples desire to utilize that same constitutional right.

The charge really was a "scare" device, a less-bombastic employment of the "mongrelization" threat. First of all, it is based on the false opinion that only whites oppose mixed marriages. The truth is that a Negro incurs the wrath of other Negroes when he crosses the color line in marriage, often to a greater degree than a white is scorned by other whites. It is a matter of pride with a lot of Negroes, especially women, and for this reason Negroes often heap as much misery upon interracial couples as do whites.

As indicated in an earlier chapter, there also is considerable doubt that statutes forbidding miscegenation actually are the deterrents they are intended to be. There is considerable evidence that more interracial lovemaking occurs in states barring mixed marriages than in states where they are legal. Twenty-nine states still prohibit such unions. In his book, *Inside U.S.A.*, John Gunther wrote: "The whole subject is cloaked in hypocrisy." He estimated that fifty per cent of American Negroes are mulattoes. In his book, *The American Negro*, Melville Herskovits states that less than twenty per cent of American Negroes are wholly of African descent. All this leads Gunther to conclude: "A lot of people have been intimate with a lot of people."

The theory that offspring of interracial couples are inferior is significant in that it has been accepted by several states as a basis for anti-mixed-marriage laws. Supporters of the California statute quoted a Georgia ruling:

> *The amalgamation of the races is not only unnatural, but is always productive of deplorable results. Our daily observation shows us that the offspring of these unnatural connections are generally sickly and effeminate, and that they are inferior in physical development and strength to the full blood of either race.*

This is nothing more than "old wives' talk," countered counsel for the plaintiff, and they presented or cited physiologists and anthropologists who refuted the state's charge. These experts held that "the progeny of marriages between persons of different races are not inferior to both parents." The majority of the court accepted this viewpoint.

Expert testimony also played a major part in arguments over whether colored races are more subject to certain diseases. The state's argument was that Negroes have a weakness for tuberculosis and that to permit whites and Negroes to marry would be to sanction the gradual weakening of the white race's relatively great resistance to tuberculosis.

Proponents of intermarriage argued that there is no proof of the physical inferiority or weakness of any race. On this issue a majority of the court agreed that: "Most, if not all, of the ailments to which the state refers are attributable largely to environmental factors."

Moreover, the majority agreed, marriage is an individual right, not a group right. If the intention of the statute was to prevent marriage of diseased people, the court reasoned, it ought to require medical examinations and prohibit marriages on the basis of such examinations, not on the basis of color. Even were it true that a large number of Negroes are more subject to tuberculosis than whites, the majority held, it is a violation of the constitutional rights of whatever Negroes are not more subject to the disease to limit the marriage rights of *all* Negroes on grounds of physical weakness.

The state showed that more Caucasians are listed in United States catalogs of distinguished people than members of other races. This was suggested as proof of the mental superiority of Caucasians. The plaintiff's counsel argued, and was upheld by a majority of the court, that "it cannot be disregarded that Caucasians are in the great majority and have generally had a more advantageous environment, and that the capacity of the members of any race to contribute to a nation's culture depends in large measure on how freely they may participate in that culture."

By this time the court's opinion was set. It voted, 4 to 3, that the ninety-eight-year-old statute forbidding interracial marriages was unconstitutional. The right to marry is fundamental, the majority held, and "since the right to marry is the right to join in marriage with the person of one's choice, a statute that prohibits an individual from marrying a member of a race other than his own restricts the scope of his choice and thereby restricts the right to marry."

The court conceded the point that persons who intermarry not only incur the wrath of society themselves, but in some cases bring grief to relatives, also creating racial tensions. Such grief and tensions are products of a prejudiced society, and not of any basic wrongness of the marriage, the majority reasoned. It held that to forbid mixed marriages because of such griefs and tensions would be to give judicial sanction to the subordination of constitutional right to prejudice and the whims of society.

Nor was the majority much impressed with the argument that intermarriage is chiefly among the lower elements of society. The dissenters quoted the Rev. John La Farge, who wrote, in *The Race Question and the Negro:* "In point of facts as the Negro group becomes culturally advanced, there appears no corresponding tendency to seek intermarriage with other races." This statement was interpreted as saying that "decent Negroes don't even want intermarriage, so there must be something indecent about it."

The majority ruled, however, that there is no law prohibiting marriage among the "dregs of society" so long as both "dregs" are of the same race. Thus it ruled that no statute could exist under which the determination of "unmarriageable dregs" is made on the basis of race.

Despite its rejection by the California court, the "dregs" argument has been, and is, a popular one. It is an offshoot of a theory fashioned in the minds of super-race zealots who have set the white woman up as an inviolate goddess of society. They have perpetuated the belief that only the degraded among her ranks could ever consider marriage to a Negro. This idea has become submerged in our everyday living, and, as such, has become a part of millions of Americans who consider themselves free of racial prejudices. It is only when they see this goddess at home on the "wrong" side of the tracks that they realize that there is a final human frontier that they are yet to cross.

During the last decade there have been several marriages of prominent persons of both races which tend to belie the "dregs" theory. Some of the better-known Negro members of recent mixed marriages are actresses Lena Horne, Anne Brown, and Josephine Baker, writers Richard Wright and George Schuyler, singers Herb Jeffries and Billy Daniels, musician William Grant Still, and N.A.A.C.P. executive Walter White.

There has been enough factual basis for the "dregs" theory to permit the white-goddess complex to grow undetected by the American conscience. For decades social disapproval of intermarriage has been so strong that few but the so-called "dregs" who had no social status to lose would dare to cross the line. With what has been a visible easing of social alarm, persons of position high enough to ignore the existing, but weaker, disapproval of society also are intermarrying. It is in the middle classes of both races, where individuals are too proud to be frowned upon by society and not important and self-secure enough to be indifferent, that fewest mixed marriages occur. Even this generalization does not apply in such urban centers as New York City, where "society" is so many-sided that interracial couples can live almost undisturbed among people who approve, or at worst tolerate, their marriage.

Dunaway, like a great many Americans, had a very narrow concept of a mixed marriage: some college-bred white debutante with a craving for jazz music gets mixed up with an illiterate, horn-tooting Negro dope-peddler; or a many-degreed, cultured Negro man marries a white prostitute "just because he likes white women." The California decision, while leaving much room for future arguments, broadened the concept and looked at the true and basic issue of whether two persons of different races but of similar economic, cultural, and social status should marry if they feel so inclined. It looked, with emphasis, on the fact that no such marriage takes place unless both parties to it feel the desire. Thus it becomes a question of the freedom of two individuals, for the court rejected all the arguments that such a marriage poses any basic threat to society; it settled the case on the basis of individual liberty.

Yet, Americans who never have heard of Freud speak and act as if sex is something dearer and more basic than constitutions or judicial concepts of human liberty. They turn even to the Bible, as the New Orleans woman did, and read the twelfth chapter of Numbers. They see where God turned Miriam to a leper because she and Aaron spoke harshly of Moses after he married an Ethiopian woman, and it worries them.

"I know that I'm a Christian," said the New Orleans woman, "and I believe what the Bible says. But I read that chapter and I just sit and wonder."

I found others who at least were thinking about the issue, although the power of rationalization kept them from worrying, even about what the Bible said.

I was chatting with an official of a little tombstone-company in New Orleans, and he brought up the mixed-marriages angle of the whole race-problem. Give the Negro too much leeway and there would be a batch of mixed marriages, he said, "and God didn't never mean for colored blood and white blood to mix."

"Oh, let's don't blame all this on God," I chided him politely. "It says in the seventeenth chapter of Acts, verse 26, that 'He hath made of one blood every nation of men to dwell on all the face of the earth.' Now how can you accuse God of making any 'colored' and 'white' bloods?"

"Oh, that can't mean what it implies," he said. "You know, these translations have got the Bible all out of kilter."

I thought about all this as I sat in car 1161, in a seat the porter doubted I could get because it was too close to the white women of the South. The fact that I did get the seat and nobody screamed to be let off the train seemed to me a tiny indication that the oldest taboo of the Old South also might be weakening under the wear and tear of time and the emergence of reasoning among basically reasonable men.

CHAPTER XV

READIN', RITIN', AND REVOLUTION

In the autumn of 1948 a crisp bonfire blazed on the University of Oklahoma campus at Norman. Students whooped around the blaze to the chant of revel yells. They were not cheering a great University of Oklahoma football team. They had built a bonfire out of what copies they could find of the Fourteenth Amendment to the United States Constitution. This was their way of protesting the admission of a Negro student.

Even at that time there were signs that the protest was but a vain cry of pained disbelief. Across the campus another group of students demonstrated. Theirs was a welcome to G. W. McLaurin, a retired Negro professor and the first Negro student in the University of Oklahoma's history. According to a campus survey, the latter group more accurately expressed student opinion. Sixty per cent of the student body had voted in favor of admitting Negroes, even on an unsegregated basis. A year before, only forty per cent had favored admitting Negroes.

Something was happening at Norman. It was the same thing that was happening at schools throughout most of the South. Colleges, more than any other element of the Southland, had become caught in the turmoil of the times. Young minds, eager to learn and understand, were being swept up in the vortex of a nationwide movement for racial amity, and it had begun to appear that not even bonfires and rebel yells would be able to stall the forces of change.

But the fight was not nearly won that autumn day in 1948 —neither at Oklahoma, nor Texas, nor Louisiana, nor Ten-

229

nessee, nor a lot of places in Dixie. By that time the battle was an old one, being fought with the federal courts as the battle-ground.

By February 1951, when I reached Norman, the conflict had all but vanished, and in its aftermath I found the closest thing to a New South that I yet had seen. It had started in Little Rock, where rising optimism was engendered in the knowledge that more than one hundred Negroes are studying in the graduate center of the University of Arkansas. There were vestiges of Jim Crow: separate toilets and classes were provided for Negroes. The state could maintain this much of segregation, because Arkansas officials had been smart enough to admit Negroes before federal courts ordered them to; thus there was no court pressure to make them move faster than they considered expedient for political or other reasons.

But what had lifted my spirits from the dismal ebb caused by arguments about train tickets and having to pay for filthy sandwiches was the personal friendship that sprang up across racial lines among scores of students.

I called on Mrs. Edith Irby Jones, a medical student and the first Negro admitted to the University of Arkansas. She described herself as "just another student." A few students had congratulated her on her first day in the medical school, she said, but classes seemed a little strained. When it came time to work in laboratories, students would pair off by choice. The instructor was hesitant to group students alphabetically for fear of pairing her with an unwilling student. She was always a little nervous until one of the students said: "Mind if I work with you?" Soon the tension vanished, and now everybody works with anybody, she said.

On a desk was a pile of snapshots, some of them of white students. "Who's this?" I asked, referring to a picture of a white woman with some books.

"That's Mary Arthur White," Mrs. Jones explained. "Each morning she pulls up in front of the house in an automobile of rather doubtful running ability. She takes me to school every morning.

"During the last cold spell the car stopped on us," continued Mrs. Jones, young, attractive, and newly married to a teacher at Arkansas A.M.&N., the state school for Negroes. "Mary and I took the bus and she said to me: 'What the heck, we'll sit together,' and nobody said a word.

"We hold cram sessions together, and quite often some of the fellows (all white) join us. We used to pitch in and cook up a batch of food for those study periods."

Miss White's home is in Butterfield, Arkansas, Mrs. Jones said, and she had visited her chum's home.

I had left Minneapolis with the feeling that if a New South existed, or if there were any promise of a New South, students and former GI's would play an important role in its development. Here was some assurance that this feeling was correct, for the relationship between Mrs. Jones and Miss White was something unheard of when I left the South. There was no such thing as a Negro visiting a white person's home as a guest. Here were the builders of a dream.

Then I remembered the perennial argument about "forced" relations and how they "do more harm than good." "We did it ourselves; there wasn't no coercion involved," crowed a minor city politician when I told him what had happened in Mrs. Jones's case. That was why I decided to go to Norman. There the education controversy had been so publicized as to marshal opinion at a fever pitch on both sides; and the coercion had come from the nation's most "coercive" body—the United States Supreme Court, with the armed forces theoretically behind its orders.

I boarded a bus for Norman in Oklahoma City and sat near the rear, as the law required me to do. There were three Negro men and two Negro women on the bus. They were somewhat better dressed than most college students, and I knew that this was insurance against anyone accusing them of being filthy and undesirable as classmates. I chatted across the aisle with one who identified himself as John H. Cooper.

The bus made several stops after it left the depot. At one corner two white men got on. There were several seats up front, but they came to the rear. One white man sat beside me and the other on the long seat at the very back of the bus. I watched the driver as he glanced into the rear-view mirror. He ignored what I thought was a violation of law, and when we got off the bus and out of hearing distance of the white students I asked Cooper if segregation was the rule on the bus. It was law, he explained, but many white students were carrying on a campaign to banish segregation on buses between Oklahoma City and Norman.

"Most drivers don't care," he said, "but there are two who really raise hell. I expect a ruckus almost any day, because some of the white vets frequently tell these two drivers: 'We all fought so we could sit where we Goddam please.' Most of them budge only if the driver gets off for the cops."

These were students on the campus where the bonfires and name-calling and rebel cheers flared so vigorously two years before. The ashes of that bonfire had scattered with the winds, and so had all organized feeling against Negroes, apparently. I walked about the campus and what I saw was no different from what I had seen at the University of Minnesota. Negro and white students walked to class together, chatting as they went. They sat side by side in classes, worked side by side in laboratories. They ate together in the Student Union building.

Students and professors shook their heads and said they wondered where the initial opposition sprang from. Even to them it seemed as if it might never have been any other way. "The interracial setup seems to be completely accepted," said Professor Cameron Meyers of the school of journalism.

I had coffee in the Union with a few members of the journalism faculty. We sat and talked, not about the race problem, but about newspapers and reporting and the problems of our profession. I realized that I was able to relax in the presence

of white people for the first time in more than a month.
I joined three whites and Mrs. Ada Sipuel Fisher, the
woman who started the fight, for lunch. I listened to them talk
school talk, classroom talk, examination talk, and I realized
that the quest for knowledge and the problems of attaining it
gave them a bond far stronger than are the divisive forces set
about by pigmentation. This was it. This was the miracle of
the Southland. This *was* a New South.

> *A cultural revolution has been in operation on this
> campus in reference to the Negro question* [wrote col-
> umnist Larry Kaufman in the campus newspaper, the
> Oklahoma Daily]. *Court rulings and changes of heart in
> officialdom brought about by these rulings have since
> seen several Negroes enter* [this] *university. At first they
> were admitted grudgingly on a segregated basis. Many
> loyal, 100 per cent "my-ancestors-came-over-on-the-ship-
> after-the-Mayflower" Americans insisted that riots and the
> like would spontaneously break forth. Negroes live in
> Wilson center* [a men's dormitory], *eat in Wilson center.
> What happened to the race riots?*

Perhaps it had been a revolution to white Oklahoma,
steeped in decades of legalized segregation. But it hardly had
been a revolution to Negroes. It had taken them five years,
filled with meetings, pleadings for money and other help,
and court fights into which the N.A.A.C.P. poured thousands
of dollars, for the Oklahoma Story to get so near its climax. It
had taken five long years and there still were clean-up battles
to be fought.

It was on January 14, 1946, that Mrs. Fisher first applied for
study at the University of Oklahoma law school. There were
no law classes at the all-Negro Langston University in Langston, Oklahoma, where Mrs. Fisher had made a brilliant record
as an undergraduate. Roscoe Dunjee, aggressive editor of the
Oklahoma *Black Dispatch*, an Oklahoma City Negro news-

paper, felt that the time was ripe to do something about Jim Crow education in his state. Mrs. Fisher was the student to make the fight, he decided, and law was the field, because there could be no hiding behind a separate-but-equal argument since there were no separate facilities. Dunjee got Amos T. Hall, a Tulsa attorney, to help him push the fight.

They told Mrs. Fisher to apply, knowing that she would be rejected. It was at this point, however, that Oklahoma Negroes got their first and least-publicized break in the college controversy. Dunjee and Hall knew that the case might never get to court if Oklahoma did what many states were doing. Rather than admit that a Negro is rejected because he is a Negro, many schools still quibble about the eligibility of Negro applicants so as to keep the case from ever reaching court with race as the issue. Dunjee went to Dr. George L. Cross, University of Oklahoma president. Cross is a native Yankee, born in Woonsocket, South Dakota, and educated in South Dakota and at the University of Chicago. Dunjee had a feeling that Cross was sympathetic to Negroes fighting segregation and Jim Crow education, for Dunjee had heard reports that Cross often had been embarrassed at educators' conferences when the question of Jim Crow schools came up.

"We have no choice but to turn down Mrs. Fisher," Cross told Dunjee. "It is state law, backed by the regents. But is there anything that I can do personally?"

There was. Dunjee asked Cross to give him a letter stating that Mrs. Fisher was qualified to study law at the university in all ways except skin color. Cross provided the letter and Dunjee pushed the case into court with the issue of race clearly defined.

As expected, the case eventually was decided by the United States Supreme Court. In January 1948, that body ordered Oklahoma to provide Mrs. Fisher with equal facilities at once. The state refused to admit her to the University of Oklahoma, however. It established a Langston University law school in

Oklahoma City. A staff of three teachers was provided, and students were to have access to the state law library.

Mrs. Fisher refused to enter the school, holding that its facilities were in no way equal to those provided at the University of Oklahoma. Dunjee blasted the new institution in his editorial columns as a "Jim Crow school," and the N.A.A.C.P. took the case back to court. After a stormy session in Cleveland County District Court, Judge Justin Hinshaw ruled that the facilities were equal. The N.A.A.C.P. appealed.

By this time, G. W. McLaurin, a man in his late sixties, had moved into the dispute. Already holding a master's degree, he applied for study at the University of Oklahoma leading to a doctorate in education. McLaurin was rejected on grounds that the state still forbade Negroes and whites to attend the same school. McLaurin went to court, and federal jurists ordered the state to allow him to enter the university or to set up equal facilities immediately.

A new graduate school on the heels of setting up a law school for Negroes? This would cut deeply into the pocketbooks of Oklahomans. It was clear now that the state would pay dearly to maintain segregation in education, and there was doubt among many that any amount of money could preserve segregation. The legislature amended state law to permit Negroes to enter white state schools on a segregated basis. This applied only to courses not given at all-Negro institutions.

On October 13, 1948, McLaurin attended his first class. Newspapers told the nation that fifty-seven years of Jim Crow had ended at the University of Oklahoma. But the thing that struck most Americans was the obvious reluctance with which Oklahoma ended it. Many newspapers carried a picture of McLaurin seated in a small anteroom that had formerly been a broom closet. This was his classroom. Since it adjoined the main classroom, McLaurin could hear the lectures and take part in discussion.

Oklahoma papers watched for student reaction. They reported that white students "had only praise for the onetime Langston professor." Students called him "just another student," and after a week "nobody was ill at ease. McLaurin was participating in discussions just like the rest."

But McLaurin had a separate toilet. He had a separate library. Each was marked COLORED, but the signs never lasted long. White students told newspaper reporters that they removed the signs because "we just didn't like the distinction." The snack bar, known as The Jug, was open to white students most of the day. At noon, however, whites were barred and the snack bar was reserved exclusively for McLaurin. This segregated treatment, McLaurin charged, was a violation of his rights under the Fourteenth Amendment. He went back to Court.

State officials were confident. Certainly, they thought, if it had been legal to segregate Negroes into schools that did not approach equality, no Supreme Court would rule out segregation where facilities obviously were equal, and primarily the same.

But trouble was coming in droves now—even before the new McLaurin case could get to the Supreme Court. Regents were advised that Negroes would have to be admitted to all graduate courses not provided at Langston. Ten new courses were opened to Negroes, with the provision that separate classes, or instruction at separate hours, be installed. About seventy-five Negroes enrolled for these classes, and the problem became acute. The university started looking for ten new faculty members to teach thirty classes, some of which would consist of only one Negro student.

While university and state officials wrangled with this problem, they got more bad news. On September 14, 1949, Julius Caesar Hill, a Tulsa Negro, walked on campus, took his luggage to the men's dormitory, and asked for his room. When counselors gave him an "are-you-crazy" look, Hill showed them his receipt for advance payment on a room. Sure enough, counselors found, Hill had applied for a room and had been accepted. The application had slipped through because Hill put down "American" in the spot asking his race.

Counselors refused to honor Hill's receipt. But the regents met that afternoon and ordered President Cross to find two permanent dormitories for not less than fifty Negroes. Hill demanded immediate housing, declaring that he would not commute to Oklahoma City, even for a single day. Hill did not get housing that day. He was on campus bright and early next morning, repeating his demand for housing. He said he had stayed in Norman overnight, standing by his refusal to commute to Oklahoma City. This caused a lot of lifted eyebrows. Where had Hill stayed? Norman had an ordinance forbidding Negroes to live in the town or to remain there overnight. The university hastened to find housing for Hill.

Regents anticipated another problem. By keeping Negroes out of Norman and away from the university they had precluded the possible problem of Negro spectators at University of Oklahoma sporting events. No Oklahoma Negro had seen the University of Oklahoma football team play at home, unless some servant got a peek from under the stadium. The regents set aside a portion of the stadium for Negro students. They made no provisions for nonstudent Negro spectators, however.

It was the first of the month in race relations: the bills for segregation began to pour in. President Cross asked for $100,000 extra in state funds for additional classroom facilities. His office estimated that Negro housing would require another chunk of money.

It had become a matter of dollars and sense, and even the legislature could see it. Mrs. Fisher was likely to win her court fight for entry into the law school sooner or later, and it was poor judgment to pour money into the Negro law school, which had only one student and stood a good chance of being closed by court order. The legislature cut off funds, and the Negro law school was to end on June 30, 1949. On that date Mrs. Fisher would have to be admitted to Oklahoma's white university. She sought to register in early June, noting that the registration deadline at the University of Oklahoma was two weeks prior to the closing date for the Negro law school. The regents again rejected her application, declaring that a separate school would exist until June 30 and that she was not eligible for admittance to the white school until July 1. Cross ignored this ruling, however, and admitted Mrs. Fisher two weeks early so she would not have to wait until fall to start work.

Negro enrollment continued to rise and school administration problems seemed never to cease. On October 28, 1949, that old bugaboo of social equality reared its head. A Negro couple petitioned the dean of students for permission to attend the homecoming dance. Lionel Hampton's Negro band was to play. Lyle Griffis, commander of the campus American Legion club, said Negroes could attend but they could not dance. An area to accommodate about fifteen Negro spectators was roped off. Word spread fast, however, that white students would ask Negroes to dance. Newspapers had reporters stationed at the dance, but a tense situation was averted because Negroes ignored the dance.

The problem of separate classroom facilities still had not been solved. There was indecision as to what constituted separate classes, and the attorney general's office persisted in passing the buck to school officials, not wanting to be blamed for a decision that would cost taxpayers more money. Finally, Negroes were assigned specific rows in classrooms. Signs were put on these rows, but each day the signs were gone. White students were destroying them. University officials have admitted that it cost more than $5,000 to replace these signs.

This was the only outward sentiment shown toward Negroes now. The anti-Negro displays had ended. Like columnist Kaufman, I wondered what had happened to the predicted riots. One professor, himself a native Georgian, told me what he thought was the answer:

"It all is a matter of association. There were plenty of students here who thought they opposed the entry of Negroes.

They had associated with no Negroes. They swore that they would leave school if the color line was broken. We had parents visit the campus and say that they would remove their children if Negroes were admitted. Negroes are here, and so are the whites who threatened to leave. What happened? They simply got used to Negroes before they could muster up a protest, or courage enough to go home.

"To me that proves that the people of the South respect law. There are those who shout that all the army's bayonets will not make them give up segregation. The final test always shows that the people of the South are neither so belligerent nor so lawless as their past blind following of custom would indicate."

This same viewpoint was expressed by Leif Olsen, editor of the student newspaper. I reminded him that the issue had been dragged out in the courts for five years, which indicated considerable resistance from somewhere.

"As you can see, it wasn't the students," explained Olsen. "The old heads—regents and legislators—were the real s.o.b.'s. Besides tearing down Jim Crow signs, students ignored them wherever they found them. They made a point of eating with Negroes at tables in the Student Union that supposedly were forbidden to white persons. When Mrs. Fisher finally was admitted to the law school she got a rousing welcome from two hundred white students who met her at the train."

Then came June 5, 1950, when the United States Supreme Court solved a lot of the problems that had piled up. It ruled out the separate toilets, eating-places, classes, classrooms, and housing, declaring that Oklahoma could not segregate in any manner the Negroes it admits to its white colleges. In a unanimous opinion, the court declared unconstitutional the Oklahoma law that set McLaurin apart from white students. This modified segregation, the court held, violated the Fourteenth Amendment, which bans any difference in treatment by the state based on race. Once a Negro is admitted, the court ruled, he must receive the "same treatment at the hands of the state as students of other races."

This was the broadest and most penetrating ruling ever issued in this country on segregation. The court acknowledged that McLaurin had use of the same classroom, library, and cafeteria as other students, and it added that there was no indication that the seats to which he was assigned in those rooms had any disadvantage of location. But it noted that McLaurin could wait in line in the cafeteria and stand and talk with fellow students, but he "must remain apart while he eats." This signified, said the court, "that the state . . . sets McLaurin apart from other students." This was found to "inhibit his ability to study, to engage in discussions and exchange views with other students, and, in general, to learn his profession.

"Our society has grown increasingly complex, and our need for trained leaders increases correspondingly," the court continued. It added that McLaurin's case "represents perhaps the epitome of that need for he is attempting to obtain an advanced degree in education, to become, by definition, a leader and trainer of others. . . . Those who will come under his guidance and influence must be directly affected by the education he receives. Their own education and development necessarily suffer to the extent that his training is unequal to that of his classmates. State-imposed restrictions, which produce such inequities, cannot be sustained."

The court considered the argument that students would set McLaurin apart if the law were ruled unconstitutional. Jurists called this "irrelevant." The court said there is "a vast difference—a constitutional difference" between restrictions imposed by a state prohibiting the commingling of students" and any refusal of individual students to commingle. "The removal of the state restrictions will not necessarily abate individual and group predilections, prejudices and choices," said the court, "but at the very least, the state will not be depriving appellant of the opportunity to secure acceptance by his fellow students on his own merits."

That was that. On the very same day—June 5, 1950—the same court ended another long dispute by ordering the Univer-

sity of Texas to open its all-white law school to Herman
Marion Sweatt. It did. And what happened afterwards at the
University of Texas is much the same as what happened at
the University of Oklahoma. Almost everybody adjusted and
the riots never occurred.

Now more than one thousand Negroes are studying in the
colleges and universities of seventeen Southern states. What responsible educators said, five years before, could be done only
with grave consequences had come to pass without bloodshed
and with ultimate general satisfaction.

Across the South, administrators of white schools now survey
their institutional practices in the light of the educational
renaissance. Some have said: "Let's face it—we must open up."
Others, bullheaded and dogmatic, still hide behind cries of
damyankee meddling and threats of blood in the streets.

In October 1950, Dr. M. D. Collins, state superintendent of
Georgia schools, warned that admission of Negroes to schools
in his state would have "more serious repercussions than you
could possibly imagine; it would be tragic."

Less bullying was Dr. J. M. Tubb, Mississippi's superintendent of education. The breakdown of segregation, he said, would
only "retard the fine progress we are now making in the
field of education." Similarly, Dr. A. R. Meadows, Alabama
superintendent, said admittance of Negroes to white institutions would set education back many years.

Notwithstanding the continued and stronger existence of
the same forces that pried open the universities of other Southern states, Dr. Perry B. James, president of Athens College,
Athens, Georgia, was adamant:

"I do not foresee any possible chance of admitting Negroes
to [Georgia] colleges and universities in the near future and
the sooner we realize this, both regionally and nationally, and
begin providing schools to meet the needs of the Negroes, the
better off they will be and the quicker we will arrive at a
sound solution to this problem."

Negroes had heard that one before: "separate but equal."

They immediately began a drive to end segregation in Georgia's schools. They could look at what happened in Norman with the feeling that there lies the only sound solution, notwithstanding Georgia's threat to close down the public and state school systems if segregation is ruled out anywhere along the line.

But the millennium has not quite arrived in Norman. There is at Langston a university for Negroes, equal in almost no way to the University of Oklahoma. Negroes still must go to Langston for courses given there. Many are reluctant to do so, as was Mrs. Fisher to attend the all-Negro law school. Negroes—and Oklahoma officials—know that once the N.A.A.C.P. has ended its fight on graduate schools, the point of issue will be undergraduate schools. The Clarendon County, South Carolina, lawsuit challenging segregation in public schools is an indication that the attack on undergraduate colleges will come from both higher and lower levels.

Oklahoma apparently foresaw this, even before the final McLaurin decision. State officials called the June 5 ruling "a victory for the attorney general's office" because the court did not declare, absolutely, that the principle of segregation is in violation of the Constitution.

Fred Hansen, assistant Oklahoma attorney general, filed a brief in the McLaurin case that, in effect, warned the court not to rule out the separate-but-equal provision. He said:

> It would mean abandoning of many of the state's existing educational establishments; crowding of other such establishments, and in preventing practically all of the approximately 1,600 Negro school teachers now employed in separate schools and colleges of Oklahoma from hereafter securing employment in schools and colleges of the state.

This is more than a warning to the courts. It is a warning to Negro teachers, many of whom already are fighting, either outwardly or covertly, to preserve the Jim Crow system. With no view for, or trust in, the long run, Negro teachers of the South, and many other Negroes with vested interests in a dual system of life, make it clear that they do not intend to fight for changes that will relieve them of their jobs. So in Oklahoma and elsewhere future battles to end segregation in education will be fought cautiously, opposed from many sides.

"But the fight will go on," said Jesse Tarver, an undergraduate in the University of Oklahoma school of pharmacy. "It has to go on. Education has to be equalized all along the line to erase the handicap of going to inferior public schools and then being allowed to go to a white college. Your early poor training shows in a lot of ways."

Tarver sat midway in the Norman city bus and I sat beside him. White students sat on the back seat. One white student sat with a Negro. I asked Tarver how he could explain what I saw in a town that forbade Negroes to stay overnight.

"Since they had no Negro residents they didn't need a segregation ordinance," he said. "Suddenly we're here. Many white students have vowed to see that segregation never becomes policy on city busses."

I asked a young white woman from Bartlesville, who was a leader in the fight for Negro equality, what motivated her actions.

"My home town is narrow and my family is narrow," she said with almost no emotion. "Naturally, when I got here I was narrow. Some of the students and professors influenced me greatly, as did some of the books I've read. Now I feel a little ashamed of some of the things I've said and done. I feel I owe civilization a little something."

She paused for a few seconds, cocking her head to one side and staring into space. "There is one thing that worries me," she confessed. "Can we students keep our scruples. We can afford to have our ideals now; we are under no economic pressure. There may be pressure from parents, but there isn't the social pressure in a college community that you feel once you move out into a job or family life.

"What has happened here has done things to a lot of us, but I wonder . . . I wonder if we believe in it enough to beat off the pressures that are sure to come."

CHAPTER XVI

DIGNITY AND GOLD CARS

I SAT alone on the side of my bed in the all-Negro Little-page Hotel in Oklahoma City. I looked out the window at deepening twilight, watching a light wind whip paper bags and dust down the street. I felt a sort of mental tiredness, a fatigue of the soul that came from probing into the mores of the South for more than a month.

I looked at my suitcase, scarred by travel and rough handling, loaded with assorted railroad and airline tags and gayly colored redcap tickets. There was tangible evidence that I had covered several thousand miles of the Southland. There was evidence that I had crossed the fading boundary of the Old South and now sat at the gateway to the great Southwest and West. Then I realized that I had much more than the suitcase to remind me of the old and new paths that I had cut through Dixie. I had the fresh jubilation provided by students and teachers in Norman, the optimism regenerated by an unsegregated ride through Georgia, the buoyant hope engendered in the oaths of a vast number of whites who swore allegiance to a new social and economic order.

As I sat on the side of the bed, watching the street light's amber glow reach out into the spreading darkness, inner conflict, of which I had seen so much, seized me. I argued with myself that the new optimism far outweighed the unpleasantries in Macon, Washington, New Orleans, or the rebuffs encountered at regular intervals.

During this self-debate I hurried to a taxi and the train for Kansas City, Missouri. I had decided, all of a sudden, that I had seen enough. I was ready to leave the South. There was

245

one more train leaving for Kansas City that night, on the Missouri-Kansas-Texas line, and I decided to take it.

Upon arrival at the station I learned that the train was a local. I saw that it had no Pullman car and only two coaches. All Kansas City passengers would have to change at Parsons, Kansas. Although disappointed, I decided to take the train. I bought my ticket at the window in the waiting-room for Negroes, being in no mood for outer conflict. I was patient when the agent expressed reluctance to take my traveler's check. I realized then that the South had almost won. I had grown weary of determining "my place," and then deliberately seeing if I could stretch the color line. I had almost reached the point of buckling under to the conditioning process, of doing "as the Romans do," and abandoning the role of a crusader.

When I boarded the train all this changed. I became a Negro with a chip on my shoulder. The coach nearest the engine had seats with immovable, one-piece backs. It was an old, uncomfortable car. White headpieces on the seat were not quite filthy, but they obviously were soiled. The other coach had individual reclining seats. It obviously was cleaner and more comfortable.

"I don't know if they segregate on this train, but this is one night Rowan won't be Jim Crowed," I thought. Determined, I took a seat in the coach with reclining chairs. Before I got the seat warm the conductor stood in front of me.

"The Kansas City car is up front," said the fragile-looking, frowning man, who appeared to be in his sixties.

"Oh, they're both Kansas City cars—everybody changes in Parsons," I said, as if to inform him.

He paused briefly, then added: "Well, the colored car is up front."

"There isn't any *colored* car now, either," I said, looking directly at him for the first time. I cited a case decided about two weeks before in Richmond, Virginia, where the circuit court of appeals ruled that segregation of interstate passengers is illegal in coaches as well as in diners and Pullman cars.

"Well, I want you to move to the other car. That law applies only to coaches coming into Oklahoma," he said.

"I'm very happy here," I replied, noticing that about fifteen white people were now in my coach. There were about eleven men and four women. They sat silent, apparently interested in how the conductor and I would resolve our controversy. The thought that some of the men in the car might intervene on the side of the conductor made me uneasy. I could see the door of the other car and knew that only four Negroes had entered it. I knew that numbers and tradition were overwhelmingly against me; but for the first time I had law on my side. I resolved to show no timidity, to stand firm to the point where it appeared I might get my brains beaten out, and only then would I yield. I turned my face to the window and looked out as if to tell the conductor that I was ignoring him, that I had heard all I wanted to hear about Jim Crow.

"A guy said he wouldn't move the other night," snapped the conductor, everything about his face red except where the cheekbones protruded. "Well, when I got the police he moved."

"Don't get me wrong," I answered. "I didn't say I *wouldn't* move. I said not of my own will. If you get the police I'll probably move, too; but somebody will pay. Your railroad will be sued; you will be sued; and the whole United States government will know about it."

That was supposed to be the double dare. I knew that railroads had paid out so much money in lawsuits involving Jim Crow within the last decade that they were becoming punch-drunk. I knew, also, that the mention of the United States government would give the conductor the idea that he was fooling with somebody important. I reached for my briefcase and began writing what actually were notes for an article based on the experience. The act also was designed to accentuate the "very important person" hint.

The conductor watched silently for a few seconds, then asked: "You a government man?"

"I am not at liberty to disclose what I do," I said, resorting to the line that had been so successful in New Orleans. The conductor mumbled some unintelligible words and stalked off the train, across the tracks, and into a building adjacent to the depot.

I laughed a false laugh and mumbled to myself that I sure as the devil *wasn't* at liberty to disclose what I was doing. The last thing I wanted revealed was that I was a reporter for a "meddlin' damyankee" newspaper.

I became more nervous with each second. I checked my watch and saw that it was nearly twenty minutes before the train was to leave. I scolded myself for rushing to the depot, for not waiting until the train was about to depart before boarding. I continued to write notes, going about it in what I thought would appear to be a most secretive and governmental manner. A white man walked to the men's room, just to see what I was doing, I was sure.

I saw the conductor returning with a tall fat man who wore a brown suit. They conferred outside the car, mumbling in soft tones. Then the conductor blurted: "Give him a Goddam gold car of his own and he still wouldn't want to move into it!"

The policeman strode in rapidly, almost catching me off guard, straining to hear what they were saying.

"Say, fellow, I'm a policeman. The conductor says you refused to move when he ordered you to."

I was angrier than I had been throughout the trip. I sat silent for a few seconds as I reached into my pocket for my ticket. I answered by holding it up toward a pudgy face on which my eyes hardly would focus because of my anger, and adding: "This says Oklahoma City, Oklahoma, to Kansas City, Missouri. That's crossing two state lines. This train goes to Parsons, Kansas, and that's crossing one state line. Under the circumstances, the law says I can ride where I please."

"Show me some credentials," he demanded.

"You show me some credentials."

"Boy, I said I'm a policeman."

"I don't care what you say. I see nothing to indicate that you're a policeman."

I could tell by his taken-aback look that I had my bluff in. My unexpected show of law knowledge and nerve had caught him unprepared. He presented a card identifying himself as "Floyd Parks, peace officer."

"I see—now, what credentials do you want to see, Mr. Parks?" I said, with overdone politeness.

"The conductor says you work for the government—probably the post office," he explained.

"I am not at liberty to disclose what I do, but I don't work for the post office. If you want my name here it is." I handed him my naval reserve card.

He studied the card as if to read it—in fact, much too closely for my comfort. "You a secret Navy agent?" he asked.

"Sir, I am not at liberty . . ." I ripped through that mysterious, noncommittal answer again, hoping that it was as suggestive as I wanted it to be.

"Well, fellow, I just wanted to make sure there would be no trouble," Parks said in softer tones. He handed me my Navy card.

"Trouble? I'm a peaceful guy," I retorted. "And I'll move if you and the conductor will sign a statement saying that I was moved by you at the conductor's insistence." Already I was writing a statement to that effect.

The conductor had remained on the platform between the two cars. Parks returned to confer with him. After a whispered few words they stepped to the ground and talked for a few minutes. I felt that I was winning, but still was quite concerned. I watched Parks lift his arms, palms up, as if to tell the conductor there was nothing he could do. Then Parks walked away. Neither he nor the conductor said another word to me. I kept my seat as far as Parsons, where we changed trains, none of which are segregated in Kansas.

Just after we left Oklahoma City the conductor entered our

car to take up tickets. He had lost face, and it showed all over him. This man obviously had lived and guarded some six decades of segregation. Aboard the train he always had been "captain of the ship," with his word law for any Negro passenger. Suddenly, all this had ended, and it had ended in the most crushing of ways: before other whites who, I was sure the conductor felt, now could only look down on him. I held my ticket out as the conductor passed, but he refused to take it. He would let me ride free, but he would not be a party to the ending of segregation. I smiled and stuck my ticket in the top of the seat beside mine. When he walked back up the aisle he paused behind my seat. He reached over and punched my ticket, never touching it.

My anger, tempered with laughter, faded rapidly. I continued to write my report of the incident for the *Tribune*, never ceasing to make my writing look "official," however. The conductor glanced at me writing, and walked to the end of the car, where he turned out the lights. Perhaps by this time I had become supersensitive, for I felt that his turning out the lights was a deliberate little bit of revenge. Again I laughed, not aloud.

I sat, still a bit nervous, and chilly as I realized that I had perspired rather freely during the argument. I turned over in my mind the highlights of my journey: McMinnville—good little Southern town, as we used to call it. I knew that I could never live there again. Never. And the people I grew up with would hate me for saying as much—that is, the people who never got out of McMinnville, or the South, to taste anything better. I thought of how touchy they were of criticism about the way they live, and how they grope for ways of proving that nothing significantly better exists in the North.

"When them white reporters gives a party, I bet they don't ask you and your wife," a former football teammate said to me.

I remembered how deliberately I chose words for my answer. I wanted so much to be convincing. "Most do, a few don't," I replied. "Even when some don't I never think that it is because I am a Negro. I feel that it is because I am not the kind of guy who appeals to them, for reasons other than my race. But most of them do ask us. We go to their houses, they come to ours. We go to the somewhat formal parties where everybody stands erect and holds his liquor with two fingers, and we go to some where everybody takes his shoes off and sits in the floor with his beer."

I got only the stares of the incredulous, and a story from a friend who expressed his disbelief by telling me about a friend of his who went to Chicago. "He went to this bar and ordered a Coke. They served him, but they charged him seven dollars for it, just to say they didn't want him there. This talk about the good old North is a whole lot of hooey."

I thought of Washington, and how easy it was to view the Capital as a hopeless symbol of man's inhumanity to himself and to his brother. I thought that if I had my choice of the place where Jim Crow and all its concomitants were to be erased, my first choice would be Washington.

And I thought of Charleston, and a man called Waring, and the cross of ostracism to which they nailed him, and the dissent he wrote, which could be the salvation of little black school-children with undernourished minds in tumbledown shacks all over the South.

I thought of a night train through Georgia, and bewilderment in Laurel, and the misfortunes of an American in New Orleans. And I thought of a University of Oklahoma white woman worrying about retaining her scruples about the treatment of other human beings outside school.

I asked myself what I had found in six thousand miles of the Southland. I asked myself what I really had been looking for. Then I remembered the remark by the conductor: "Give him a Goddam gold car of his own and he still wouldn't want to move into it!"

In his way the conductor had answered my question. Or he had made me see the answer, because he had posed one of the *big* questions in race relations: What does the Negro want? I

knew that the answer to this question embodies everything that
I had sought in a New South, everything that had eluded me
during five weeks of activity that kept my nerves and emotions
in jangled uncertainty.

There is no single answer to the question of what the Negro
wants. I had seen vividly during my journey that on almost
no issue is Negro opinion so solid as some Negro "political
bosses" would have their political bosses believe. Negroes'
views are determined by economic status, education, place of
residence, religion, and all the other factors that influence the
opinions of other Americans.

Amid the shanties of scores of towns I had heard near-
impoverished Negroes say: "I don't want social equality. What
I want is opportunity—food, clothing, and shelter for my
family. I want my children to live better than I did." This
poorest-of-all Negro means it. Economic security is the current
limit of his goal. He honestly has no designs on the white
man's living-room—or his daughter.

I heard something different from "middle-class" Negroes
who have reached the poorer class's goal of basic economic
security. This middle-class Negro wants economic equality—
the same pay for the same work, the same job for the same ability, the same promotion for the same industriousness and effec-
tiveness. This Negro has begun to taste freedom, and he longs
for more of it. That is why, in America, the Negro crying loud-
est about racial injustices quite often is not the trampled-
down individual white Americans think he ought to be to
shout so loudly. Men become addicted to freedom, and the
fuller their veins become of it the greater becomes their need
for it. That is why men fight and die for it—yes, even men who
have tasted but little of it. That is the reason for the Paul
Robesons who curse the freedom from which they gained so
much: the more we taste of the sweetness of democracy, the
more impatient we become for the whole fruit. Weak men
addicted to the drug of freedom lose themselves and their
power of reason in the agony of being without it.

That is why the middle-class Negro, in possession of the basic necessities of living, will demand economic equality. And he will demand political equality—the right to vote, representation for taxation.

Social equality? In public the middle-class Negro probably will say that he doesn't want it. In private he may admit that he does. In each case he means that he has no burning desire to visit the country club or to have dinner with his firm's board chairman. But it is an economic, not racial, barrier to which he yields.

Negroes in the top economic, educational, and cultural brackets want something else. They have reached the latter two goals and, since man must always aspire, they look ahead. Such a Negro may say that he does or does not want social equality. Usually he is being expedient, and always he means this: "If social equality is sitting at the dinner table of white friends who invite me there, I want the right to be there. If it means living in a neighborhood in my economic bracket, although it be a predominantly white area, I want the right to be there. If it means worshipping God without worrying about the color of the person kneeling beside me, I want the right to do that."

In short, this Negro refuses to recognize any racial barrier, whether imposed by tradition or statute. If a white man chooses not to ask him to dinner, so what? That is an individual predilection, and there are Negroes who do not choose to ask him to dinner. Personal preference, for whatever reason, he honors; but other individuals must be left free to associate with him as they see fit.

I weighed these thoughts against the conductor's remark, and I knew that all these goals had a central core: *dignity*. An illiterate Negro in a hovel can achieve a measure of dignity by seeing his children clothed, fed, and sheltered. A middle-class Negro achieves a standard of dignity by seeing his labors and talents well rewarded, by knowing that he is a part of his government and his community. The elite, highbrow Negro achieves dignity when he realizes that he can climb the highest hill in the land and be seen as an American capable of scaling the heights, and not as a Negro—who has reached an unusual level for a Negro.

I knew that the conductor was right. Had the Jim Crow car been gold I would not have wanted to move there. Apparently no white passenger minded my riding in the same car; even if he had, I felt, his was the freedom to go elsewhere. I was not protecting my back from a stiff, immovable seat, or my head from a soiled headpiece. I was protecting my dignity.

As my train hurtled through the night that seemed so eternal, out of a land where it seemed I had lived two lifetimes, I wanted America's Noah Brannons to know that a green youngster from a country town in middle Tennessee had returned to his native Southland, looking for a simple little thing called dignity. Then I wanted them to think about the word and realize that it is neither a simple nor a little thing. I wanted them to realize that dignity has become, and must remain, an extremely important American word. In explaining the why and wherefore of World War II to Brazilians in 1947, General George C. Marshall said:

"We fought for the dignity of the individual."

CHAPTER XVII

NO HIDIN' PLACE

To cross the Mason-Dixon line going North is never quite the same as going South. Not if you are a Negro. There is not much difference in tangible things that we write down in a ledger. No things like laws that give the northbound traveler sudden freedom. No rights that are inviolate and may no longer be taken away. No, these are not the things that mark the magic boundary that supposedly separates two ways of life. The difference is in the mind and spirit and nerves. It is the dissolving of tension. The depressing feeling of living with *all* the odds against you begins to let up. The fear of physical harm lessens. Militancy becomes less synonymous with foolhardiness. You begin to feel that you can "talk back."

That is what I thought when I got off my train in Kansas City. This, I told myself, is the difference between Kansas City and Knoxville, St. Louis and Savannah, Louisville and Little Rock. But I knew that the difference is neither so great nor so glaring as night unto day. Only the conditioned Negro mind, sensitive to the lesser subtleties of human affairs, can measure this change. This same Negro mind knows that the step across the boundary really is a barely discernible transition from flagrant displays of bigotry to the more subtle, surreptitious variety of prejudices. You begin to realize that you have found freedom only because freedom is a relative thing.

I was hungry when I reached Kansas City. I knew that the Fred Harvey restaurant at the train station was one of the few places in the city that would serve patrons of any race.

"They don't bar anyone there," I had been told, "but they'll Jim Crow you graciously if you allow it."

255

I stood at the restaurant entrance for several minutes. Each time a Negro entered, the hostess met him with a broad smile. She led each Negro to a rear table where the employees eat on changing shifts. That was what I had been told would happen. I walked in and she smiled at me, asking: "One, sir?"

I nodded, yes, and she asked me to follow her. I followed a few steps behind until it was obvious that she was taking me to the rear table. I stopped and sat at the counter near the front. She took several steps before realizing that I no longer was following her. She turned, and this time I smiled graciously. She did not bother to give me a menu, as she had done for other patrons. My waitress was very courteous, however. Probably only the hostess and I realized that another small battle was being fought in a sort of cold war of the races.

It continued in St. Louis, where I got caught downtown in a snowstorm. I didn't know which streetcar to take to my hotel. I stood on a corner for fifty-five minutes and watched white taxi-drivers go a few feet past me to pick up a white fare. Finally a Negro cab-driver picked me up.

I knew that what happened to me was important primarily because it was multiplied in our land a hundred thousand times daily in a thousand cities and towns. Sure, St. Louis has her reputation for subtlety. I recalled the swimming-pool riots of nearly two years before, when policemen were sent to guard pools and lockers after the courts ruled that all pools had to be opened to Negroes and whites alike. The city then set aside separate days on which girls and boys could swim. On several occasions, Negro girls would return to lockers that they locked before going swimming. When they opened their lockers black cats would jump out. This occurred despite the fact that policemen were guarding the entrances, locker-room custodians were in the room, and the lockers had to be opened by someone. Here was a subtle official protest to Negroes swimming there.

But St. Louis was not alone then, and it is not alone now. America's Noah Brannons would have to realize that. They would have to see that *virus prejudice* is in the national bloodstream, and that "doctoring" promises a cure only when men in the farthest, biggest cities and the nearest, smallest hamlets become "doctors." I had seen hope for this even in the Deep South, and that hope existed in St. Louis. The pools were open, and a generation of subtleties would never change that. This was another of the chinks in old racial armor which I had seen so much of in the South of 1951. True, I had not found a "New South," for I had found too few new ideas in the minds of the South. Only among a courageous few of a passing generation, and among wisdom-seeking youth who stand to control a coming generation, had I found an admission that racism has been the Southland's mental illness, her epidemic. I had begun to have a glimmering of hope that an increasing number of the people were quietly desirous of a cure.

Despite this hope, I knew that I was leaving the South, land of my birth and childhood, never to return. And as I looked at the hundreds of Negroes milling about the train stations of cities along the boundary, I knew that I was not alone. Thousands of other Negroes were, and are, leaving the South.

Even as far South as Birmingham I had walked into the waiting-room to buy my ticket to Montgomery, where I stopped briefly en route to Laurel, and the room was crowded with Negroes. I was concerned about whether there would be enough seats aboard the train to Montgomery.

"Don't worry about the crowd," the agent said as he handed me my ticket. "They're all going north."

So it is in scores of cities. Negroes with an eye to the promised land of the West and the industry of Northern cities are flocking out of peanut patches and cotton fields and off the overworked land of tenant farms.

I looked at the throng in St. Louis: old men with gray hair and bent backs, the productive days of their lives already spent; young women with babes in arms, clothes in shopping-bags, pasteboard suitcases held together with twine, spirits held together by the promise in a letter from a relative reporting that

white families of the North pay twenty dollars a week for a
cook; young men with no luggage, no change of clothes—just a
cheap new suit on their backs and a few saved dollars in their
pockets, chasing down the report that Detroit needs men to
build tanks to defend democracy.

These, I felt, were twentieth-century pilgrims, many of
whom would find no Plymouth Rock north of the Mason-
Dixon line. But their departure made them happy in the
sense that a daydreamer is happy; and it made the white
South happy, for the white South long has argued that the
excessive number of Negroes in Dixie accounts for the racial
conflict. It is easy to extend democratic privileges to a few,
but it is impractical for a large number, I was told several times.
The speaker always made it clear by either implication or
plain statement that "you end up with Negroes bossing whites,
when there are too many Negroes with white man's rights."
So this migration, which reached an almost staggering rate
during World War II, is supposed to be the cure-all. The white
South forgets, however, that the Negroes who leave are those
with a spirit of venture, with "get up and go." Because of this
loss in men with the initiative and self-confidence needed to
pick up everything about their set lives and stumble into a
strange, fast, new environment, the South will suffer in the
long run. But the South cannot be expected to realize this
until it concedes that no society prospers, or even survives,
unless each of its members is producing to the limit of his
capability. For many reasons, the Negro never has been
allowed to contribute his utmost to society, either in the North
or South.

I knew what would happen to these modern pilgrims, venturing into a North to which I returned not because I could
praise it and profess an honest love for it; not because I felt that
it was steeped in the tradition of human equality; but because
I was choosing the lesser of two evils. To put it positively,
I was returning North because I knew that it held a brighter
immediate future for me—one those pilgrims hoped it would

hold for them. After all, there had been enough opportunity-channels open in the North for a barefoot boy who daydreamed at the food of the Cumberland Mountains, with nothing but daydreams in view, to be working for a daily metropolitan newspaper less than a decade later.

But this had not blinded me to the evils of the North, and I knew that because of these evils many of these pilgrims would not be so lucky as I had been. Some would get caught in the undertow of big-city brutality—brutality that I had seen in many forms and had learned to despise. Others would find themselves too accustomed to the paternalism of the South and thus grossly unprepared for the hard knocks of a dog-eat-dog society, especially when that society is ridden with moral dishonesty and racial subterfuge.

As I watched these migrants in Kansas City, St. Louis, and Cincinnati, I realized that although I was leaving the South my report to America's Noah Brannons had not ended, for part of the story of what it means to be a Negro is in the minds and souls of citizens across the nation—in the doings of the people of the state and city that I had left to begin my report.

I remembered a November night in 1948, my first on the job at the *Tribune,* when two white reporters asked me to have dinner with them at the Commerce Club. We went there and sat for several minutes, but no waitress came. Finally one of my companions went to the manager and asked why we were getting no service.

"They've stopped serving meals," was the message my companion brought back. We looked about us and saw waitresses serving meals to other patrons. We walked out and I asked my companion for the truth, a truth that I would not find shocking, for I had faced it scores of times by then: "It was because of me that they wouldn't serve us, wasn't it?" He replied that it was. We went to another restaurant and ate without unpleasantness.

Even with the Commerce Club I had a recourse: I could have sued, for a Minnesota law makes it mandatory that individuals be served in such public places without regard to race, creed, and the like. But the first day on the job was no time to get involved in a racial controversy, I decided, so I let the matter drop. My two companions did not, however. Without ever mentioning it to me, they spread the word among fellow workers, many of whom ceased to patronize the Commerce Club. Those who didn't stop were forced to, a few days later, when the Commerce Club burned down. Strangely enough, a new policy apparently went up with the new building, for I have visited the Commerce Club several times since and have received service, sometimes with a smile.

Racism of the poorly concealed variety comes in many forms in the North, I remembered, and it is only a vigilant few who prevent the disease from spreading. It is common knowledge among Minneapolis Negroes, and a considerable number of whites, that Negroes are far from welcome in Charlie's Café Exceptionale, and that Negroes must be served in a private room or, with only the rarest of exceptions, not at all.

One day I was asked to lunch with a few white friends. We called Charlie's for a reservation, and were informed that they didn't reserve tables for lunch, but that there was plenty of room. On our way to the café we discussed its racial policy and decided that two Negro members of our party should go in first. We did, and I asked for a table, informing the headwaiter that two others would join us later.

"There are no tables available. You may have a private room," he said.

"What do you mean, no tables?" I asked.

"All reserved," he said.

"But we were just informed a few minutes ago that you don't reserve tables for lunch."

"Must have been a mistake. You can have a private room," he replied.

I rejected the private room and stepped toward the door so my white friends would know to come in. They passed by as if they never had seen me before, and asked the waiter for a table.

"Oh, yes, your reserved table . . ." said the waiter, leading them into the dining-room.

"What do you mean, reserved table?" asked the white couple. "Why is it you have a table for us but didn't for our Negro friends?"

The half-startled, half-angered waiter suddenly decided that he was mistaken about who they were. He thought they were another couple with a reserved table. They, too, would have to use a private room. We all walked out and went to another place where the food was no less tasty and the atmosphere, if not quite so ritzy, was less expensive.

The practice at Charlie's is no secret, not even among official Minneapolis. When Senator Humphrey was mayor of Minneapolis he became angered by reports of this policy and asked William Seabron, a Negro social worker, to have lunch with him. They went to Charlie's.

"I'll have my regular table," Humphrey said to the head-waiter, not even waiting to see if he would try the private-room story, and he and Seabron walked into the dining-room. That was the first, and last, known time that a Negro has eaten at Charlie's without being ushered into a private room.

This happens, not in Mississippi, but in Minnesota, at the top of the nation, as far as an American of any color can get from the Mason-Dixon line. And it is part of my report. It is more important, as a part of this final report to all Americans, because of the way citizens of the upper Midwest reacted to the report, as run in the Minneapolis *Tribune*.

Reaction was overwhelmingly favorable—far more favorable than I had dreamed it might be. Less than an hour after the first edition carrying the first article was on the streets, a parking-lot operator called to let me know that he was "on you people's side." I could use his parking-lot without charge as long as I lived and was able to own a car, he said. There were hundreds of letters to the paper, more than five hundred to me personally. "Shame, shame on our nation," cried the vast majority of them. There were pages of sympathy, and some two hundred promises that the writer or caller would "pray for you and your people." I was mailed the cross of a Catholic order by a woman who said God is on the side of the Negro and eventually justice must win out. Transplanted Southerners—an architect, a Bible-school student, a truck-driver, a housewife—called to say that I had written the truth. One such Southerner, a woman who works behind the bar at a tavern near the *Tribune,* told reporters: "Only two people ever told the truth about the South. That's that colored reporter for the *Tribune,* and Erskine Caldwell."

To me that was unwelcome praise, for in that remark was the significance in the way Minnesota, Iowa, Wisconsin, and North and South Dakota residents had responded to the articles. To them I had simply written the "truth about the South." Naturally, some of these residents objected to the articles, a few with bitterness and for many reasons. A North Dakota chain-grocery-store manager said nobody ever would convince him that Negroes do not stink, and he would always favor segregation of the races. A South Dakotan called me "a left-wing Democrat, trying to embarrass the Republicans." A Minneapolis Negro said I was "playing footsie with a Republican newspaper in a plot to embarrass the Democrats." Two weekly Minnesota newspapers figured it all was a scheme to promote passage of a fair-employment-practices-commission bill that was to come up before the Minnesota legislature. But above the muddle of conflicting criticisms stood a throng of indignant citizens, crying that the South "still is fighting the Civil War." They felt nobly democratic in contrast to the Georgia about which I had written. They could praise the report as "the truth about the South."

So there arose the same kind of righteous indignation that swept across the nation when hoodlumism erupted into law-defying violence in Cicero, Illinois, or when an American who gave his life in defense of his country was denied burial in a Sioux City, Iowa, cemetery because he happened to be an Indian—an American Indian. These indignant ones were the people who asked me for speeches, who wanted to know more about the indignities suffered by an American Negro who returned to his native land.

As I had feared, only a very few viewed my report as part of a shadow cast by their own lives. As I moved about the state, in the wake of my report to a sailor whom I remembered although I had lost all contact with him, I had to remind Minnesotans that although Noah Brannon was a real, living man, to me he had become but a symbol. A symbol not of Texans who dislike Negroes out of ignorance, or of prejudiced people south of the Mason-Dixon line, but of Americans everywhere whose tainted souls and thoughts and acts put our whole nation south of freedom. I reminded them that a decade earlier a Negro lad had leaned against the bank building in his Tennessee home town, dressed in an overcoat so close to tattered that his classmates named it "Strings." This lad had waited for the men who guarded the gates of opportunity to let him pass through. A decade later, when this same Negro sits at a desk a thousand miles away in a shiny newspaper building in downtown Minneapolis, he has escaped "Strings," but not the implications of that overcoat.

This reporter sits at his desk when word comes in that "a flood is sweeping Mankato"; or "there's been a terrific explosion at Rochester," or "there's a big train wreck at Winona." On orders from the city editor, he jumps into his car and heads for Mankato . . . or Rochester . . . or Winona . . . or any of hundreds of towns in the upper Midwest. As this Negro reporter drives along he wonders how long he will have to stay in the town. If overnight, will the hotel rent him a room? Will he be able to buy food at the restaurants? That is, eggs without shells in them, coffee without salt in it? Does Montevideo, Minnesota, really have an unwritten law that no Negro can remain in town overnight? What about Hibbing and some other Iron Range towns—are they that way, as reported? These are the things this Negro must wonder about—along with whether or not he will do adequately the job assigned him. He knows that, to some extent, he is at the mercy of the people about and for whom he writes. Therefore the people of Montevideo have become custodians of the gates of opportunity, just as the people of McMinnville once were. A reporter who can't get a story is of less value to his paper than a reporter who can, and it makes no ultimate difference if one reporter fails because, as a Negro, he is resented by news sources, or if he is barred from a hotel room or a town, and denied access to the news. It simply means that an editor must send a reporter who *can* get a hotel room or remain in a town overnight; thus the Negro has suffered an abridgment of opportunity that is just as effective as if he never got the job.

That is what I told the people of Minneapolis and St. Paul and other Minnesota communities.

So I knew that my report, or any subsequent report, could have little lasting effect until the people realized that hatred is the common denominator of small people everywhere. Prejudice is no ailment of the toe, or of the Southern extremities of mankind; it is near-gangrene of the body, the whole body, and what is needed is a wonder drug, a tonic for the national bloodstream, not amputation of any apparently less-healthy part of the body.

But as I talked of the two-facedness of the North, the wickedness of sordid tenement rows in Harlem, brutal riots in Detroit, inhumanity on Chicago's South Side, and biased employers in Minnesota, I had to remember that there was a difference between all these things and what I had written about the South. I could stand in an open meeting of Minnesotans and talk about Minnesota prejudices, and white citizens would come and listen without fear of direful consequences. This was not true of the South that I had left. There I would not have dared to say the things that I had written, and citizens would not have dared to come and listen. After the *Tribune* began to run my articles on the South the word reached Mc-Minnville. White people, reportedly led by policemen, distributed cards with the Klan cross and the words, STOP CARL

ROWAN, on them. I got a message from "a McMinnville policeman" that he had a "friend in Minneapolis who is going to fix
things for you." This was an attempt at the intimidation that
is possible in the South. It is possible wherever little men are
backed by big laws, and that is the difference in the North and
the South. The McMinnville policeman, accustomed only to
McMinnville's way of doing things, was not aware of this difference, for "fixing" a Negro does not come so easily where
enough people have respect for human dignity to have it
entered in the lawbook. So in the North the fight is against
small men who manifest their hatreds and antipathies by guile
and trickery; in the South the struggle is against little men with
the towering club of law, and it is impossible, often, to nego-
tiate either with law or little men with towering clubs. The
North, in resorting to subterfuge, has at least negatively acknowledged my rights, leaving me to contend only with the
wily nonconformist. I have a fighting chance. The North may
not always play by the rules, and that makes it a bad sport;
but the South refuses to make any rules in which I am recognized as part of the game.

Yes, there is a difference, both in the way two sections of our
country invoke their prejudices and in the way they protect
them. Yet there is a commonness in the way group animosities
are perpetuated. Snobbery, everywhere, is the running-mate of
bigotry. Charlie's café turns the unwelcome sign to Negroes
because its operator wants to run a place for the "elite," and
a generation of snobs has not become accustomed to thinking
of the adjective "elite" as applying to the noun "Negro."
Charlie's is a going enterprise. So is snobbery. Both will remain
so as long as there are enough people who worship the dream
of being a part of something "exclusive," even though the
exclusiveness exists only in a narrow mind.

But it is not in our cafés alone that we have set snobbery
up as a twentieth-century bail. We have worshipped this false
god in our work, and in our play, in our moments of supposed
worship to the Almighty, upon our sickbeds, and in the hal-

lowed earth in which we all go to rest and hope to meet our maker. And we have rationalized these practices with a facile blindness not unlike lynchers rationalizing their deed.

Ultimately we stand in the midst of chaos and bemoan our disunity. Each of us blames the people for a decaying national morality; seldom do we blame *we, the people.* Bigotry is not a disease of the people; it is a disease of individuals, and eradication of the disease is an individual responsibility, for the only ultimate cure is self-administered.

But we need men of courage. We need men like the Catholic priest who sat silent in a meeting of the Omaha Urban League and heard how white youngsters had stoned a Negro family as it left a home that it was about to buy in an all-white neighborhood. Whitney Young, Urban League executive secretary, was concerned about what might happen when the family tried to move into the house. He asked board members what the League might do.

"I know what to do," said the priest, who told the group that the neighborhood into which the Negro family had bought was predominantly Catholic. "What time are they moving in?" he asked.

The priest was told the proposed moving-time. He advised Young and other board-members not to worry. "I know what to do," he repeated.

At the appointed time the Negro family arrived with some of their furniture. Older neighbors pulled back curtains to peek. Youngsters eased away from their homes toward the Negroes, ready to hurl stones and insults. But before the first stone was thrown the youngsters saw a frocked gentleman walk off the porch of the home that the Negroes had bought. It was their priest, who had made himself an unofficial, one-man welcoming committee. He shook hands with the Negro man and helped him carry the first piece of furniture into the house.

Youngsters dropped their rocks in shame and turned toward their homes for advice from parents, who obviously had encouraged the first stoning. But the peeking faces disappeared in sudden embarrassment. A Negro family had found a new home outside the blight and rubble that had been marked "for Negroes only." A few weeks later they also had some new friends—among the very neighbors who had expressed such great unhappiness at seeing them buy the house.

That is not an incident of great rarity. Men of such courage are acting and speaking out with growing frequency, although the number of such men still is far below the need. After the Korean War broke out, the 47th "Viking" Division, composed primarily of Minnesota guardsmen, was recalled to active duty. Among those returning to war was a white Minneapolis newspaperman. He learned that a Negro woman who was a member of his church was about to get married, and that she and her fiancé were looking for a home. He was asked if he would consider renting them his house. "Why not?" he said. "Why shouldn't Negroes live in it? That is a right they're calling me back to fight for." So he rented his home, in an all-white neighborhood, to the Negroes. Hours after the word got out a few members of the neighborhood had drawn up a petition seeking to bar the Negroes. They started out with the petition and found some signers. Then they went to one home where the father said he positively would not sign, and he lectured the petition-bearers.

"Do you want your property's value to drop to where you'd have to sell it at a loss?" demanded the petition-bearers.

"I didn't buy my house to sell; I bought it to live in," was the reply, and the door was shut. This nonsigner also was a member of the Methodist church to which the Negro woman and the white reporter belonged. He called the pastor.

Despite the knowledge that opinion in the neighborhood was against Negroes moving in, this minister began to walk the streets of the neighborhood, calling on members of his church. He told them that the Negroes in question were respectable citizens with every legal and moral right to live in the house. He would be very unhappy to know that any member of his church was trying to bar them from the neighborhood. Soon a priest and a rabbi were out giving the same lecture to their followers. Their argument was morally convincing, but a few residents were unwilling to relinquish the property-values argument. Then a white man who not long before was president of a group of real-estate men, who have been the chief propagandists about Negroes lowering the value of property, got in a word. The property-values argument is all propaganda and no fact, he said. His word carried weight with even the most recalcitrant. The Negroes moved in. At last reports no buildings had caved in, no new, neighborhood maladies had sprung up, and harmony existed in the area to no less a degree than when the Negroes moved in.

So my search for the New South really had brought into perspective the near-omnipresence of racial animosities. I remembered a spiritual that was popular in churches during my boyhood:

> *I went to the rocks to hide my face;*
> *The rocks cried out, "No hidin' place."*
> *There's no hidin' place down here.*

So there was the real dilemma, the awful dichotomy of human affairs. Everywhere I saw the need for courage, for moral strength, and for reasserted belief in the Golden Rule, which for too many Americans has fallen into the unsophisticated, unglamorous, and laughed-at category of "Sunday School talk." Yes, the need is *everywhere,* and the South knows it, and therein grows the dilemma. Therein lies the barrier to a New South, indeed to a New America, for we lose our ideals in the muck of rationalism by acknowledging that "Everybody does it." Instead of progress from the South, we get talk about the mote in the North's eyes; from the North we hear wailings about the beam in the South's eye. This self-pride becomes a cataract through which neither the North nor the South can see the matter in its own eye. So we justify all that exists in the South, where written law is the antithesis of our Constitution and our democratic ideals, by saying: "Well, at least they're honest about their prejudice." This is the same way that we pour our hearts out to a mobster who, because of some questionable code of honor, "is not a squealer—I can say that for him."

Perhaps we need new codes of honor as well as a New South, for with all of Dixie's "honesty" in making her hatreds readable, the result still is the searing of human souls and the warping of human minds. And we do need a New North; but we will have very little of this New North until we are nearer a New South, for despite the forces of division we are still one nation, and the mores of the North must to some extent reflect the mores of the South. Our boundary is too vague and too fluid for it to be otherwise. Hatred has but one source, and that is the diseased mind. Many are the minds of the North that embrace hatred; but in greater number are the minds of the South that both embrace and endorse it. We must discourage the endorsements to rule out future embracers.

And the future is our great hope. There are those among us who fear it, and many of us black folk live in it: almost all of us put our faith in it—never, however, accepting the Hegelian dream that history cures all ills as it creates all of them. We are not yet masters of our own fate, but we intend to grope and grapple with the present, and try to put a mold of our making on the future. And even the white South believes that, in large measure, we will succeed. Said the Jackson (Mississippi) *Daily News*:

> . . . there is a new Negro in our land and the Southern lawmaker, or citizen, who fails to realize that fact is being stupid at his own cost. The new Negro has more education. He has better health. He has better clothes. He reads more newspapers. He is adopting the white man's customs, the white man's speech, the white man's standards and the white man's shibboleths. Now it doesn't make sense to assume that this new Negro is going to be content in the

cabin of his slave grandfather. And it doesn't make sense to pretend that is where he ought to be. His eyes are on better things, materially considered. He is going to have a car and drive it. He is going to buy a home and live in it. He is going to step into citizenship and exercise its rights and demand its privileges. Indeed, our use of the future tense is merely to gentle the recalcitrant of our readers to the fact that the new Negro is doing these things. The new Negro is not a man of tomorrow. He is a man of today.

These are enlightened words from a paper in Mississippi, where, all but the liars will agree, the Negro is *not* a man of today. And too well does the Negro know the old proverb that "tomorrow never comes." But today is a long day for the Negro, and perhaps only the dawn is at hand. The wheels of justice *are* turning, and everywhere that old despot, custom, is on the run.

There is turmoil in the South, and it, too, has moved into the national bloodstream. This is how the late Samuel Chiles Mitchell, professor of history at the University of Richmond, explained the South's turmoil:

The 19th Century had three dominant ideas: liberty, industry and democracy. The ante-bellum South set its face against all three. Not liberty, slavery! Not industry, plantation agriculture! Not democracy, a contrived system of aristocratic rule! And in the pursuit of these false ideals the South lost the better part of 100 years.

But North or South, black or white, we are but one, and we all lost those hundred years. We all race to catch up. This is our hour of bedlam, and through the dust and haze of turmoil I hope America's Noah Brannons—the people who "did not know"—can see what it means to be an American Negro. In our common hour of tribulation, as we stumble to a common destiny, I only hope the Noah Brannons really care.

CPSIA information can be obtained at www.ICGtesting.com
Printed in the USA
LVOW06s1939291215

468297LV00001B/60/P